Palgrave Macmillan Studies in Banking and Financial Institutions

Series Editor: Professor Philip Molyneux, Bangor Business School, Bangor University, UK

The Palgrave Macmillan Studies in Banking and Financial Institutions are international in orientation and include studies of banking within particular countries or regions, and studies of particular themes such as Corporate Banking, Risk Management, Mergers and Acquisitions, etc. The books' focus is on research and practice, and they include up-to-date and innovative studies on contemporary topics in banking that will have global impact and influence.

Titles include:

Steffen E. Andersen
THE EVOLUTION OF NORDIC FINANCE

Roberto Bottiglia, Elisabetta Gualandri and Gian Nereo Mazzocco (*editors*)
CONSOLIDATION IN THE EUROPEAN FINANCIAL INDUSTRY

Dimitris N. Chorafas
BASEL III, THE DEVIL AND GLOBAL BANKING

Dimitris N. Chorafas
CAPITALISM WITHOUT CAPITAL

Dimitris N. Chorafas
SOVEREIGN DEBT CRISIS
The New Normal and the Newly Poor

Violaine Cousin
BANKING IN CHINA

Vincenzo D'Apice and Giovanni Ferri
FINANCIAL INSTABILITY
Toolkit for Interpreting Boom and Bust Cycles

Peter Falush and Robert L. Carter OBE
THE BRITISH INSURANCE INDUSTRY SINCE 1900
The Era of Transformation

Franco Fiordelisi and Ornella Ricci (*editors*)
BANCASSURANCE IN EUROPE
Past, Present and Future

Franco Fiordelisi, Philip Molyneux and Daniele Previati (*editors*)
NEW ISSUES IN FINANCIAL AND CREDIT MARKETS

Franco Fiordelisi, Philip Molyneux and Daniele Previati (*editors*)
NEW ISSUES IN FINANCIAL INSTITUTIONS MANAGEMENT

Kim Hawtrey
AFFORDABLE HOUSING FINANCE

Jill M. Hendrickson
REGULATION AND INSTABILITY IN U.S. COMMERCIAL BANKING
A History of Crises

Alexandros-Andreas Kyrtsis (*editor*)
FINANCIAL MARKETS AND ORGANIZATIONAL TECHNOLOGIES
System Architectures, Practices and Risks in the Era of Deregulation

Caterina Lucarelli and Gianni Brighetti (*editors*)
RISK TOLERANCE IN FINANCIAL DECISION MAKING

Roman Matousek (*editor*)
MONEY, BANKING AND FINANCIAL MARKETS IN CENTRAL AND EASTERN EUROPE
20 Years of Transition

Philip Molyneux (*editor*)
BANK PERFORMANCE, RISK AND FIRM FINANCING

Philip Molyneux (*editor*)
BANK STRATEGY, GOVERNANCE AND RATINGS

Imad A. Moosa
THE MYTH OF TOO BIG TO FAIL

Simon Mouatt and Carl Adams (*editors*)
CORPORATE AND SOCIAL TRANSFORMATION OF MONEY AND BANKING
Breaking the Serfdom

Victor Murinde (*editor*)
BANK REGULATORY REFORMS IN AFRICA

Anders Ögren (*editor*)
THE SWEDISH FINANCIAL REVOLUTION

Özlem Olgu
EUROPEAN BANKING
Enlargement, Structural Changes and Recent Developments

Ramkishen S. Rajan
EMERGING ASIA
Essays on Crises, Capital Flows, FDI and Exchange Rate

Allesandro Roselli
FINANCIAL STRUCTURES AND REGULATION: A COMPARISON OF CRISES IN THE UK, USA AND ITALY

Yasushi Suzuki
JAPAN'S FINANCIAL SLUMP
Collapse of the Monitoring System under Institutional and Transition Failures

Ruth Wandhöfer
EU PAYMENTS INTEGRATION
The Tale of SEPA, PSD and Other Milestones Along the Road

The full list of titles available is on the website:
www.palgrave.com/finance/sbfi.asp

Palgrave Macmillan Studies in Banking and Financial Institutions
Series Standing Order ISBN 978–1–4039–4872–4

You can receive future titles in this series as they are published by placing a standing order. Please contact your bookseller or, in case of difficulty, write to us at the address below with your name and address, the title of the series and the ISBN quoted above.

Customer Services Department, Macmillan Distribution Ltd, Houndmills, Basingstoke, Hampshire RG21 6XS, England

The Nigerian Banking Sector Reforms

Power and Politics

Seth Apati

palgrave
macmillan

First published 2012 by
PALGRAVE MACMILLAN

Palgrave Macmillan in the UK is an imprint of Macmillan Publishers Limited, registered in England, company number 785998, of Houndmills, Basingstoke, Hampshire RG21 6XS.

Palgrave Macmillan in the US is a division of St Martin's Press LLC, 175 Fifth Avenue, New York, NY 10010.

Palgrave Macmillan is the global academic imprint of the above companies and has companies and representatives throughout the world.

Palgrave® and Macmillan® are registered trademarks in the United States, the United Kingdom, Europe and other countries.

ISBN: 978–0–230–27841–7

This book is printed on paper suitable for recycling and made from fully managed and sustained forest sources. Logging, pulping and manufacturing processes are expected to conform to the environmental regulations of the country of origin.

A catalogue record for this book is available from the British Library.

Library of Congress Cataloging-in-Publication Data

Apati, Seth, 1971–
The Nigerian banking sector reforms : power and politics / Seth Apati.
p. cm.—(Palgrave Macmillan studies in banking and financial institutions)
Includes index.
ISBN 978–0–230–27841–7 (hardback)
1. Banks and banking – Nigeria. 2. Monetary policy – Nigeria. I. Title.

HG1601.A66 2011
332.109669—dc22 2011000542

10 9 8 7 6 5 4 3 2 1
21 20 19 18 17 16 15 14 13 12

Printed and bound in Great Britain by
CPI Antony Rowe, Chippenham and Eastbourne

To God,
the only hope of the 120,000 pensioners
who lost their life savings in
banking stocks in the great Nigerian stock
market crash of 2008

Contents

Tables

Figures

Preface

Despite all the theoretical economic explanations for Nigeria's banking reforms, on-the-ground observation suggests that the real drivers of these reforms were a complex interplay of institutional and socio-political forces.

First, a 2001 US Secret Service investigation into a Nigerian client's account revealed the need for increased surveillance of the nation's banking system by the Central Bank of Nigeria (CBN). That same year, a major foreign exchange scandal showed massive levels of abuse of the nation's weak foreign exchange laws, which led to the suspension of 21 of the 89 banks from the official foreign exchange market.

As one of the world's largest crude oil producers and the supplier of 10 per cent of the world's liquefied natural gas – and also, according to Goldman Sachs, one of the leading emerging market economies after the BRIC countries (Brazil, Russia, India, China) – Nigeria emerged as a large foreign exchange earner, a development which benefited banking in the absence of a real sector. By 2005, the increase in crude oil prices and the parallel, though unconnected, reforms in the economic and financial sectors thrust the nation into the global limelight. Nigeria became one of the continent's most sought-after destination for foreign direct investment (after South Africa and Egypt), which was itself made easier by the reforms.

However, unlike other emerging market, financial sector reforms driven by endogenous shocks and regional contagion, the reforms in Nigeria did not fit any of the classical approaches. To be effective, a reform has to be a coordinated programme of actions that are linked one to another and involve fundamentally improving the structure, practices and behaviours of an industry or government while correcting abuses, malpractices and inefficiencies with the aim of creating a new structure and form.

In developing economies (or near-emerging markets) such as Nigeria, economic institutions are inefficient, information is asymmetric and any analysis of banking systems – or, indeed, of financial sector reforms generally – inadvertently involves an analysis of the key individuals or power brokers behind the institutions.

According to Arnaldo Mauri's five-step classification, Nigeria is a mid-sized economy in either stage two or three. Infrastructure decayed in the nearly three decades of military rule, electric power was epileptic, transport and aviation were poor and GDP per head was still well below 1,000 dollars. Yet it was this same infrastructural decadence, coupled with a booming market powered by a population of 140 to 150 million, that created a sizeable market for non-manufacturing services – hospitals, restaurants and, the greatest of them all, financial services.

Despite Transparency International's 2004 rating of Nigeria as one of the three most corrupt nations in the world, portfolio managers for emerging market funds still poured money into the country. Three years later, the investment, capital-raising and infrastructure concessioning binge, funding entertainment (including movie galleries, five-star hotels and multi-purpose destination malls) had snowballed, with little investment in the real sector, manufacturing and infrastructure.

The May 2007 change of government from Olusegun Obasanjo to Umaru Yar'Adua notwithstanding – with its attendant policy somersaults and reversals of some of the controversial reforms and tariff waivers of the earlier administration – the economy still continued on a roller-coaster. GDP growth rate was over 6 per cent, consumer price inflation was reported to be in single digits (albeit based on suspicious data) and the long-term credit rating of BB– placed Nigeria on a par with Brazil and Russia (see Appendix), two of the world's leading emerging markets.

Most of these miracles were driven by an economic team which set the nation on the seemingly irreversible path of growth that earned commendations from the most dispassionate economic critics. All this changed in mid-2008, when, following the global credit crisis, the nation's GDP growth forecast was revised downwards from 6.5 per cent to 4.5 per cent.

Despite official denial by the CBN that the nation's financial system was immune to the crisis, macroeconomic data for the last quarter of 2008 started revealing cracks in the banking system. The sustainability of banking growth, and indeed that of the entire economy, was now thrown into question.

By early 2009, it had become crystal clear that the nation's financial system was at major risk and the regulators were culpable. The great stock market crash of 2008 and the resultant banking crisis of 2009 were actually the third phase of a larger and longer financial crisis, which the Nigerian nation had overlooked. The first phase was the unbridled licensing of banks in the 1980s and 1990s, which eventually overwhelmed regulatory capacity and led to bank failures in the 1990s. The second was the collapse of the regulatory collaboration between the nation's regulators, a situation which had worsened in the period from 2004, resulting in monetary and banking policy running at variance with securities market behaviour. Obviously the manifestation of the problem was peculiar to each stage, but the basic mechanics were the same.

Every era of banking history is defined by its signature challenge. And the manner in which those challenges have been handled has made heroes and destroyed others. Even though every regulator's answers seem to be appropriate for their time, lessons from Nigerian banking history have always revealed the inadequacy of each set of reforms soon after the 'reformer' is out of office.

The mystique of most reforms is that they acquire a dynamic of their own and result in far-reaching outcomes beyond the contemplation of the reformers. In Nigeria, whether the economic and banking reforms have actually effected any long-lasting impact is now debatable. Three possible hypotheses exist for the future: steady growth, volatile growth (like Indonesia's) or a sudden meltdown. Whether Nigeria's economic and financial sector growth rates will be sustainable in the medium to long term, or whether the country will end up with a mild case of meltdown (like the Asian economies in the 1990s), or whether it will be in some intermediate state are the three scenarios the economic models offered.

This book is a humble, fact-based attempt to generate thought-provoking ideas on the prognosis of Nigeria's banking reforms.

Foreword

Nigeria as a country has suffered and continues to suffer disappointments from many fronts: government, banks and their regulators, leaders or impostors and opportunists who made their way to the corridors of power. The focus of Dr Apati in this book is on banking in Nigeria and the various challenges it has faced, the loss of integrity in the system and the progressive abandonment of its effective role in the economic development of the country. Even though this book is about banking, it reveals the impact of a culture of corruption on almost all, if not all, aspects of national life. During the 1980s, for example, the military rulers saw banking as a way of making easy money for themselves and promoting loyalists. The number of banks was increased phenomenally from 24 to over 100 without regard to the limited resources of the regulators for their supervisory functions. The issuance of banking licences was abused and became a 'smart' way of gaining access to foreign exchange at the official rate, which was then sold off at parallel market rates. The Naira continues to lose value, with occasional slight appreciation. Corporate governance in banks was not taken seriously, as some of them were operated like private empires. Consequently, large insider deals were made, and managing directors enriched themselves in some of these banks to an unimaginable extent. The regulators of the financial system (Central Bank of Nigeria, the NDIC and the SEC) were not proactive enough to intervene in a timely manner to save the financial system from avoidable crisis. The stock market crashed after the privileged hawks had had their day. The problems were either covered up or went on unnoticed for so long that the former CBN Governor assured the nation that Nigerian banks were solid post-consolidation. Dr Apati reviews in some detail the limited success of the consolidation exercise, while the fragility of the system became evident when five of the 24 banks had to be rescued and their Managing Directors sacked.

The banking industry has abandoned its traditional role in the overall development of the economy. Rather than give credit support to credible entrepreneurs at all levels, including the grassroots, banks felt comfortable with easy money-making through commissions earned on various deals, even questionable ones. While small- and medium-scale enterprises are regarded as engines of growth, this does not seem to be the focus of banks. Government and central bank policies are not strong enough to compel the banks to play their role as appropriate. Sometimes, the policies are also restrictive and oppressive. For example, the government encourages investment in agriculture but makes loans easily obtainable by large corporations, leaving the peasant or small-scale farmers with nothing. Dr Apati has been painstaking in his analysis of the banking system, with which he has worked for about two decades. His experience as an advisor in the financial milieus not only of Nigeria, but extending to the West Africa subregion, makes his views credible and respected. He has structured his presentation in an easy-to-read and understandable format. He educates on banking reforms generally in emerging markets, while making a case for banking reform in Nigeria with analysis of its political dimensions.

In order that the reforms might have the desired impact, the author devotes some attention to the regulators, offering solutions on how to restructure and strengthen them for their onerous tasks and responsibilities. The author concludes with a roadmap to sustainability of banking reforms.

This book is highly recommended to various groups of people. To the general interest reader, to students of economics, history and political economy, financial analysts, politicians and academics, this is a rich source of information. Lastly, it might provide a soul-searching opportunity for those who have profited from the lapses and corruption of the system. Some might decide to plough back some of their wealth to the local economy.

Philip Latilo,
Former Secretary-General
West African Bankers' Association

About the book

As one of the world's largest oil producers, Nigeria benefited from increased investment flows from Western and Asian multinationals, as well as the international multilateral agencies, to record double-digit growth in its banking sector in the 1990s and early 2000s. Taken together with the hundreds of billions of dollars misappropriated by the oligarchs, who control everything from oil and gas to telecommunications, the accelerated growth of banks has been at the expense of other sectors of the economy.

With the return to democracy in 1999, the military-turned-civilian 'dictator' drove major reforms in the economy at such a phenomenal rate that he received IMF and World Bank commendations, and attracted Western-trained economists (including a World Bank managing director) to return to Nigeria to run its affairs. The overall objective was to make Nigeria one of the world's 20 largest economies, in the process overtaking other oil-rich states such as Indonesia, Venezuela and Malaysia.

Central to the political and economic reforms was the cleansing of Nigeria's banking sector, which had become a transit point for global money-laundering and which needed to be sanitized for the country to receive further US support.

Despite this, institutional vested interests continued to control the nation's money and capital levers, thereby limiting the macroeconomic benefits of the much-publicized reforms.

Drawing from the examples of the US, Malaysia, Egypt and others, the government increased bank capitalization to nearly $200 million and forced financial sector industry consolidation by reducing the number of banks from 89 to 25.

This book examines the impact of banking industry consolidation and financial sector reforms in the world's largest black economy.

Was the consolidation successful? Did it positively impact Nigeria's economic reform programme? And how did the IMF, the World Bank and the US contribute to the outcome?

The author draws on about 20 years' experience working with global multinationals in Africa's oil-rich zone to address these key questions and examine the political economy of banking sector reform in one of the world's fastest growing economies.

1
Banking Reforms in Emerging Markets: An Introduction

1.1 Background

After the successful democratic elections in Nigeria in 2003, the key priority for the Obasanjo-led administration was to institute – and follow through with – far-reaching, multi-faceted reforms in all sectors of the economy. During its first term (1999–2003), the administration had been unable to drive through any large-scale reforms in the major sectors of the economy successfully due to the institutional challenges created by the previous sixteen years of military rule.

By 2003, President Obasanjo was able to assemble a cohesive team of Western-trained economists, some of them with experience in multilateral institutions such as the World Bank, in order to develop an economic blueprint, a reform strategy, and a more concerted strategic approach to reform. These reforms were expected to cover decentralization and macroeconomic balance and efficiency, including the optimal use of increasing oil revenues in a federal state. Decentralization was the arrowhead of the reforms and involved decentralizing some hitherto protected industries, privatizing government holdings in business concerns, and strengthening the non-federal arms of government.

The impetus for the reforms was psychological, domestic and international. First, President Obasanjo recalled the Nigerian economy, and its supporting physical infrastructure, as a functional state when he left power as a military ruler in 1979: in sharp contrast to the comatose system he encountered when he regained power as a civilian president twenty years later. Second was Nigerians' domestic yearning for change after 16 years of military rule. Third was the clarion call for reforms by international investors, in particular the multilateral agencies and the US government, who insisted on comprehensive socio-economic reforms as a *sine qua non* for any large-scale investment in Nigeria and as a prerequisite for moral support of the new administration.

The economic reforms were comprehensive. They straddled seven main areas: the civil service; power; transport; the legal system; the ports; telecommunications; and financial services (mainly banking). However, the political manoeuvres of the idle rich, who had sponsored Mr Obasanjo's electoral campaign, burdened him with inept nominees to the cabinet and other executive positions in the federal government, limiting the success of his reforms during his first term in office.

By the end of the first term, it had become obvious that financial sector reforms, which were initially synonymous with banking, were most likely to have the greatest and quickest impact, at least in the short term. Inflation had reached 10 per cent (increasing later to almost 14 per cent), the GDP growth rate was still at a mere 3–4 per cent (barely 1 per cent ahead of the population growth rate) and official unemployment (although the figures were unreliable) was worsening.

Inflation and unemployment had become the two albatrosses of the economy. Inflation, manifested in wildly fluctuating prices, created widespread uncertainty. Unemployment, on the other hand, created a large army of dependants, bred corruption and fed booming crime.

Battling inflation was the key priority. This required dealing with several factors, including the fiscal deficit, interest rates and the money supply. In Nigeria, tackling interest rates alone would not have had sufficient impact on the money supply problem due to the large scale of black market money exchanges, money laundering, money trafficking, and a whole array of other economic crimes. The only solution, it seemed, was wholesale reform of the financial sector, in particular the notorious banking sector, which, uniquely, had been growing rapidly, at an average of 44 per cent per annum, in an economy which, for the most part, was gradually collapsing.

The key assumption was that reforming Nigeria's financial system would be a catalyst for economic growth – or at least reduce the leakages and economic sabotage for which the banking sector was notorious.

This chapter examines the basis of the argument whether financial sector development leads to economic growth, or vice versa. Subsequent chapters examine the theoretical basis and the empirical evidence for the relationship between financial development (or financial sector reforms) and economic growth, the case and process of reforms in selected developing economies and the evidence peculiar to Nigeria, where one of the nation's largest banks, 'the soul of the nation', was the starting point for systemic banking reforms. Section 1.2 deals with some academic background to the financial reforms. Accordingly, business readers may choose to skip the remainder of this chapter and go straight to Chapter 2.

1.2 Financial sector development and economic growth

The theoretical framework

The importance of the financial sector is that it facilitates the savings and investment functions of the economy, and thus leads to economic growth. Financial intermediaries transfer resources from savers to investors and are therefore important in the process of economic growth. It is assumed that, for this important role in the economy to happen, efficient financial systems must be in place. However, there are divergent views as to the role of finance in the economy and the transmission mechanisms for growth.

The theoretical basis for the role of finance in economic growth hinges on several hypotheses, mainly developed in Western countries by Western economists. Key among these are the Keynesian investment hypothesis (1936), the Miller–Modigliani finance irrelevance proposition (1958, 1961), the McKinnon–Shaw (1973) financial repression model and the efficient market hypothesis (EMH) (Fama 1965, 1970). While the first two models are specific to the level of the firm and focus more on stock markets and developed economies, the McKinnon–Shaw model relates to the macroeconomy and the effects of underdeveloped capital markets in developing countries.

The Keynesian proposition of the 1930s suggests that investment decisions (and therefore economic growth) are determined mainly by the level of confidence, the expected level of demand and the rational behaviour of investors. This implies that the workings of the financial sector are insignificant for investment decisions and, therefore, economic growth. Keynes also argued that investment determines savings and, for that reason, investment decisions are more important than savings decisions.

Similarly, Miller and Modigliani (1958, 1961) suggest that the most important decision for maximizing shareholder wealth concerns investment, and that all other decisions (financing and dividend) follow from this. As a result, the value of a firm is only materially affected by the projects it decides to take on. Relating this to the macroeconomy implies that the financial value of a firm and its economic growth are independent of each other. This suggests that real output in the economy does not depend on financing activities in the economy but that these activities develop as a result of increased investment processes and opportunities.

However, the assumptions on which the Miller–Modigliani propositions are based are simplified and, in practice, financing decisions can affect stock market valuation and growth when these assumptions are relaxed. These assumptions include the existence of perfect capital markets, with no taxes or transaction costs, rational and consistent behaviour by market participants, and fixed financing and dividend decisions. Thus, the Miller–Modigliani proposition enables us to understand what might occur when these assumptions apply. In essence, therefore, not only do financing decisions matter when these assumptions are relaxed, but the types of finance (capital structure) used also become important. Extending this to the macroeconomy suggests that finance might be important to economic growth. The behaviour of banks could have a significant impact on overall growth and thresholds may exist for the relative effects of financial development indicators.

The McKinnon–Shaw financial repression hypothesis relates to developing economies, where capital markets are underdeveloped and government intervention in the running of financial markets is extensive, thus suggesting a repression. The McKinnon–Shaw traditional framework (following from Schumpeter 1934) is based on the classical growth model, which assumes that financial liberalization leads to financial deepening in the economy, which in turn precedes increased savings, investment and output. They assume that savings determine investment and that full utilization of resources is always guaranteed. Therefore, the McKinnon–Shaw model suggests that government intervention in the financial sector through interest rate controls, high reserve requirements and allocation of credit reduces competition, and this in turn reduces savings, investments and economic growth. Consequently, financial liberalization is preferred to government intervention, since it is believed to promote efficient financial systems. A liberalized financial system leaves the forces of demand and supply to determine prices, allows free entry into the market and provides a wide range of financial services. Additionally, innovative financial instruments are invented, together with more responsive pricing, in the presence of competition. In other words, the McKinnon–Shaw model considers the role of finance as significant in the economy, in contrast to those of Keynes and Miller–Modigliani.

However, the McKinnon–Shaw model ignores the role of the stock market and the need for complete institutional reform of the financial sector in developing economies (ADB 1994, Inanga 1995, Oshikoya and Ogbu 2002). It also assumes that liberal interest rates will always lead to increased private savings by economic agents. However, evidence from developing economies suggests that savings could be insensitive to interest rates, and that most people save for safety rather than for investment or returns (Emenuga 2002, Mwega 2002). As experience from South-East Asia has shown, financial liberalization can result in negative growth, and government intervention can serve to increase economic growth (as evidence from South Korea and China suggests). Therefore, financial liberalization as proposed by the McKinnon–Shaw model needs to be accompanied by wider economic and institutional reforms.

Furthermore, the theory of the role of stock markets in promoting economic growth is based on the 'efficient market hypothesis' (Fama 1965, 1970). This proposes that prices are correctly set in efficient markets and that such markets are best able to allocate capital to appropriate sectors in the economy. Moreover, efficient stock exchanges not only provide an avenue for investors to trade in shares with minimal transaction costs and inefficiencies but also create investment opportunities by providing funds for projects. Stock markets also provide an avenue for corporate control, for example through takeovers and mergers, since stock exchanges regulate the activities of companies and set minimum requirements before they can be listed. Thus, efficient financial systems promote financial development, which in turn leads to economic growth. Inefficient stock markets lead to financial crises and distortions in the economy.

The traditional theory of growth, supported by McKinnon and Shaw (1973), suggests that the main transmission mechanism is capital accumulation, including labour. However, growth cannot be sustained if capital accumulation continues without a corresponding increase in productivity (Valderrama 2003). This is the result of diminishing returns: the addition of an extra unit of capital means that, in the long run, additions to capital lead to diminishing marginal productivity and, with it, stagnant or declining growth.

However, this traditional theory has been superseded by a new growth theory, which centres on the use of technology or advances in technology to drive productivity and hence increase economic growth. This is based on the assumption that technological advances lead to sustained growth by compensating for the diminished returns from capital accumulation.

Empirical evidence on the finance–growth nexus

Empirical evidence relating to the impact of financial development on economic growth is wide and varied. Most research identifies a relationship between financial development and economic growth. However, the problem is causality (that is, the chicken and egg problem) and the different impacts on developed and developing countries. Does financial development explain economic growth, or does economic growth give rise to financial development? And are there thresholds beyond which the relationship becomes insignificant? The earliest disputes in the literature of causality can be traced to Schumpeter (1934), Robinson (1952) and Goldsmith (1969).

Of particular interest in recent literature is the variation between the impact of financial development on developed and developing economies. These studies (Patrick 1966, Demetriades and Hussein 1996, Arestis and Demetriades 1997, Al-Yousif 2002, Bekaert *et al.* 2003, Rioja and Valev 2004) suggest that the impact of financial development varies from country to country and across time periods. In particular, Patrick (1966) noted that the direction of causality changes over the course of development. For example, while Tsangyao (2002) found no significant effect from financial development on economic growth in China, Ghali (1999), in a study of Tunisia, concluded that financial development indicators have a significant effect on economic growth. This implies that there is no one impact of financial development on the economy. Graff (2003) suggests that the effects of financial development matter more in developing countries. Rioja and Valev (2004) hold that capital accumulation is the channel through which financial development affects economic growth in low-income countries. Middle- and high-income groups are affected by productivity growth. Beck *et al.* (2000) and Benhabib and Spiegel (2000), using cross-country sectional data and time series data respectively, suggest that financial development has a significant impact on both productivity and capital accumulation in all the countries studied.

As economies differ, so also do the effects of financial development on them (Saint-Paul 1996). The implication from various researches is that the impact of financial development is dependent on a country's legal and socio-political framework, as Levine *et al.* (2000) tried to incorporate in their finance–economic growth model. Shan and Morris (2002) suggest that the effects of financial development indicators on growth vary according to the industrial structures and cultures in an economy. De Gregorio and Guidotti (1992), La Porta *et al.* (1998), Levine (1997), Koivu (2002), Driffill (2003), Graff (2003) and De Haas (2004) suggest that economic development is stimulated by financial development, especially if the financial system is rooted in a sound legal system with proper controls. They reason that sound legal systems increase some banks' money or credit supply, which may actually serve to increase financial development.

Thus, Wachtel (2001) suggests that 'countries with better contract law, more informative accounting, and accurate financial reporting will have more developed financial systems and more growth,' while Khan (2000) proposes that the issue of the direction of causality can be resolved by examining the relationship between the legal environment and financial development. The positive impact of financial development in certain countries can be traced to simultaneous political and legal reforms. For example, financial reforms in an economy with high levels of corruption will not have a positive influence on growth because corruption stifles investment and leads to decline in growth (Mauro 1995).

Studies in this area also propose a threshold at which the impact of financial development becomes significant to the economy. Greenwood and Jovanovic (1990) noted that financial development aids growth in a mature economy. Rioja and Valev (2004) held that 'the strong contribution of financial development does not occur until a country has reached a certain minimum level.' Park (1993), however, in a study of financial development and economic growth in South Korea and Taiwan, suggests that, beyond a certain stage, the effects of further financial development may be insignificant or even negative for economic growth. By contrast, Rousseau and Wachtel (2002) and Lee and Wong (2005), consider inflation as the threshold beyond which the effect of financial development on economic growth could change. In particular, Rousseau and Wachtel (2002), in their study on the effect of inflation on the finance–growth relationship across 84 countries from 1960 to 1995 using five-year rolling panel regressions, found that below a threshold inflation rate of 6–8 per cent the effect of financial development on growth becomes significantly positive. This suggests that threshold effects tend to be country specific, as inflation rates vary across countries.

Furthermore, research has also focused on the various financial indicators, testing for the relative significance of each variable in predicting the impact of financial development on growth. In particular, the focus of these studies is on the relative importance of market-based compared to bank-based indicators. According to Pagano (1993), the term financial development is a 'generic notation' and, therefore, the impact of its various components must be examined. Atje and Jovanovic (1993) held that stock markets were a more significant variable than banks. This has major implications for countries like Nigeria, where the focus of regulation has been on banking, and securities market regulation has been weak until very recently. Indeed, Caporale *et al.* (2004) and Thangavelu and James (2004) suggest that the causality between financial development and economic growth holds good only when a proxy for the stock market is included in the model, implying that stock market indicators are more important to economic growth. Baier *et al.* (2003) noted that the inhibition of stock markets in an economy reduces or hinders economic growth.

Others, however, refute the assumption that the mere opening of a stock exchange leads to economic development. Financial sector development, according to this school of thought, must be all-encompassing, including the banking, insurance and securities markets, and an institutional framework must be in existence. Kassimatis and Spyrou (2001), for instance, observe that stock markets affect economic growth only in countries where there is financial liberalization, and that it would be unwise to open them where repression still exists. Minier (2003) holds that stock markets need to grow to a certain level before they begin to affect economic growth. This also supports the assumption that other institutional factors affect financial development and, in turn, economic growth, and that thresholds exist for the effects of financial development on economic growth. Singh (1997) observes that stock markets are not as important in promoting growth in developing countries, mainly because of the volatility of these markets. In addition, Morck *et al.* (1988) and Shleifer and Summers (1989) suggest that stock markets inhibit economic growth by making shareholders uninterested in the running of an organization. Shareholders can dispose of their shares easily, which encourages short-termism, a behaviour that could be detrimental to creating the culture of systematically developing large indigenous corporations in developing countries.

On the other hand, Arestis *et al.* (2001) assert that banks, rather than stock markets, promote economic growth, and that results obtained in contradiction to this are due to deficiencies in the use of the data. Similarly, Jayaratne and Strahan (1996), in their study of reforms of branch banking in the US, concluded that they led to increased economic growth. These conclusions are based on the theory that the banking sector developed in order to ease the problems of information asymmetries in stock market operations, especially in emerging stock exchanges (Park 1994, Patrick 1994). However, Demirguc-Kunt and Levine (1996), Demetriades (1997) and Levine (2002) do not support the existence of any differences between market-based and bank-based proxies for economic growth, indicating that both promote growth.

In summary, therefore, the literature and the theory agree on the important role of finance in an economy, but the extent to which this is relevant remains a source of dispute. Thus, Levine (1997) and Valderrama (2003) suggest that examining the determinants and implications of an economy's financial structure can lead to a clearer understanding of the extent of the importance of financial development in the economy. This book attempts in part, in later chapters, to understand the determinants of the banking structure in Nigeria.

1.3 The case for reforms: financial repression and financial sector reforms

In emerging market countries such as Nigeria, the financial system can be distinguished from the financial sector. Park (1994) defines the financial system as 'an economic sector that uses productive factors to provide the services of a payments system, financial intermediation, and access to securities markets'.

In the extreme case of an economy in which financial intermediaries are non-existent, savings, investment and economic growth are hindered. The problems of adverse selection and moral hazard[1] in the presence of information asymmetry, coupled with huge transaction costs, make it difficult – if not impossible – to allocate resources efficiently from savers to lenders.

Financial repression in developing economies is characterized mainly by interest and exchange rate controls, directed credit programmes to fund allocation to particular sectors of the economy, government ownership of financial institutions and a lack of independence for the central supervisory and regulatory body. This was the case in Nigeria and many West African countries up until the 1980s. Financial repression results in low rates of savings, high rates of inflation, negative real interest rates, high budget deficits and a lack of competition, given that the government is both owner and customer of the banks and crowds out the private sector. This invariably leads to mismanagement, corruption and a huge profile of non-performing loans (since lending decisions are based on political instead of commercial or financial considerations), which cannot be checked or controlled by a government-dominated central bank. A season of hasty reforms usually follows, aimed at correcting the 'financial disintermediation' or 'dysfunctional intermediation' of the past, but often with limited success (Ikhide and Alawode 2001, Mwega 2002, Senbet and Otchere 2006). As Mwega (2002) suggests, 'financial sector reforms are particularly difficult because of the powerful vested interests that have been created through high government intervention over the years'. Brownbridge and Harvey (1998), in a study of the impact of financial reforms in African economies, found that 'the greater the structural changes in the banking system caused by government intervention, the more difficult it was to achieve the objectives of financial liberalization by simply reversing the earlier policy changes'.

Based on the McKinnon–Shaw financial repression hypothesis, financial sector reforms emphasizing liberalization and the withdrawal of government control have been implemented in various developing economies, with differing results. The core objectives of these reforms are manifold: to increase financial intermediation in the economy with the aim of increasing savings, investment and output; to reduce financial sector repression by liberalizing interest rates; to institute transition from direct to indirect monetary policy; to restructure the balance sheets of banks and restore their solvency; and to develop financial markets (Brownbridge and Harvey 1998, Emenuga 2002).

Evidence (Villanueva and Mirakhor 1990, World Bank 1994, Ikhide and Alawode 2001, Mwega 2002, Senbet and Otchere 2006) suggests that results obtained from financial sector reforms depend on the sources of the reforms. That is, they are either reactive, the result of discrete events, shocks or general distress in the financial sector, as in the case of Nigeria in the Structural Adjustment Programme (SAP) era, or they are proactive, to avoid any future systemic disruptions, as in Nigeria in 2004. Also important are the scope (how varied and wide the reforms were), the type (interest rate controls, supervisory allocation of credit to various sectors or recapitalization of financial institutions), and the timing and appropriate sequencing or ordering of the reforms. The existence of an independent, determined, well respected and competent supervisory and regulatory body is also significant. Additionally, the general socio-political, institutional and legal frameworks must be taken into consideration (Brownbridge and Kirkpatrick 2000).

Financial liberalization under the World Bank-sponsored SAP in African countries in the late 1980s to 1990s suggests that reforms did not produce the expected results. The problems were manifold: a weak private sector; a dearth of information about the creditworthiness of borrowers; problems enforcing contracts, leading to an increased risk of loan default; huge government deficits usually funded by the financial sector; and high inflation, interest and exchange rates (World Bank 1994, Ikhide and Alawode 2001, Mwega 2002, Senbet and Otchere 2006).

As a result, the government still remains the largest borrower, crowding out the private sector and limiting the effects of interest rate liberalization (World Bank 1994, Mwega 2002, Beck *et al.* 2005). In particular, Brownbridge and Harvey (1998) and Mwega (2002), in separate studies on specific African economies, found that reforms were undertaken in the context of macroeconomic instability, persistent market failures and weak supervision. The World Bank noted in 1989 that 'Successful sequencing for financial liberalization requires achievement of macroeconomic stability [control of inflation] and fiscal discipline [reduction of fiscal deficit] in addition to improved legal, accounting and regulatory systems for the financial sector; a tax system that does not discriminate against the sector; and care of sequencing, for example such that capital inflows from liberalization do not offset macroeconomic stability' (World Bank 1989). In particular, Ikhide and Alawode (2001) emphasize the need for financial repairs before reforms, and that reforms should take place within a stable macroeconomic environment. Dornbusch and Reynoso (1993) advise returning to core macroeconomic fundamentals, such as realistic exchange rates, balanced budgets and a favourable economic climate. Chapple (1990) suggests reducing fiscal deficits, and then liberalizing, first, the financial system and, then, the trade and capital accounts. Similarly, Villanueva and Mirakhor (1990) suggest that 'only countries that can boast of macro-stability plus adequate bank supervision should proceed directly with financial liberalization'. Emenuga (2002) notes that 'financial sector reform should start late in the adjustment timetable.'

In addition, various studies suggest that financial liberalization, usually defined by an increase in real interest rates, does not achieve the intended objective because private savings are not sensitive to interest rates (Nissanke *et al.* 1995, Mwega 2002). However, even if they were, it would guarantee neither investment nor economic growth unless the savings were channelled into productive activities (Emenuga 2002). But, measuring the effects of financial reforms is problematic, since it is all but impossible to separate the effect of such reforms from others taking place in the economy simultaneously. Additionally, the dearth of data from the pre-reform years makes it difficult to measure their long-term impact.

A further consideration is that, if reforms are forced on an economy by external multi-lateral or donor institutions as a pre-condition for injecting funds into that economy, they will fail. This is because they are seen as an extension of imperialist rule, lacking local legitimacy (Lipumba 1994, Mwega 2002). Such reforms are seen as a means – to be reversed as soon as possible– of obtaining foreign aid. In such instances, financial reforms will lead to negative interest rates and, with them, a reversal in economic growth. In Sierra Leone, for instance, the impact was a decline in real interest rates coupled with an increase in inflation rates. This was the result of wider macroeconomic instability occasioned by export product supply shocks. However, improved economic growth was experienced (–0.5 per cent to 3.2 per cent) due to increased foreign direct investment in the form of loans and grants as reforms were implemented with the aim of accessing foreign aid.

As a minimum, therefore, an efficient and well developed financial system, as practised in the US and Europe, should have the following characteristics: monetization of the economy; development of a commercial banking system with an independent central bank; development of other financial intermediaries (including the stock market, pensions, mortgages); and integration of the formal and informal financial markets (ADB 1994). A breakdown of initiatives for economies in sub-Saharan Africa would include the following aims: develop the quality of financial markets by strengthening bank balance sheets and capital ratios; introduce innovative financial instruments; improve competition in the banking sector by privatization and encouraging foreign ownership; develop primary and secondary markets for t-bills and government stock; develop capital markets; encourage real time-based payment systems; encourage specialized banks and other financial institutions to fill specific niches and improve regulatory capacity.

The Central Bank of Nigeria (CBN) appears to have been successful in developing a viable commercial banking system up to the 1980s. However, these nascent successes appear to have been challenged in the 1990s, and what remains to be seen is whether the CBN will be able to continue to act as a determined and effective regulator. The integration of both the formal and informal financial markets is probably a more deep-seated and cultural issue that transcends the financial sector and is a reflection of the state of the economy.

Therefore, the state has a role to play in financial sector reforms in developing economies, both in designing and sequencing reforms and in integrating the formal and informal sectors. These must be based on the peculiarities in each economy and the extent of market failures, macroeconomic instability and the size of the informal sector. In other words, there is limited benefit from the one-size-fits-all programme defined by an external agency, which is often proposed by the World Bank and the IMF (Mwega 2002). Appropriate intervention policies will depend on the cause and the context of each country's experiences (Hawkins 1999). For example, for successful financial sector reforms in Indonesia (and other East Asian countries) the issue of corporate debt restructuring, bankruptcy procedures and bank ownership structure had to be addressed (Hawkins 1999, Djiwandono 2000). Additionally, the focus was more on recapitalizing and restructuring than on other forms of liberalization. For this reason, Senbet and Otchere (2006) note that the multiple functions of the financial system need to be taken into consideration before reforms are implemented, in the process emphasizing the role of the stock market. However, they suggest that the mere opening of a stock exchange does not in itself lead to economic growth.

Reforms in Anglophone West Africa

Reforms undertaken in the SAP and post-SAP eras in Nigeria between 1986 and 1994 and between 1997 and 2001, for example, were undertaken in the absence of fiscal reforms, resulting in huge deficits. This led to various policy reversals, including re-purchasing government shares in recently privatized banks, setting up parallel exchange rate regimes and reintroducing interest rate controls one year and deregulating again the next. Moreover, financial liberalization did not achieve its objective of market-driven interest rates. Although the economy grew from –2.7 per cent to 5 per cent over the period, measures of financial liberalization and deepening grew worse. Moreover, real deposit rates, real savings, and the rate of inflation efficiency and depth in financial intermediation, and credit flow to the private sector declined over the same period. The growth in real GDP in the 1990s cannot, therefore, be attributed to financial reforms (Ikhide and Alawode 2001, Emenuga 2002, Ayadi and Hyman 2006). On the other hand, it has also been shown that reforms in the 1990s gave birth to new sources of risks. These included greater competition leading to slimmer margins, the entry of new banks without the necessary expertise to manage risks in a liberalized environment, greater incidences of fraud, and the risks arising from foreign exchange-denominated transactions, such as lending in foreign currency and contracting foreign exchange liabilities.

As a result, part of the need for the recent reforms in Nigeria (from 2004 to date) was the perception that small banks were too vulnerable to large defaults, and too prone to unaccountability and corruption. Recent experience in Nigeria suggests the fallacy of this hypothesis and the absence of any positive evidence to support this size-based argument for banks.

However, for Ghana, in the SAP period between 1983 and 1990, real GDP grew from 3 per cent to 5.6 per cent, with increased credit to the private sector and gradual macroeconomic stability. In the same period, the ratio of money supply to GDP declined from 17 per cent to 15.5 per cent. This contrasts with Nigeria, where reforms were implemented hastily and were 'partial in scope, destitute of other concomitant adjustment measures, and inconsistent'. Emenuga (2002) suggests that the positive impact experienced in Ghana was due to consistency in implementation, which was properly paced alongside other structural reforms.

For Sierra Leone, the impact was a decline in real interest rates, coupled with higher inflation and a decline in financial deepening. This was the result of wider macroeconomic instability occasioned by export product supply shocks. As with the reforms in Nigeria, the process was too slow to achieve the desired result.

In spite of similar socio-political and economic environments, the varied results obtained from reforms can be attributed to the speed and scope of implementation, together with associated policies.

Reforms in Asia: Indonesia and India

Unlike the West African countries, the reforms in Malaysia, Thailand and Indonesia (1997–9) were reactive in nature and born out of the necessity of reviving the financial system (and indeed the economy, which had been thrown into crisis as a result of external currency shocks) due to both the prevailing crisis in Asian markets and internal weaknesses in the economy (Djiwandono 1999, Hawkins 1999). To cushion the after-effects of distress, asset management companies and deposit insurance corporations were formed.

The major internal weaknesses in Indonesia were the size of corporate debt and a weak banking sector that was largely managed and owned by the corporate world. Indonesia was the worst hit, and also had the highest rate of corporate debt-to-equity ratio. Even after previous reforms, the banking sector could not support increased financial intermediation, as the small – but healthy – banks could not finance major lenders, and the large – but weak – banks had internal structural weaknesses on which to focus. This suggests that banks are unable to perform their financial intermediary role effectively in the absence of an ability to perform other functions such as sharing risk, providing liquidity, promoting governance, promoting contractual efficiency, and facilitating global integration (Senbet and Otchere 2006). Recapitalization and restructuring were, therefore, seen as means of driving financial reforms in order to avert further economic crisis. Unlike Nigeria in 2004, recapitalization in Indonesia arose out of systemic distress and was carried out in several planned stages. In addition, bank restructuring and recapitalization was a complex and expensive process as it was mostly funded by government securities.

For India, the need for the 1994 reforms was born of a wider need for economic growth and competitiveness in international markets. Reforms were part of a comprehensive set of structural and economic changes aimed at enhancing productivity and efficiency and increasing international competitiveness. Reforms and restructuring in India were long overdue because the operational efficiency of banks, characterized by a low capital base, low profitability and a high proportion of non-performing loans, was in decline.

Restructuring was designed to remove the external constraints bearing on the profitability of the banks, improve their financial health by introducing appropriate prudential norms and strengthen the financial system (including improving the competitiveness of the banking system).

Reforms in India were similar to those in other Asian countries. Recapitalization of nationalized banks was for the most part implemented through the sale of government bonds and the investment of recapitalized funds in government securities in different phases and tiers. Issuing share capital reduced government stakes in the banks.

Additionally, interest rates were deregulated in 1997–8. New banks, including branches of foreign banks, were allowed into the economy. Competition gave rise to a range of para-banking activities, including leasing, merchant banking and mutual funds. Increased banking supervision with well-defined ratios and strategies for monitoring and measuring banks' capabilities (CAMELS and CACs) was also put in place.

Summary

Unlike the Asian and the West African countries, where the systemic reforms were often made in reaction to crises and the impetus for the reforms was clear, the regulatory authorities confirmed that the Nigerian banking system was sound and that the nation was witnessing increased foreign direct investment. Consequently, the 2004 reforms came as a shock to the financial system, so much so that even some members of the CBN board were unaware of the details until they were announced on 4 July 2004 by the governor, Professor Chukwuma Charles Soludo.

Moreover, not only had the economy witnessed several previous attempts at banking sector reforms, which had met with mixed success, but the new governor, a macroeconomist and author, was himself aware of their limited efficacy.

Most evidence suggests that the *ex-ante* case for aggressive, consolidation-centred banking reform in Nigeria was either weak or non-existent.

Although the reform of the banking sector was identified, *ex-post*, as a possible step to increased efficiency in the level of banking intermediation in Nigeria (Hesse 2007), the available evidence shows, at best, a positive association between increased concentration and lower interest spreads, which cannot be objectively attributed to the banking reforms.

Indeed, evidence from economic history suggests that other factors besides rationalizations led to the 2005 banking sector reforms.

These extraneous factors will be examined in subsequent chapters.

1.4 The soul of the nation: the 'Big Four' experience

Upon assumption of office in 1999, the Obasanjo administration appointed a new governor of the Central Bank of Nigeria immediately. Before his appointment, Chief Joseph Sanusi had been managing director of the nation's largest two banks: United Bank for Africa (1990–2) and First Bank of Nigeria (1993–8). Before that he had been the deputy governor of the CBN, in charge of monetary and banking policy (1989–90).

His tenure at some of the 'Big Four' banks, including the United Bank for Africa (UBA), was instrumental to his understanding of the banking system and the inner workings of banks in Nigeria. For most of the two decades from the 1970s to the early 1990s, the Nigerian banking sector had been dominated by four large banks: First Bank of Nigeria (formerly Standard Bank); United Bank for Africa; Union Bank of Nigeria (formerly Barclays Bank); and Afribank. These were some of the largest banks in West Africa.

The licensing of new privately owned banks in the early 1990s created intense competition and rivalry. Many of the 'Big Four' banks lost market share, whilst the newer banks resorted to all manner of practices, not just to win customers but also to circumvent Central Bank regulations. The need to modernize the 'Big Four' banks was aptly demonstrated by UBA, which was bought out in 1992 by private sector players led by Hakeem Bello-Osagie, the *de facto* crown prince. Investigations into the bank's operations revealed a link between the bankers and the ruling military class. When the government decided to sell its shares in UBA, a buyout team led by Bello-Osagie took management control of day-to-day operations although they only owned 446,250 shares as a direct shareholding (*UBA Annual Report and Accounts 2002*). They were even more powerful than the South African company, Stanbic Nominees, which held about 744 million shares, or about 44 per cent of the bank's entire share capital.

For 10 years from 1992, the management of the UBA was controlled by Bello-Osagie and his proxies. However, in early 2002, following regulatory investigations, a change of management was secured by the Central Bank. This change, in itself, carried the seeds of a large-scale merger three years later.

These investigations, together with other ongoing investigations, suggested the prevalence of sharp practice in the nation's banking sector. It was common for banks to pretend that they wanted to import goods from overseas in order to obtain dollars from the CBN at a cheap rate, only to sell them on the 'black' or parallel market at a higher price. One of the Nigerian banks was, for instance, indicted for setting up a non-bank finance company, as a cover for its illegal activities. Most of the foreign exchange obtained was simply sold to this non-bank finance company – a practice popularly known as round-tripping and a major criminal offence. Following extensive investigations, the CBN accepted the recommendation of a probe panel that a fine of ₦1 billion (US$8.5million) be imposed on the offending bank. Other recommendations included the enforced removal of the bank's chairman. The CBN investigation into the bank was ordered by the presidency following a complaint that the US Treasury had been short-changed in a fraudulent transaction, leading to a loss of US$350,000. The Nigerian government was concerned to have Nigeria's name removed from the list of nations unwilling to cooperate in the fight against money laundering and other financial crimes, and, predictably, it took very decisive action.

But, as well as the outcome of the investigation into large Nigerian banks by the Central Bank, led by Chief Sanusi, two other conclusions emerged: the banking sector was rife with malpractice; and, more importantly, the CBN itself needed to be reformed.

2
The Nigerian Banking System: The Case for Reforms

2.1 Introduction

In Nigeria, the structure of the banking industry has not altered significantly in over two decades, despite considerable alteration in the banks' volatile performance and conduct during this period.

One of the oldest arguments in industrial economics is whether to adopt the structure–conduct–performance paradigm or the performance–conduct–structure paradigm. In its simplest form, the latter argues that the performance of any industry will shake out the weak players and impact on their conduct and market behaviour, thereby determining the market structure.

This chapter attempts to explain the sources of growth and its key drivers. It will also ask why banking blossomed at the expense of other sectors, and why the structure did not change. I will also examine issues such as corruption and foreign exchange abuses.

2.2 The military, corruption and the banking sector

Based on estimates from the World Bank[1] and the Economic and Financial Crimes Commission (EFCC),[2] an estimated US$300 billion to US$400 billion was stolen from the nation's oil revenues following independence. This figure is realistic, given that by September 2006, within three years of its establishment, the EFCC had recovered over US$5 billion, almost all of it from cronies, associates and relatives of government functionaries and public officers who had served the country in the preceding ten years.[3]

Given that the military had ruled the country for 30 years, the bulk of this looting had been perpetrated by them. Though inconclusive, inductive evidence further supports the reasonableness of the US$400 billion figure. For instance, an estimated 24 per cent of the shareholding of one of West Africa's largest companies was linked by the EFCC to the son of a former military head of state. A parallel case was the celebrated arrest of a former governor of Lagos State and retired army brigadier, who was investigated and prosecuted between 2005 and 2006 in connection with the channelling of some of the estimated US$13 billion that was looted and stashed abroad by the late head of state, General Sani Abacha.

In contrast to similar oil-rich countries, such as Indonesia, Nigeria had simply squandered the money it made from selling its oil resources. A significant amount of these funds – an estimated US$280 billion between the early 1980s and 2000 – had flowed through the Nigerian banking system.

Though no documented proof exists for the calculation, experts such as Michael Peel, an associate of Chatham House's African Programme, suggest that crude oil estimated to be worth US$3.5 million or more is stolen each day from the Niger Delta by conspiracies of government officials, militia, the military, and innocent-looking expatriates, with the proceeds being laundered through the banking system. Even though most of the proceeds of Nigeria's legitimate oil sales were held in European and US banks, the government borrowed heavily against future oil revenues, and most of the borrowed money was converted into the local currency before being wired out of the country again. In all instances, Nigerian banks earned residual income from these transactions even though little value was created in the domestic economy.

Under military rule, the reckless spending of petrodollars led to increased business for the banks, including the government funds that were kept with them and later siphoned abroad to pay phoney companies for large-scale, bloated projects. Over the last few months of the transitional military regime, before Mr Obasanjo assumed power for the second time, Nigeria's foreign-exchange reserves shrank from over US$6 billion at the end of 1998 to US$4 billion at the end of March 1999, confirming the large-scale perception of the link between the military rulers and extravagant spending. At the end of the banking consolidation exercise, about ₦350 billion (US$3 billion) in additional equity had been injected into the banks as fresh capital from both local and foreign investors, including public officers. Though granular data is not available, a good proportion of it was from diverted public funds, as evidenced by the purchase of over 3 million units of banking stock (valued at approximately US$700,000) by a serving inspector-general of police who was tried for stealing about ₦17 billion (US$144 million) of public funds.

The logic for the campaign against money laundering was captured in the EFCC chairman's statement in a lecture at the Financial Institutions Training Centre (Ribadu 2006a): 'We are working to reduce corruption in the country. If we clean the banking sector, we may have helped to clean other sectors.'

The stench in the Nigerian banking sector, as with many other developing countries, had been widely recognized prior to 2004, but the tenacity of the EFCC and the determination of the head of the anti-sleaze organization had established the quantity of stolen funds and mapped the route along which the money flowed. An elite force with a special mission to battle the dark side of the banking and financial system, the EFCC had been modelled as a cross between the Metropolitan Police anti-fraud squad and the Secret Service, but with the target of policing economic and financial crimes. Globally, including in Nigeria, financial crimes are treated separately from others, such as white-collar crimes because modern technology has made it easier to perpetrate them without detection by the regular police. Consequently, many governments have created specialist units for policing financial crime. In Nigeria, the final straw that led the Obasanjo administration to set up the EFCC was threefold. First, increasing pressures from the US, following the US Secret Service investigations that had been forwarded to the Central Bank of Nigeria leading to indictment of a major Nigerian bank. Secondly, the wish to facilitate Nigeria's removal from the Financial Action Task Force's list of non-cooperating countries and territories; and, thirdly, the need to repair the international community's perception of Nigeria, which had been damaged by an avalanche of stories of both true and fictitious financial crimes.

These financial crimes occurred mainly in three forms: procurement-related corruption, which resulted in contract inflation, non-existent or uncompleted contracts, and kickbacks; stealing or outright diversion of public funds; and other conflicts of interest. The proceeds of corruption almost always had to pass through the banks, with a few banks conniving with the looters to launder their stolen funds. Money-laundering, often referred to as the world's third-largest business, was probably becoming a fast-growing industry in Nigeria. Classified into three layers – placing, layering and integration (hide, move and invest) – Nigeria's banking laws made it easier for stolen loot to be wired out of the country through spurious trade finance transactions and allied outward money-laundering. While it was cumbersome to track the integrity of outward transfers, it was easier to track inward ones.

The culpability of Nigerian banks in outward money-laundering of looted public funds was also demonstrated in the celebrated case of the EFCC versus Tafa Balogun, in which the latter, a former inspector-general of police, was charged with money-laundering. Outward money-laundering was remarkably easy for an import-dependent country such as Nigeria, which could justify phoney payments to bogus or non-existent foreign companies for spurious or overinflated transactions in foreign currency.

These outward transfers also included payment for over-valued or unnecessary technical and management fees, questionable intellectual property acquisition, and advance fees for several white elephant projects that were 'kickbacked' to the overseas account of the government official concerned. Corruption had been rife in Nigeria since the civil war of 1966, but became worse with the return to democratic rule in 1979.

In 1979, when the first Obasanjo administration handed over power to the civilian regime of Shehu Usman Shagari, the nation's sovereign debt was US$3.2 billion (*This Day*, 12 August 2006), a substantial increase over the less than US$500 million debt that had prevailed up till the end of 1976. However, between 1977 and 1979, with the downturn in Nigerian oil sales after the Arab oil embargo at the same time as the Western banks were awash with liquidity from the glut of petrodollars, external borrowing became an easy option for the government. Consequently, a naïve administration continued the aggressive spending of the military era on infrastructure development. Internal evidence from Chief Falegan, a member of the negotiating team for Nigeria's jumbo loans during the Obasanjo regime, suggests that the Nigerian delegations to the loan negotiation meetings in Europe and America often had weak negotiating skills and were in a relatively disadvantaged position compared with their Western counterparts. Effectively, the Obasanjo government ended up taking these, sometimes avoidable, loans at ridiculous rates. During this period Nigerian banks also expanded rapidly, as they were often the disbursing agents for the loans.

Following the precedent set by the Obasanjo military administration, the Shagari civilian administration, under the new wave of logic that Nigeria was 'under-borrowed', coupled with the illusion of a resurgent oil boom in early 1980, increased planned expenditure from ₦8.3 billion to ₦23.7 billion. By 1985, the year that General Babangida took over government, the debt stock had risen to US$18.5 billion. By 2005 it had risen to an all-time high of US$35 billion. After paying more than US$43 billion in the period 1967–2005 (*ThisDay,* 13 March 2005) in interest and penalties for default, the country still owed US$35 billion in early 2005. Based on statistics provided by the Debt Management Office (DMO), Nigeria's external debt rose from US$32.9 billion in December 2003 to US$34 billion in 2004. Compound interest was part of the cause of this staggering debt profile. Eighty-five per cent of the US$35 billion was owed to the Paris Club of creditors from the world's richest countries and 7–8 per cent was owed to multilateral institutions, including the World Bank and IMF.

Overall, Nigeria's debt profile was the result of years of brazen accumulation of capital expenditure on poorly appraised white elephant projects, especially in the 1980s, most of the debts having been accumulated under the Obasanjo and Shagari regimes between 1976 and 1983. However, the problem with the first Obasanjo regime and the Shagari regime which followed it (and, indeed, the Babangida regime of 1985–93) was not just that the country borrowed a lot of money, which mostly ended up in private pockets through kickbacks and abandoned projects, but that there was a preponderance of ill-qualified people in charge of the nation's finances.

The Babangida administration, in contrast, appeared intellectually top-heavy, even though it had rather an odd mix of leaders in the Ministry of Finance, through which CBN reported at that time. With a senior lecturer in sociology as minister of finance, and an accountant as governor of the CBN, the nation's economy and banking sector lost direction. With the benefit of hindsight, it was overly optimistic – if not impossible – to expect a sociologist and a manufacturing accountant, no matter how well intentioned, to effectively control macroeconomic variables in a highly inflationary and rapidly expanding economy.

With such a combination of non-professionals, who did not understand the delicate nuances and intrigues of the international financial community and were not respected by the banking community on Broad Street, the stage was set for a systematic rape of the nation's economic resources by the military dictators and, worse still, by the new-generation bankers who had worked professionally in the US and knew how to evade detection.

According to the director of the Debt Management Office, only 2 per cent of loan-based projects came to fruition: 60 per cent were registered as totally failed; 15 per cent as marginally functional; and 10 per cent as never even beginning. And yet 100 per cent of the funds passed through the banks, with the result that the banking sector raced ahead of the real sector. Essentially, only the European countries and the Nigerian banks benefited from the borrowing binge, resulting in fast growth for the Nigerian banks. But every insider knew that the source of this growth was external, that it was unsustainable and that it was only a matter of time before the crisis that was beginning to hit the real, or manufacturing, sector would descend on the 'glamorous' banking sector in one fell swoop.

The jumbo loans, multiple debt negotiations, and multi-currency project financing deals for steel and river basin development projects (most of which never saw the light of day) also fuelled the emergence of a new generation of banks to support these 'quick' projects – merchant banks. Many of these merchant banks were one-location shadows or skeletons of the London investment banks. With limited overheads, the commercial and merchant banks collected extravagant upfront 'arrangement fees' for projects that never took off.

Corruption had several ways of artificially bloating the income and profitability of the Nigerian banking sector. The first was that corrupt money often had to be laundered through several transactions, as compared with, say, a single direct-wire transfer for remittance of legitimate funds. For each transaction, the bank imposed charges, thereby bloating the bank's income from multiple or repeated transaction fees. The second was that corruption often goes hand in hand with 'settling', 'motivating', 'gratifying' or 'compensating' the bankers who 'facilitate' the transaction, inadvertently creating a crop of wealthy bankers who were largely benefactors of an opaque payments system. Most banks took advantage of the preponderance of irregular deals to charge excessive fees on 'irregular' or otherwise illegitimate transactions, knowing fully well that the principal or client was unlikely to complain, least of all to the regulatory authorities. The third was the inflated amount spent on imports. Most imports during the 1980s did not contribute in real terms to the economy. According to His Royal Highness, Oba Oladele Olashore, a former managing director of both First Bank and Afribank (Ribadu 2006b), the country failed to receive as much as 25 per cent of the value of her huge expenditure on imports. This suggests that banks were making artificial fee incomes and commissions on bogus import finance and trade transactions. Leading commentators on the administration and management of the Nigerian debt are near-unanimous in concluding that a significant portion of the nation's loans ended up back in the originating Western countries. The bulk of these missing funds were repatriated either as proceeds from kickbacks, bloated commissions, outright misappropriations, or sheer loot and invariably through fund transfers effected from or through Nigerian banks.

With a weak regulatory capacity to monitor these abuses, one major setback caused by the Babangida administration to the nation's financial system was the proliferation of banking licences. Two possible reasons could be suggested for the widespread issue of these licences by the centralized regime of Babangida (with a former World Bank technocrat, Dr Kalu Idika Kalu, as minister of finance). Though specious arguments were put forward about the under-banked nature of the country and the need to democratize access to credit, there were other, more subtle, considerations.

2.3 Size and structure of the Nigerian banking system

Despite key changes in the Nigerian banking industry since the 1960s, there had been little or no change in the market structure. By industry structure, we mean the key indices of the industry in its entirety, such as its contribution to the overall economy, interdependence with other industries and input–output relationships. Market structure, on the other hand, focuses on firm-level analysis, inter-firm behaviour and concentration ratios, and the basis of competition between individual market players or corporate agents (See Tables 2.1 and 2.2).

The banking industry in Nigeria, like many other industries operating in competitive conditions, has always been dominated by a handful of firms. A few banks have been extremely large, resulting in a highly skewed size distribution and a banking industry structure that was antithetical to growth. According to Sutton (2005), industry structure influences at least three main parameters.

The first is price competition, which impacts on both input and output prices. As in most industries, the nature of price competition in banking is related, though not necessarily in a causative manner, to the level of market concentration (See Figures 2.1 and 2.2). The second is the long-term investment bias of the industry players, or the incentive for any single firm to invest significantly in additional fixed asset acquisition or sunk costs. In fragmented or low-concentration industries, significant investment in capital helps a firm either to lower its average costs or to strengthen its bargaining power through economies of scale. The third is the attractiveness of the market to new players, who may invest in or acquire existing players.

According to Sutton (2005), the entry of new players can either be 'simultaneous' or 'sequential'. In Nigeria, it is envisaged that the

Table 2.1 Size of the Nigerian banking industry 1960–2007

	Financial institutions		
Year	**Commercial**	**Merchant**	**Total**
1960	12	1	13
1970	14	1	15
1971	16	1	17
1975	17	5	22
1980	20	6	26
1985	28	12	40
1990	58	49	107
1992	66	54	120
1995	64	51	115
2000*	90	0	90
2001*	90	0	90
2002	90	0	90
2003	89	0	89
2004	89	0	89
2005	25	0	25
2006	25	0	25
2007	25	0	25
2008	24	0	24

*Universal Banking came into effect in 2000/2001.
Source: Data from CBN Annual Reports, various years.

sequential entry of new players in a market-led consolidation would have more radical effects on industry and market structure than the near-simultaneous entry afforded by regulatory-driven consolidations. While no conclusive empirical modelling of the Nigerian banking industry has been published, we can borrow ideas from 'structural estimation' or 'single industry studies', given the high degree of information that exists about the banking industry, which permits a single-market study.

From a single market perspective, the Nigerian banking industry between 1960 and 2008 evolved along the structure–conduct–

Table 2.2 Banking sector indicators 2000–8

CBN banking sector indicators 2000–6									
Efficiency measures (per cent)	**2000**	**2001**	**2002**	**2003**	**2004**	**2005**	**2006**	**2007**	**2008**
Net interest margin	54.82	55.74	56.48	55.87	54.37	5.59	60.15	52.25	54.80
Yield on earnings assets	5.71	9.10	6.42	4.74	14.17	9.85	8.35	n/a	n/a
Return on assets	3.43	4.73	3.47	2.67	3.12	1.85	1.61	3.89	3.95
Return on equity	47.62	55.81	36.60	25.52	27.35	12.97	10.60	23.84	22.01
Efficiency ratio	72.53	65.96	49.60	49.02	77.03	39.97	71.43	65.90	31.77
Concentration ratio (assets)	0.41	0.39	0.39	0.39	0.39	0.44	0.51	0.40	
Earnings and profitability of banks (₦ billion)	**2000**	**2001**	**2002**	**2003**	**2004**	**2005**	**2006**	**2007**	**2008**
Interest income	197	296	386	349	412	340	339	1,178	1,787
Interest expenses	89	131	168	154	188	147	135	562	808
Net interest income	108	165	218	195	224	193	204	616	979
Non-interest income	84	117	118	161	184	159	171	577	700
Operating income	193	282	336	356	418	352	375	1,193	1,679
Operating expenses	132	186	250	282	322	290	270	786	1072
Profit before tax	60	96	86	74	96	72	108	407	607
Non-performing loans (₦ billion)	**2000**	**2001**	**2002**	**2003**	**2004**	**2005**	**2006**	**2007**	**2008**
Non-performing loans	100	126	182	236	316	356	222	388	464
Total loans	567	639	721	915	1,133	1,477	2,081	3,802	6,170
Ratio of non-performing loans to total loans	0.18	0.20	0.25	0.26	0.28	0.24	0.11	0.10	0.08

*Concentration ratios refer to 5-firm concentration ratios.
Source: CBN Annual Reports and Banking Supervision Reports, various years.

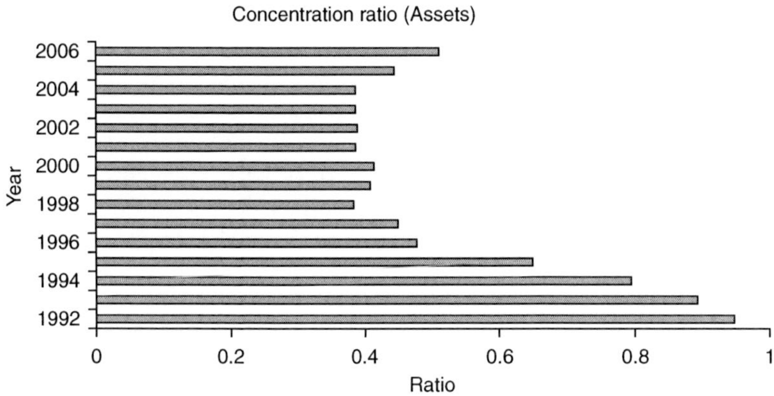

Figure 2.1 Bank concentration ratio (assets)
Source: Beck et al., pp. 597–605.

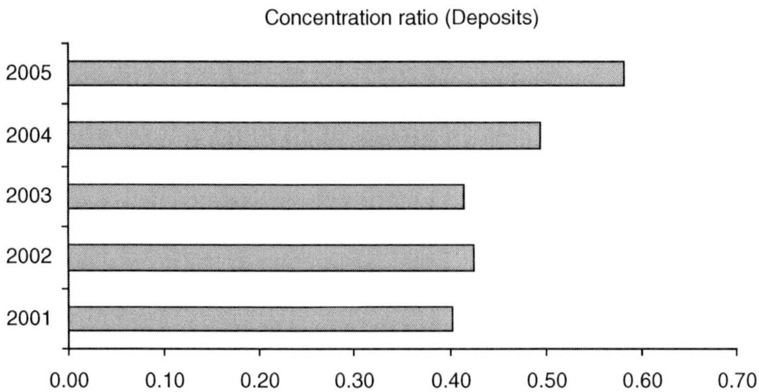

Figure 2.2 Bank concentration ratio (deposits)
Source: IFC WB Group Private Sector Resources–Concentration Ratio (Deposits). http://www.financial-indicators.org/sector_banking.php?country=NGA

performance paradigm as proposed by Bain (1956). Even though we cannot suggest a one-way causation, the pattern suggests that the structure (concentration of the industry in a few players) has always influenced the conduct or pricing behaviour of the banks, which has led to the supernormal profits or performance of the banks. While there is no documented evidence of price-fixing or formal collusion, various interviews with leading bank executives suggest that, up until the late

1990s, there was an unspoken tendency – if not an informal understanding by the 'Big Three' banks – not to engage in confrontational pricing. Consistently with the Bain theory, this, coupled with an ill-equipped regulator, led to high profits.

Predictably, these supernormal profits, which were above the cost of capital, were sustained in this high concentration market and were not eroded by the entry of new players, largely for three reasons. The first was the existence of barriers to entry into the lucrative public sector banking of government funds. The second was the economies of scale enjoyed by larger banks. The third was the 'excess' demand for banking services by a fast-growing but relatively unsophisticated population in an era of finite supply.

By 2003, however, the cumulative effect of licensing new entrants in the 1990s, some of whom had become mature players with relatively strong executive leadership, led to a fall in market concentration of assets from about 50 per cent in 1996 to between 40 and 43 per cent. Accordingly, there was an industry-wide parallel drop in interest rates and profit margins, which is consistent with most economic models.

This systemic drop in industry profitability, with a concomitant sharp rise in non- performing loans, put several of the marginal banks at risk, providing another justification for the much-advocated banking reforms.

2.4 The great foreign exchange debate: 'free funds' and the FX era

This section discusses the introduction of a dual exchange rate system in Nigeria, the import licensing regime in 1984, and the great question of whether the parallel markets and the official market exchange rates would converge. Next, I discuss the suspension of almost a quarter of the nation's banks (20 or 21 out of the 89 banks) from the CBN's official foreign exchange market in 2001, based on allegations of 'free funds'. Banks suspended included STB, Diamond Bank and FSB International, with some of the banks concerned taking the Central Bank of Nigeria to court.

Finally, we examine the argument as to whether the official exchange rate and the parallel market rate would converge, and how banks profiteered recklessly from foreign exchange (FX) arbitrage, taking advantage of lapses and weak surveillance by the regulators.

Between 1960 and 1986, Nigeria operated a fixed exchange rate system, which pegged the value of the *naira* to one or more of the international

Table 2.3 Banking performance in Nigeria: reduced returns versus increased concentration

CBN banking sector indicators 2000–8									
Efficiency measures (per cent)	**2000**	**2001**	**2002**	**2003**	**2004**	**2005**	**2006**	**2007**	**2008**
Net interest margin	54.82	55.74	56.48	55.87	54.37	5.59	60.15	52.25	54.80
Yield on earnings assets	5.71	9.10	6.42	4.74	14.17	9.85	8.35		
Return on assets	3.43	4.73	3.47	2.67	3.12	1.85	1.61	3.89	3.95
Return on equity	47.62	55.81	36.60	25.52	27.35	12.97	10.60	23.84	22.01
Efficiency ratio	72.53	65.96	49.60	49.02	77.03	39.97	71.43	65.90	31.77
Concentration ratio (assets)	0.41	0.39	0.39	0.39	0.39	0.44	0.51	0.40	
Concentration ratio (deposits)		0.40	0.43	0.42	0.50	0.58			
Earnings and profitability of banks (₦ billion)	**2000**	**2001**	**2002**	**2003**	**2004**	**2005**	**2006**	**2007**	**2008**
Interest income	197	296	386	349	412	340	339	1,178	1,787
Interest expenses	89	131	168	154	188	147	135	562	808
Net interest income	108	165	218	195	224	193	204	616	979
Non-interest income	84	117	118	161	184	159	171	577	700
Operating income	193	282	336	356	418	352	375	1,193	1,679
Operating expenses	132	186	250	282	322	290	270	786	1,072
Profit before tax	60	96	86	74	96	72	108	407	607
Non-performing loans (₦ billion)	**2000**	**2001**	**2002**	**2003**	**2004**	**2005**	**2006**	**2007**	**2008**
Non-performing loans	100	126	182	236	316	356	222	388	464
Total loans	567	639	721	915	1,133	1,477	2,081	3,802	6,170
Ratio of non-performing loans to total loans	0.18	0.20	0.25	0.26	0.28	0.24	0.11	0.10	0.08

Source: CBN Annual Reports and Banking Supervision Reports, various years.

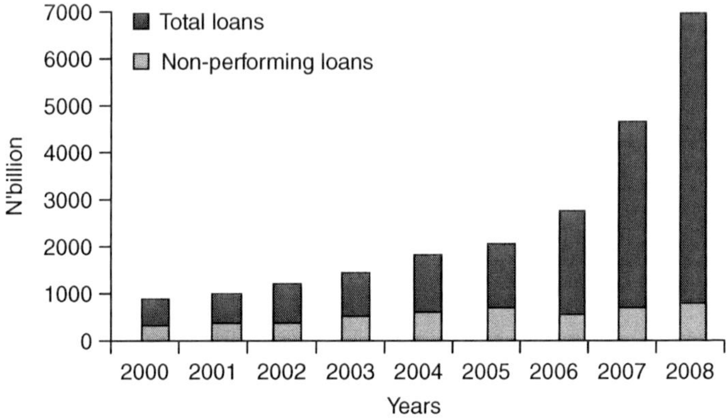

Figure 2.3 Ratio of non-performing loans to total loans
Source: Data from the CBN annual reports. Graph by the author.

currencies. During this era, there was little or no free foreign exchange 'market', as there was only a foreign exchange 'stock', and therefore no room for arbitrage or active local currency speculation. However, in the early 1980s, the collapse of world oil prices and the resulting sharp decline in oil export revenues led to negative trends in economic growth, which occasioned the Economic Stabilization Act of 1982, together with its austerity measures and counter-trade policy. By 1986, when it became obvious that the short-run fiscal stabilization measures were not effective and that government revenue as a percentage of GDP had fallen from 24 per cent in 1980 to 12 per cent in 1985, the inability of the federal government to defend the fixed exchange rate of the *naira* against selected international currencies in the face of declining foreign exchange reserves was also obvious. Two main options were open to the Nigerian government. The first was to accept the IMF Structural Adjustment Facility, including its stringent terms and conditions. The second was to reject it but adopt a variant of the traditional structural adjustment programme (SAP), to be developed and implemented domestically.

The objectives of the SAP, which was the option eventually chosen, were to:

- restructure and diversify the productive base of the economy so as to reduce dependency on the oil sector and imports;
- achieve fiscal and balance of payments viability over the medium term; and
- promote non-inflationary economic growth.

Achieving these objectives hinged on a number of policies (Nnanna), which included:

- setting up a Second-Tier Foreign Exchange Market (SFEM) as a mechanism for a realistic exchange rate and, consequently, the alteration of relative prices to enhance efficiency in resource allocation;
- further rationalization and restructuring of tariffs in order to aid industrial diversification;
- liberalization of the external trade and payments system, which meant the removal of price, trade and exchange controls;
- elimination of price controls and commodity boards;
- deregulation of interest rates; and
- rationalization and restructuring of public sector enterprises and the overhaul of the public sector.

The deregulation of the foreign exchange market by the introduction of SFEM in 1986 led to a parallel market because the quantity of foreign exchange sold by the CBN in the official market was inadequate for all end users. Though the CBN introduced several measures intended to stabilize and ease the availability of foreign currency (such as designating branches of the central bank to sell foreign exchange to eligible importers), there was a fundamental question as to whether there would be any likely convergence[4] of the exchange rate.

The absence of a convergence augured two things for the banks. The first was that the gap between the official rate and the parallel or black market rates meant that banks, in an era of porous monitoring, could make economic rent by arbitraging foreign currency between the two markets and earn an undisclosed parallel market premium. The second was that, in an import-dependent economy, where there was a standing parallel market and an unmet demand for foreign currency, deposit money banks could make supernormal profits by trading mainly in foreign exchange, without concentrating on asset creation or developing their credit analysis competencies.

Needless to say, the total number of banks in the country increased almost threefold, from 40 in 1985 to 107 in 1990. Predictably, the performances of the banks also increased significantly after 1986, compared with their profit margin in the 1970s and early 1980s. In the early 1970s, banking was not the money-spinner it was to become in the 1980s and 1990s. This was confirmed in a statement by a former chairman and chief executive of one of the leading banks in Nigeria in the 1970s and 1980s, Gamaliel Onosode, who said that that there were no rich bankers in his generation. With the exchange rate at par with sterling and, at the time, stronger than the dollar, there was no possible arbitrage or artificial income to be made by playing the currency markets. If anything, taking an option on the *naira* would most certainly have been an out-of-the-money bet, or what bankers call an unattractive bet.

Additionally, with the collapse of the manufacturing industries in the 1980s due to worsening electricity problems and a gradual devaluation of the *naira*, there was a tectonic shift in power in the economy from manufacturers to traders. In the 1970s, when the government had an import substitution policy and provided fiscal incentives for manufacturing, being the chief executive of a large manufacturing conglomerate was probably the most enviable position in the organized private sector. Bankers were at the beck and call of manufacturers. Besides, the country had just emerged from the civil war and there was a deliberate policy to finance growth in manufacturing. SFEM changed all that.

SFEM was the second-tier foreign exchange market. The Foreign Exchange (Monitoring and Miscellaneous Provision) Decree No. 17 of 1995 fully established the autonomous foreign exchange market (AFEM) and repealed the Exchange Control Act of 1962 and the Exchange Control (Anti-Sabotage) Decree 19. The new decree also allowed foreign investors to repatriate their capital, profits or dividends – less tax – and to open domiciliary accounts. In 1997 and 1998, the exchange rate system was further liberalized and a dual mechanism was instituted. Again, the dual exchange rate system created a rent-seeking economy, in which bankers and cronies of government officials abused the system by arbitraging foreign exchange. Although all official transactions (except those approved by the president) were supposed to be pegged at the official rate, several imperfections still existed. This, coupled with the marked volatility in the exchange rate of the *naira*, caused the government to replace the AFEM with the Inter-bank Foreign Exchange Market (IFEM) in October 1999. Under the new system, oil companies were allowed to place their foreign exchange funds with deposit-taking commercial banks, in contrast to the AFEM policy, which had specified that such funds must be lodged with the CBN.

The creation of an active market in foreign exchange for commercial banks outside the 'official' AFEM sources unwittingly led to the creation of a 'free funds' market. Technically, free funds are foreign exchange funds sourced from non-CBN sources outside the official CBN market. They are not subject to any officially stated exchange rate band, and hence they are not officially fully disclosed. Since these funds were not purchased from the CBN, but from the 'free' or 'unrestricted' foreign currency inflows and cash holdings of companies, banks and individuals, many banks simply did not fully disclose the amount traded and the applicable exchange rate. Additionally, the scarce foreign exchange in the 'free funds' market traded at a premium, with many bank treasurers asking for and collecting brokerage fees from willing buyers who generally issued a separate cheque for the undocumented brokerage, or wired the commission to a secret or offshore 'nostro' account, which was never disclosed. Ultimately, the young treasurers and managing directors in many banks became the *grands nouveaux riches*, leading to the emergence of a new wealthy class who bought choice property in rural England, reminiscent of the old wealth of the immediate post-colonial era of the 1960s. In reality, what was called 'free funds' was usually foreign exchange obtained from the CBN at reduced IFEM rates for specific customers and specific purposes, and then sold at a premium on the parallel markets. This was often done through a sister company of the bank, which applied for the funds and then diverted them for other purposes.

Many bank treasurers made a fortune out of this, ostensibly on the pretext of making money for the banks employing them. As many of these opaque transactions were recorded in third party books, it was difficult for the banks to know how much the expediter, in this case the treasurer, made for himself, how much he gave to the counterpart as brokerage, and how much was the true net income made for the bank. By mid-2001, however, delays in the settlement and delivery of foreign exchange, and a major foreign exchange loss in the 'free funds' market by the daughter of a former federal police chief and chair of the National Drug Law Enforcement Agency, led to the indictment of First City Merchant Bank (FCMB) and its subsidiary, City Securities Limited. Sanctioned by CBN, FCMB subsequently challenged the indictment and filed a lawsuit in November 2001 in the High Court of Lagos State seeking to restrain several commercial banks from making any representations to CBN and related agencies about FCMB's involvement in any 'free fund' transactions related to the plaintiffs.

Without prejudice to the innocence or guilt of the parties involved, the case afforded the CBN the opportunity to understand the process by which commercial banks transacted foreign exchange business in Nigeria – a process they had been unaware of, or had simply turned a blind eye to. Following detailed investigations, the CBN suspended 21 of the 95 banks from the foreign exchange market in April 2001 for allegedly engaging in foreign exchange malpractices, which included inter-bank 'round-tripping'. While 'free funds' were not necessarily illegal (if accurately disclosed), 'round-tripping' certainly was.

Two of the 21 suspended banks, Diamond Bank and NAL Bank, had formerly been managed by people now on the board of the CBN. Private sector bank chiefs had a hands-on approach to bank supervision. They knew the dirty tricks of avoidance, non-compliance and outright violation of banking regulations, and knew how to investigate them. Unsurprisingly, the two banks – Diamond Bank and FSB International – filed individual suits at the Federal High Court seeking an injunction to restrain the CBN from implementing the sanctions. Although the injunction was granted, it was glaringly obvious that internal controls at both the commercial banks and the Central Bank were weak. It was also obvious that the CBN's surveillance capacity needed to be strengthened in the short term, and that banking sector reform was needed in the medium term.

3
Restructuring the Regulator

3.1 Background

Before 1983, the Nigerian financial system was, or appeared to be, sound and stable. However, as the oil boom declined and foreign debt increased (largely due to the poor management of the oil earnings in the 1970s), the military regime succumbed to pressure from the IMF and the World Bank, under its recommended Structural Adjustment Programme (SAP), to correct the problem of 'an inadequate number of licensed banks' (Stein *et al.* 2002). Unfortunately, no deliberate strategy was employed to strengthen the supervisory capacity of the Central Bank of Nigeria (CBN). This conceptually plausible but contextually naïve theory of the World Bank resulted in the military regimes in Nigeria selectively pursuing financial liberalization measures while creating moral hazards through their numerous agents in the financial system.

Accordingly, the Central Bank, which was the only banking regulator before the establishment of the Nigerian Deposit Insurance Corporation (NDIC), was overwhelmed by the task of supervising an increasing number of banks while simultaneously contending with interference in its day-to-day operations from politicians and military rulers.

In this chapter, we will examine the imperative for restructuring the regulator in Nigeria's political economy.

3.2 The origins of the regulatory challenge

In most free market economies, the efficiency of the reserve bank (as the central bank is called in some countries, such as the United States) and the success of any monetary policy agenda it pursues are largely interwoven. According to the Central Bank Act, 1958, its mandate was:

- issuing the legal tender currency;
- maintaining external reserves to safeguard the international value of the currency;
- promoting monetary stability and a sound financial system; and
- acting as banker and financial adviser to the federal government.

After the inception of the CBN in 1959, the central bank adopted a fixed parity exchange rate regime between sterling and the *naira*. This exchange rate policy continued until 1967, when the value of the *naira* was pegged to the dollar following the devaluation of sterling.

After several oscillations between the US dollar and sterling, the *naira* was pegged to a basket of the currencies of the country's 12 major trading partners, including the UK and the US. The oil boom of the 1970s created an impetus for development. Accordingly, control of monetary aggregates and the use of monetary policy to check fiscal excesses and achieve sub-sectoral economic objectives became the focus. As most of the nation's revenue was the result of the windfall from crude oil exports and not from internally generated revenue (for instance, taxes), there was an increased burden on the CBN to balance the government's objective of rapid economic growth across geographic regions and specific, non-oil, sectors (including agriculture) with the need to control inflation.

This was the beginning of a regime of direct monetary control of economic aggregates to achieve sub-sectoral objectives rather than the conventional use of the all powerful rediscount rate. By the mid-1970s, credit ceilings on the deposit money of banks and prescribed sectoral credit allocations to preferred sectors, particularly agriculture and manufacturing, were key features of the new regime.

The rationale for these guidelines was ostensibly to diversify the economy by providing accessible credit to entrepreneurs and to direct the bonus revenue to sectors considered critical to rapid development, even at rates below the minimum rediscount rate. But, this preferential incentive system, which was supposedly designed to redistribute and/or achieve efficient resource allocation among all sectors of the economy (including the orderly growth of the financial markets), also sowed the seeds of a deceptive banking system and the promotion of sharp practice in the financial system.

First, the monetary authorities (and the civil servants who made the decisions) had no inkling of the behavioural impact of their decisions.

Secondly, the CBN, by such direct controls, had inadvertently imposed upon itself administrative responsibility for monitoring compliance at the *micro-level* and ensuring that those sectoral limits were adhered to. Ironically, the authors of the new policy in the Federal Ministry of Finance and the CBN itself had been too clever by half, since they had neither the quality nor the number of personnel effectively to track the compliance of the 24 commercial banks with their 770 branches. Worse still, the CBN itself, whilst having barely adequate resources to monitor the banks in question, kept changing the sectoral ratios and credit limits year after year, without planning for the increased resources it would take to run a central bank handling non-core central bank functions.

In retrospect, two facts became evident. First, the increasing burden on the CBN created a moral hazard because its officials had to monitor a system for which they were ill equipped, thereby laying the foundation for sharp practices as a result of only superficial compliance by commercial bank staff. Secondly, the ineffectiveness of these policies created a problem of adverse selection: subsequent empirical evidence revealed that the flow of credit to the preferred sectors did not meet the prescribed preset targets and failed to impact positively on investment and output in those sectors. In short, the commercial banks possessed factual information on their sectoral credit disbursements whilst the CBN lacked both the technology and the personnel to access it. The information asymmetry between the two parties created a compounded adverse market process in which neither the target sectors nor the most qualified companies or individual borrowers in that sector obtained the required credit. The skills gap in the commercial banks further compounded this problem, as they inevitably lent funds to borrowers who were most likely to default on loan repayments; the ultimate guarantor of some of those loans being the CBN itself.

In 1981, the unexpected crash in global crude oil prices turned out to be the first crisis. It revealed that neither the managers of the nation's economy nor the CBN were prepared for the challenges ahead.

3.3 The challenges before the regulator

The rot in the banking system began gradually and was exacerbated by the oil price crash of 1980. Following the banking failures of the 1950s and the indigenization decrees of 1972, the system was dominated by the 'Big Four' government-controlled banks (First Bank of Nigeria, Union Bank of Nigeria, United Bank for Africa and Afribank). Between the boom of the 1970s and the CBN being under the wing of the Federal

Ministry of Finance, the inefficiency in the banking system was consistently overlooked. Where banking sins abounded, regulatory grace or sheer ignorance also flourished. However, the persistent slump in the dollar price of crude oil led to a visible deterioration in the already weak infrastructural and social service base and provided the right milieu for a change in political power. Accordingly, in January 1984, the military seized power under the pretext that the nation's economy was drifting under an allegedly directionless civilian regime.

In line with their central command orientation, the new rulers immediately instituted direct control of the economy, which included an import-licensing regime. Twenty months later, however, there was another coup, which scrapped import licensing in favour of allocating foreign exchange, which appeared more transparent but still gave room for cronies of the administration to avail themselves of unlimited foreign exchange at will.

The only solution that would meet the criteria both for apparent transparency in allocation and direct access to foreign exchange for the military rulers' political patrons was the deregulation of the foreign exchange system, which the IMF had persistently advocated. Unfortunately, IMF and World Bank officials failed to understand how an otherwise well-intentioned policy could be abused for self-serving ends. Deregulation in a developing country such as Nigeria, where the surveillance capacity of the regulator was weak, could have been effective only if the regulator had first been strengthened.

For the new military regime, deregulation meant a half-hearted implementation of the IMF recommendations. The introduction of a dual exchange rate system allowed a windfall from foreign exchange arbitrage by buying US dollars at the preferential official rate of ₦22 and selling at ₦84, along with issuing new banking licences to loyalists in order to legitimize foreign exchange abuses. In other words, the much-touted deregulation of the Babangida era simply legitimized the giving of new banking licences to selected players in order for them to enjoy access to foreign exchange at preferential rates, while the rest of the populace lived below the poverty line. In essence, a banking licence was a multiple entry visa for making money. Accordingly, the number of banks rose from 20 in 1980, to 40 in 1985 and to 107 in 1990.

The (spurious) arguments for deregulation were the under-banked nature of the country (Table 3.1) and the need to democratize access to credit but there were also additional factors that influenced the decisions that the military dictators took in the financial sector.

Table 3.1 Number of banks in Nigeria 1980–92

Year	Commercial	Merchant	Total
1980	20	6	26
1985	28	12	40
1990	58	49	107
1992	66	54	120

The first was the insinuation that Nigeria had become a transit point for hard drugs, especially cocaine. For this reason, it had become imperative to set up the National Drug Law Enforcement Agency in 1990 to curtail drug trafficking and the associated money-laundering. With increased surveillance by the international community, an alternative route for the money laundering was to own a banking licence in order to make foreign currency transfers, while the bank violated basic know-your-customer policies.

The second reason for the reckless issue of licences was the abundant arbitrage that could be earned from the dual exchange rate regime. Obtaining a banking licence was tantamount to minting money. In a country with high illiteracy rates, it was intuitively obvious that people would prefer black market transactions with little documentation or audit trail.

According to Professor Ariyo of the University of Ibadan:

Many of the banks that gained entrance into the industry owing to wide opportunities for profit were accused of round-tripping of official foreign exchange into the parallel market, to exploit opportunities that existed based on the wide margin [or premium] existing between the official and the parallel market rates. The participation in the foreign exchange market did require banks to set aside substantial domestic liquid resources to back up their demand for foreign exchange at the latter stages, contrary to what obtained during the era of regulation. Over time [since 1987], a number of changes came into being when the market was deregulated. One of these is the alignment of the official rate with that of the parallel market. This and other changes were geared towards requiring the banks to build up and keep a substantially huge amount of liquid resources which has been used as a policy to mop-up excess liquidity in the banking sector (Sobodu and Akiode, 1996).

The third reason was the vendettas in the military. In a country with over 200 ethnic groups, each political clique wanted its own dedicated bank for routing its own loot. This meant its own banking licence to wire stolen money abroad. Routing such monies through the bank of an enemy with a vendetta against you or your supporters would only provide fodder for your political enemies. By owning a licence, the generals and their cronies would not only have a ticket to easy money but also a cover for their illegitimate money-laundering. (This was expressly confirmed by the founding director of one of the nation's new generation banks, who ensured that he had no retired general on his board. Only one bank had two generals on its board at the same time. Furthermore, a simple correlation analysis suggests that banks with links to serving or retired generals had shorter lifespans and recorded poorer performance than banks without such links.)

In such a self-serving system, it made strategic sense for the military types to perpetuate a near-impotent central bank with a weak surveillance capacity, which only received reports from the commercial banks long after the abuses had occurred. By 1992, the issue of the competence of the CBN came to the fore, with the allegation that a whopping US$12 billion was missing from the nation's oil windfall account.

Restructuring the regulator

The Presidential Panel of Inquiry into the CBN in 1994 was Nigeria's first major attempt at restructuring the central bank. During the 16 years of military regimes between 1984 and 1999, most federal government agencies, including the CBN, were subject to executive abuse of power. One manipulative tendency perfected in the 1980s was the appointment of credible but naïve Western-trained economists to implement the self-seeking agenda of the ruling military.

By 1993, when General Sani Abacha assumed power, the inability of the CBN to account properly for the disbursement of the $12 billion excess oil windfall in the Stabilization and Dedication Accounts led to several official inquiries. These culminated in the inauguration of the Panel on the Reorganization and Reform of the Central Bank of Nigeria. Led by an eminent economist, Dr Pius Okigbo, it also included Alhaji Umaru Mutallab, Mr Paschal Dozie (both experienced bankers), Mr Y. Sankey, Mrs B. Latinwo, Chief Ufot Ekaette, Mr O. Oyefodunrin and Mr Ibrahim Ida.

Although the report was never officially released, or even found until 2009, submissions reaching the public censured the CBN for poor supervision, lack of qualified personnel, corruption, poor management of the economy, inept management of foreign reserves, lack of independence and the proliferation of two-branch banks. Overall, it found that the

CBN had failed in its primary responsibility for supervising financial institutions and managing the economy.

As part of its recommendations, the panel advocated a central bank that would facilitate the effective management of the economy, provide non-inflationary support to government, and foster a healthy financial system. It would be a bank that would be insulated, as far as possible, from the direct influence and power of office holders and could inculcate in its functionaries the ethics of hard work and transparency.

As with several other government probes, no White Paper on the report was published enunciating official policy, nor any pronouncements on the panel's findings. By 2004, 10 years after the panel had submitted its report, the official government position was that the report was missing from the office of the secretary to the government of the federation, the official custodian of such documents. However, several undercurrents of reform at the CBN had been underway since May 1999, when the Obasanjo administration appointed Joseph Sanusi as governor for a five-year term. Drawing on his experience at First Bank, where he had embarked on major restructuring, he launched Project EAGLES, an acronym for Efficiency, Accountability, Goal-Oriented, Leadership, Effectiveness and Staff-Oriented.

The stated vision for the Central Bank, then, was: 'To be proactive in providing a stable framework for the economic development of Nigeria through transparent implementation of monetary policy and achievement of efficient and effective price stability for a sound management of the financial system.' The initial two years focused on internal re-engineering and computerization, but the real changes were not seen until 2004, when the office of governor became vacant.

3.4 Politics of appointing a governor of the Central Bank of Nigeria

The efficiency of a central bank is broadly defined by three factors: its level of independence; the character of the governor; and the competence of the core central banking team. Economists are unanimous in the view that the independence of a central bank typically promotes low inflation and price stability.

Most empirical studies suggest an inverse relationship between measures of central bank independence and inflation. While this correlation does not prove convincingly that independent central banks are the causative factor for low inflation, the association still remains strong, at least for developed countries. On the other hand, countries with less fiscal discipline and less aversion to inflation may be less likely to have independent central banks.

Despite the unproven, weak or inconclusive link between the central bank and other real macroeconomic variables such as economic growth, unemployment and real interest rates (Alesina and Summers 1993), it remains encouraging for developing countries such as Nigeria to note that an independent central bank is instrumental in achieving price stability.

Six measures of central bank independence have typically been defined (Alesina and Summers 1993).

1. **Legal.** Legal independence is a function of the legislation passed by government concerning the operations and autonomy of the central bank. It covers the term of office of the governor. If this is longer than the term of the government then it is considered more independent. In other words, an independent central bank is one whose institution is at least legally autonomous and which has the legal power to insulate itself from undue political interference.
2. **Political.** This deals with the turnover of governors, the number of government representatives on the management board and whether or not the governor holds another office in the government itself. The more stable the tenure of the governor and the fewer government officials on the board or committees of the central bank, the more politically independent the central bank tends to be.
3. **Price and inflation stability.** The most important objective of any central bank is price stability, as reflected in low inflation. If the central bank is saddled with other objectives, its ability to achieve this objective will be hampered. Central banks that follow targeting methods for maintaining inflation and interest rates are in a better position to maintain price stability. This however, is not necessarily synonymous with adopting any particular inflation-targeting approach, nor does it connote the Central Bank focusing on inflation management to the detriment of overall economic growth. In summary, such central banks are perceived to have a greater likelihood of effectiveness by focusing on a few appropriate instruments to control price levels and inflation.
4. **Exchange rate policy.** According to Ally and Wikramanakanye, the role of the central bank depends on whether the exchange rate regime is fixed, managed or floating. Other relevant issues include which authority or agency of government decides the exchange rate regime,

intervention in the foreign exchange market and pricing, direct and indirect foreign exchange controls, and foreign exchange borrowing.

5. **Monetary policy and deficit financing.** The independence of a central bank is reflected in its autonomy in determining monetary policy, that is, whether or not it is the sole authority empowered by law and responsible on a day-to-day basis for monetary policy formulation, and whether or not it has the final decision in matters relating to lending to the government. Overall, the assumption is that an independent central bank can select the appropriate instruments to control prices, inflation and exchange rate stability and has limited accountability to the legislative arm of government of the country beyond keeping its activities transparent.
6. **Accountability and transparency.** Central banks with clearly defined objectives, which are predetermined, published and communicated to the public, with regular and consistent assessments of their own performance against targets, using consistent standards, are regarded as transparent. The greater the rigour of oversight from parliament, and the greater the level of scrutiny of an independent arm of government outside the executive that appointed the governor, the higher the accountability of a central bank is deemed to be. Central banks that are accountable to parliament, rather than the executive, are to be preferred. Otherwise, there is the possibility of undue influence.

Beyond the independence of the central bank as an institution, there is also the character of the governor and his key lieutenants. Most economists agree that an independent central bank is more beneficial to an economy. This is especially so where it is led by a governor who is viewed as 'moderately conservative', that is, one who is inflation-averse or risk-averse, or who simply has a commitment to price stability.

However, economists such as Schultz have noted that the appointment of central bank governors has not always been optimal in a democratic setting, even in developed economies (Schultz 1999). Presidents or heads of states often nominate central bank governors who reflect the colour of their governments. This is more the case in countries where the political scene is highly polarized, or in multi-ethnic states such as Nigeria, where the consequences of the opponent winning the election are severe. In such countries, an appointment to the position of central bank governor may have a more political coloration in line with the agenda of the incumbent. Worse still, where democratic institutions are weak, and the concept of the median or average voter representing the choice of the public is almost non-existent, the appointment of a governor is more politicized. In countries where elections are neither transparent nor free and fair, there is a good chance that the winners of the election do not represent the average voter, and are less inflation-averse than is the general public. In these instances, even if the winning party in government makes what it considers its 'best' choice, the appointment, according to this theory, is still likely to be suboptimal. The governor, even though more conservative than the government, may not be more conservative than the general public.

Typically, when an economy enjoys sustained growth, the character of the governor may have limited consequences. However, for economies like Nigeria's, just emerging from stagnation, the leanings of the governor will be instrumental in reviving the economy.

Schultz (1999) suggests that the benefits of a 'moderately conservative' independent governor underscore the philosophy behind many appointments in developed Western countries. Ordinarily, the 'moderately conservative' is typified by long-term focus, prudence in balancing targets and a leaning towards predictable, steady growth. The evidence is that a 'moderately conservative' governor, who is more inclined to maintain equilibrium, will typically not be inclined to adopt short-term economic measures to win short-term successes. However, this only works in developed countries where the economy has achieved a semblance of maturity in a democratic culture with strong institutions.

In developing countries, which are more vulnerable to economic shocks due to their dependence on imports and the volatility of mono-product commodity prices, the benefits of a conservative governor may not be significant. In general, how conservative a central bank governor should be correlates with the vulnerability of the economy to unpredictable economic shocks, and the consequent need for radical transformation. The flipside is that, where a liberal governor is appointed, he or she may single-handedly implement liberal policies, which may or may not be good for the economy. If this happens where democratic institutions are weak, the electoral system unreliable, and the views of the median voter inconsequential, the society may be stuck with an independent governor who cannot easily be removed. The independence of a governor who is merely an agent of the government may damage the economy.

'Monolithic economic establishments' may be good for economies in recession or depression that require a unified coalition of economic forces and unitary government bureaucracy to forklift the economy, as was the case with Japan. However, such establishments may also be dangerous during more stable periods, when greater balance is required in order to avoid catapulting the economy into recession.

From a simplified perspective, based on Gartner's (2004) work, we can typify four types of central banks for a developing country such as Nigeria using a dual-target model of inflation control and income growth (unemployment reduction):

1. **Growth-oriented/liberal central bank.** This is one that is less inflation-averse, or 'less conservative', than society and will take notable inflation risks to achieve economic growth.
2. **Conservative central bank.** This is one that is as conservative as the society and will theoretically try to balance out the effects of any economic shock with a quick adjustment in interest or rediscount rates in order to neutralize the impact on inflation.
3. **Moderately conservative central bank.** This is one that will not quickly raise inflation in order to achieve short-term economic growth and reduced unemployment because of the potential long-term inflationary consequences. Exceptions will arise only when the shock is assessed as almost certain to be more than temporary, and when there is a perceived need to increase inflation in order to stimulate economic growth.
4. **Arch-conservative central bank.** This is one that will raise inflation only in the face of a deep economic recession, and then only as a last resort.

Irrespective of the type of central bank, the underlying assumption is that the stronger the macroeconomic and inflation-monitoring framework, and the stronger the enforceability of the performance contract with the governing body, the less the need for conservatism. On the other hand, the weaker the macroeconomic framework and the weaker the enforceability of the contract with the governor (as is the case in many African countries), the stronger will be the need for a conservative governor.

The Nigerian evidence

Folarin Alayande in his articles 'Rent Seekers in the Banking Hall' and 'Now Let's Have Serious Banking' (ThisDay 2004) has articulated the key qualities and indicators of a successful Central Bank governor in a developing economy. Based on our review of the performance of CBN governors, five factors influence the effectiveness of a governor:

1. the independence of the CBN;
2. the character and competence of the governor;

3. the working relationship between the governor who is in charge of monetary policy, the cabinet minister who oversees the Federal Ministry of Finance with oversight for fiscal policy and national revenue mobilization, and the economic adviser to the president, who has responsibility for general economic policy advice;
4. the economic and business cycle; and
5. the external macroeconomic environment

Since the inception of the CBN in 1959, the country has had nine indigenous governors, four appointed by military regimes and the others by democratically elected civilian regimes. Before 1999, and in the absence of any enabling legislation on the bank's autonomy, it is difficult to assess their character and competence. This is particularly so under the military regimes of 1966–79 and 1984–99.

With the return to democracy in May 1999, and the reforms instituted by the new administration to improve the efficiency of all public agencies, there was a radical shift in mindset about the calibre of people to be appointed.

Between 1999 and 2004, the Obasanjo administration appointed a moderately conservative banker in the person of Chief Sanusi. However, by 2004, when the economic reforms of the administration were underway and there was a greater imperative for growth, Obasanjo's key consideration was for a liberal or growth-oriented governor. By then, Nigeria had come full circle in experimenting with various exchange rate systems. With the United Bank for Africa (UBA) investigation by the US Treasury on foreign exchange abuses, the administration needed a liberal reformist. After five years of a managed, free-floating exchange rate system, the newly elected president was also keen on reducing double-digit interest rates. Any appointee needed to guarantee that he could deliver on that promise. In return, the president would give him carte blanche to run the apex bank. Lowering interest rates was close to the heart of the president, who was known to have faced challenges himself in his earlier life as a farmer and school proprietor.

Perhaps some significant lobbying had also taken place. Professor Soludo was undoubtedly a strategist, and not only in economic planning. He had exceptional ability in building loyal relationships across the media, academia and the political class, and for managing upwards – his bosses. Three months before Mr Soludo's appointment, the Sunday editor of a leading national daily published a synopsis of articles from the *Harvard Economic Review* arguing that the selection of the governor should be based on economic expertise, contrary to the previous

Table 3.2 Nigeria's central bank governors and economic advisers

Central bank governors						Economic advisors			
S no.	Name	Birth	From	Till	Age on resumption	S no.	Name	From	Till
1.	MaiBornu	1919	1963	1967	44	1.	Okigbo	1962	1967
2.	Isong	1920	1967	1975	47	2.	Obafemi Awolowo*	1967	1970
3.	Ciroma	1934	1975	1977	41	3.	Shehu Shagari*	1970	1971
4.	OlaVincent	1925	1977	1982	52	4.	Adedeji*	1971	1975
5.	Ahmed	1940	1982	1993	42	5.	Edozien	1979	1983
6.	Ogwuma	1932	1993	1999	61	6.	Aboyade	1985	1992
7.	Sanusi	1938	1999	2004	61	7.	Asiodu	1999	2001
8.	Soludo	1960	2004	2009	44	8.	Kpakol	2001	2003
9.	Sanusi	1961	2009		48	9.	Soludo	2003	2004
						10.	Ode Ojowu	2004	2005
						11.	Osita Ogbu	2005	2007
						12.	Tanimu Yakubu Kufir	2007	2009

*Federal Commissioner for Economic Development.

practice. Earlier that year, a series of pre-sensitization – preparatory – articles by Olusegun Adeniyi were published in *ThisDay* about the need to appoint a proven economist with published views on leading economic issues. Adeniyi was a journalist of notable integrity and also a prolific author, who in 2007 became media adviser to the president of Nigeria. In that series, entitled 'Who will Save the Nation?', the columnist, borrowing extensively from a *Harvard Economic Review* article, argued that in many countries, notably the US, economists and bankers are almost always appointed to lead the central bank. Furthermore, Adeniyi noted that in over two centuries the Federal Reserve Bank had never elevated an insider to that position.

In one of those articles, he argued:

Records suggest training in economics is the first condition for anyone who wants to get on the Board of Federal Reserve [equivalent of our Central Bank]. The paper then went on to review the credentials of the present Board, headed by Alan Greenspan, who held a PhD in economics from New York University. His deputy, Roger Ferguson, also held a PhD in economics, from Harvard University. A third member, Susan Schmidt, had a PhD in economics from North Western University. Edward Gramlich had gained his own doctorate in the same discipline in 1965, while Donald Kohn had obtained his from the University of Michigan. The 15-man Board of the Bank of England was equally peopled by eminent economists, most of who held doctorates. The same was true for the Bank of Kenya, with which I also drew a comparison.

Predictably, many readers of the column assumed that there were ulterior motives for that article, and that one of the two contenders for the position – both of whom had PhDs – had sponsored Adeniyi to write it, an allegation he convincingly refuted in the same column.

Even though many of the reader comments on the underlying motive of the article were unfounded and probably baseless, the thrust of the article was clear: the next CBN governor should be a proven macroeconomist with well-defined views on macroeconomic policy and management. The strategic appointment of a former World Bank vice-president (and American citizen), Mr Fischer, as the new governor of the Central Bank of Israel at about the same time seemed especially fortuitous. Although both countries had many intellectuals in the diaspora, there were few offshore economists with prominent opinions on the Nigerian economy who could have been recalled to head the nation's central bank. Accordingly, the lessons from Israeli actions were threefold. It is important to have a 'reserve army' of offshore intellectuals – essentially on standby – who can be mobilized to execute urgent developmental campaigns. The Israelis have always sought to create a virtual economy where knowledge was resident in geographically remote, but networked, individuals.

The second part of the lesson was the imperative to network in a coherent manner so as to have a 'team' that could work in harmony. Last was the imperative to understand the language of central banking. Whoever was going to lead the CBN into the twenty-first century would have to understand the powers and hidden motives of key decision makers in the international financial community in order to prevent a recurrence of the bungles made by the nation's negotiators at the multilateral agencies and the London and Paris clubs in the 1970s and 1980s.

The Obasanjo administration had recognized, albeit implicitly, these imperatives when it sought a replacement for Sanusi. In a country with three dominant ethnic groups and a plethora of others of varying sizes, the polarization of senior government positions was always analysed along ethnic lines. Of the central bank's seven indigenous governors, only one had been Igbo.

The fact that the banking sector was in need of reform was not in contention. Inside sources suggested that a private sector banker from one of the new generation banks was being touted. Speculation had centred on Fola Adeola, immediate past Managing Director of Guaranty Trust Bank, an exceptional new generation bank in terms of service delivery, and Akin Kekere-Ekun, Director of Habib Bank, a conservative mid-sized bank. In a country with a skewed media and a gullible undereducated populace, most of whom parroted the opinions of a few rabble-rousing opportunists, the media was a major driving force of public opinion. Accordingly, in the months before the expiry of the tenure of the governor, there was wild speculation in the media about his successor and about how his disposition and constituency would affect the way in which he would attack the myriad problems of the banking sector, chief among which was the excesses in the banking system.

The banking system, before the early purge in 2002, had essentially been a feudal system in which a few bank chiefs held sway. Barrels of illicit money had been made from the dual exchange rate system, which, together with the weak import documentation regime, had permitted many bank institutions and their cronies to make money by round-tripping. During the 1990s, round-tripping had essentially been of two types: inflating import invoices to import cheap goods in order to obtain foreign exchange (forex) at the discounted government rate and make a margin on the excess forex allocated; and outright falsification of documents in which no goods were imported and the forex allocated was sold on the black market. The artificial lifestyle of the bankers also encouraged supposed bank inspectors to ask for a piece of the action.

Between 1990 and 1993, the forex abuse under the Babangida military regime was particularly glaring, due to the collateral money market glut, which led to a hotchpotch of non-bank finance houses mushrooming in the key cities of Lagos, Kano, Kaduna, Ibadan and Port-Harcourt. Interest rates – or, better still, discount rates on short-term fixed deposits – were as high as 45 per cent, with brokerage rates for sourcing these deposits often as high as 20 per cent. Most bankers had known that this trend was not sustainable and, while the cowboys played the bank rodeo game, a few of the smarter bankers made fortunes from the unregulated free for all of the non-bank finance houses, and used the proceeds as deposits to apply for proper commercial banking licences. One of the consequences of the free market system in transitional developing countries, such as Nigeria, was that capitalists had a short memory. On the plus side, one unexpected bonus from those days was that at least one of the leading new generation banks was built on the proceeds of its finance house antecedents.

Others used the illicit money to build cleaner banking institutions that would outlive the owners. The smarter bankers used the generals to obtain their licences and paid them off. The more successful of these banks did not retain any general on their board; many of those that did went into liquidation, though not solely due to the plundering by the founding directors.

Spurred on by big profits, professional bankers, mainly in their mid-thirties, had developed business plans on their desk-top personal computers after hours, and marketed these ambitious plans to retired generals and government oligarchs who, sitting on a stash of illicit wealth, were looking for ways to layer the money back into the economy and legitimize it. Banking licences had become easier to obtain with relaxed rules in the years immediately after 1990, but the young bankers, who understood that they could not trust the bureaucracy, or the vagaries and policy somersaults of the CBN, simply paid a retired general. Other, more sophisticated, new generation banks realized that obtaining a banking licence through a retired, but not tired, general was one thing; staying close to the corridors of power was another, in a country where power was a revolving door with multiple exits. It required gumshoe tactics to stay in the loop – this included collaborating with government officials, networking with cabinet-level ministers, and developing a constantly refreshed pool of public officials as informants. Not a few of those humble looking civil servants drove the flashest cars at the weekend in a country where the gross annual remuneration of directors in parastatals could not buy a Volkswagen Beetle or a Mini Cooper. It suggested that a few of them could have been compromised!

Cleaning up the system in 2004 required a radical who could not only draft bold policies but who was 'clean', that is, had no skeletons in his cupboard. Security reports on Professor Charles Chukwuma Soludo suggested that he was neither a playboy nor a wheeler-dealer. Difficult to stereotype, he did not appear to have any of those skeletons in his cupboard. Though a university don, he had made substantial income from several concurrent consulting engagements with multilateral institutions, including the UN and the World Bank, which had already made him comfortable before his government appointment.

If he were to be appointed, the test would be how he would pull the levers that might tackle the endemic inflation with which his predecessor had battled for five years. The more pressing problem, however, was regulating the foreign exchange system and controlling the steep decline of the *naira* against the dollar. In an import-dependent economy, where all foreign exchange flowed through the commercial banks, the immediate challenge was to improve CBN's surveillance of these. The banks had also been the butt of criticism as the nation's albatross of corruption and money-laundering, albeit exaggerated, which led to the popular complaint that the banking sector was being given a bad name in order to hang it. Whoever was appointed governor would have to take some forceful decisions.

Most leadership and management experts agree that the primary job of a leader is choosing and retaining the right team by creating a vision, mentoring and sustaining momentum (Alayande 2010, *Business Day* Newspapers). If nothing else, Mr Olusegun Obasanjo had proved himself to be a leader by selecting the right people when he won his second term ticket in 2003. Perhaps one could not have expected less from someone who had survived as a general and warlord in the civil war of a multi-ethnic society with over 300 languages, where your life is only as good as your last choice of a batman. As such, economic commentators trusted that Obasanjo's choice for the top job at the CBN would be well thought through. On 29 April 2004, the debonair Professor Charles Soludo, then chief economic advisor to the president, was announced as the eighth indigenous governor of the CBN. This was announced in a radio interview with the president:

> The Central Bank has done very well in the last five years in managing the monetary aspect of the economy. The macro-economy has been well managed. But I don't see the Central Bank as [managing] only the monetary aspect alone, for a country like Nigeria, that is in

> a hurry to develop, the Central Bank has a developmental responsibility and I think the time has come when that developmental responsibility must come to the fore. And I see Charles Soludo as someone who has that developmental orientation, he has worked with me, and I believe he should go there. And it is because he has what it takes. I don't care where he comes from (Adeniyi 2004).

Soludo's appointment was the first time an economist with a rigorous academic background had been appointed to lead the central bank in Nigeria. Professor Soludo had made his mark through economic modelling and consulting for senior figures in Aso Rock, the seat of power. In that capacity, he had worked closely with a few Western diplomats, the incumbent finance minister, who was a former World Bank director, and most of the institutional economists and bureaucrats, all of whom liked his work. Subsequently, he became chair of the National Planning Commission, where he had the chance to prove his mettle by leading a team that drafted what became the nation's economic strategy document, the National Economic Empowerment and Development Strategy, promising several economic targets to the president.

Most of the so-called demerits of the new governor were ill founded. The first was that he had never run such a large institution. However, most central bank chiefs anywhere in the world were similarly 'handicapped'. In the final analysis, the governor's job was about policy, not administration; hence the huge bureaucratic machinery to support him. The second argument, that he was too young, ignored the history of the CBN: two previous governors – Adamu Ciroma and Abdulkadir Ahmed – had been appointed in their early forties. As he was a relative newcomer, a humble professor of economics of only 43, whose only exposure to government had been a one-year stint as chief economic adviser to the president, few people were in a position to predict the thrust of Soludo's monetary policy. Be that as it may, Soludo's appointment was the beginning of the second and most definitive phase of the Nigerian banking reforms.

3.5 Consolidation and the challenges of bank restructuring

In July 2005, barely five weeks after his appointment, Soludo announced a reform programme for the banking sector.

Six key weaknesses were identified in the paper entitled 'Consolidating the Nigerian Banking Industry to Meet the Development Challenges of the 21st Century':

- weak corporate governance, poor compliance and poor ethics;
- late or non-publication of bank accounts;
- gross insider abuses, resulting in huge non-performing loans;
- insolvency, as evidenced by negative shareholder funds;
- a weak capital base;
- over-dependence on public sector deposits.

Out of the 89 banks, 62 (or 70 per cent) were classified as sound and satisfactory, 14 (16 per cent) as marginal, and 11 (12 per cent) as unsound. Four pillars of the 13-point reform agenda to protect the 'fragile' and 'marginal' Nigerian banking system from impending collapse were, to increase the minimum capitalization (shareholder funds) of banks to ₦25 billion (approximately $200 million); a phased withdrawal of public sector funds from banks; bank consolidation through mergers and acquisitions; adoption of a risk-focused and rule-based regulatory regime.

This was quoted as being only the first phase of the 'new agenda' to reposition the CBN, in particular, and the Nigerian financial system in general, but the recurring question remained: why did Mr Soludo think he could effect banking sector reform overnight simply by raising the minimum capital requirements? Was it simply a game of size? And was focusing on size an efficient and effective means of commencing a structured reform of the banking system?

Predictably, several banking practitioners and economists disagreed with the new CBN governor. A leading investment banker, and chief executive of a niche bank, Atedo Peterside, sponsored several advertorials in leading newspapers challenging the logic of the new governor's 'size is right' regime and expressing deep scepticism over the feasibility and timing of the recapitalization agenda.

Fundamentally, Soludo's reform strategy hinged on a 'bypass' approach, which implied making fundamental decisions that challenged the status quo without consulting the power brokers who might be hurt by his policies, in so far as he had the president on his side. There were two principal methods of effecting financial sector reform in a developing country that was not driven by external macroeconomic forces, as in the Asian experience. One was to use the 'grand campaign' approach. This would have involved an elaborate process of developing a 'financial sector master-plan' and detailing the phases of the roadmap. The other was to adopt a 'bypass strategy', which selected only a few key monetary policy instruments (which the government, through the CBN, would focus on), and included only a few stakeholders, rather than the large stakeholder group that would have been involved in the 'grand campaign' approach.

The risk with the grand campaign approach was the enormous effort required to manage multiple interest groups – many of whom could disrupt the reform process or use political means to thwart or delay its realization. An elaborate process such as this had been used in adopting the structural adjustment programme in Nigeria and many other African countries, but had proved inefficient.

The bypass approach – or the 'instrumental approach' – was more focused, even though to non-economists it could appear *ad hoc*. The strength, and therefore the success of the bypass approach, lay in identifying one or two key variables and attacking them, irrespective of which interest groups were affected or what collateral impact it might have on other, subsidiary, variables in the short term, as long as the mid-term benefits justified the means of achieving them.

One final argument for using the surprise method of Mr Soludo was to win the support of the international community and convince its members that the regime could pursue a deliberate, targeted approach to economic management that was not in thrall to the sensibilities of a few power brokers. This 'shock and awe' approach was also a calculated ploy to demoralize those interests that had stolen money and wired it offshore to send back into Nigeria, and at the same time to reduce the wanton looting of the economy.

However, beyond the obvious reason for the reform was a more subtle one. In Nigeria, the exchange rate had been the centre of gravity of the economy. Since the advent of the civilian regime in 1979, governments had survived and fallen through their management of the exchange rate. Both the Shagari and the Buhari-Idiagbon regimes had been naïve in appointing mediocrities into sensitive positions that could influence foreign exchange management, while the Babangida regime had played the exchange rate issue to its own advantage.

For almost two decades, Nigerian banks had abused the foreign exchange procedures and used the proceeds of the foreign exchange game to make themselves billionaires, and in turn funded politicians, resulting in a complex nexus of money and power, and a spiral of 'new money' power brokers who wanted to continue profiteering from the banks. Moreover, the sheer number of these banks had made it difficult to tackle the problem. Reducing their number would make supervision by the CBN more manageable, while also enabling the banks themselves to become more competitive internationally. The exchange rate had been the country's centre of gravity. Once that fell, everything else fell with it. Like a juggernaut, the Nigerian economy had a high centre of gravity that made it unstable. If Soludo could tackle the exchange rate problem within his first six months, he would prove to his critics that he possessed an excellent understanding of the economy.

Yet, beyond managing inflation and the exchange rate, the banks remained a nightmare. Several challenges still remained. First was the political hurdle of obtaining the buy-in of the various interest groups. Second was the issue whether the arbitrary figure for the new minimum capitalization of banks could be defended, and whether a single benchmark could be used for local and international banks with varying risk profiles. Third was the impact the banking sector recapitalization would have on the financial markets, especially the volatile capital markets.

4

Does Size Matter? The Quest for Transnational Banks

4.1 Introduction

Much of the argument for the banking consolidation in Nigeria in 2005 was the quest for size or scale. Size is often correlated with three things: the performance or internal efficiency of an organism, living or corporate; the behaviour of that organism in response to its environment; and the potential effect the size of an individual agent may have on the behaviour of other agents and, ultimately therefore, on the structure of its environment or industry.

In classical economics, there are three similar debates. One is the argument of economies of scale versus being 'too big to fail'. This thinking recognizes that, while larger firms enjoy lower costs and transactional efficiencies, they can become so dominant that the collapse of the firm could lead to the collapse of the industry and hence damage the economy. Contrary to the size-based argument for the Soludo-led consolidation, recent evidence has confirmed that size is a proxy for the extent of the systemic threat posed by a bank, so it could inherently be both an advantage and a disadvantage. The second argument concerns size versus competitive efficiency. This hinges on the thesis that a minimum critical mass is needed to be cost-efficient and more competitive in an existing market. The third argument is about whether small or big firms contribute more to cutting-edge innovations and revolutionary breakthroughs. While the evidence is mixed, the general observation is that, while smaller firms may be more creative, bigger firms are faster at commercializing and democratizing such breakthroughs.

In a competitive society, size is relevant at the scale of an industry. In the basic theory, size or scale brings about economies of scale – savings from reduced unit costs and accumulated efficiencies.

In a postmodern world, the real challenge is not growth versus efficiency. Growth without efficiency is risky or dangerous growth. Efficiency without growth can lead to marginalization. Neither can survive market turbulence or unexpected market shocks. A streamlined, self-sustaining growth, as in Rostow's five stages, is the optimal or preferred option as it is the one that allows both the operator and the regulator to grow at manageable rates.

Achieving size only through mergers is also an extremely risky proposition (Folarin Alayande, 'Rebuilding The Temple of Banking in 2010', ThisDay 2010), especially in instances where the regulators are ill prepared to assess or predict the disruptive post-merger effects on the entire industry. This was the case in Nigeria, where the regulators had no economic models for the *ex post* banking structure, and let the banking industry operators seize the game. Simple portfolio theory holds that a merged conglomerate can unfairly leverage a dominant position in one industry to gain market share in another. However, the forced consolidation of banks in Nigeria in 2005 ignored the risk of the portfolio effect within the banking industry and the ripple effect on the overall financial system.

While the ability to compete on a global scale was promoted as the main reason for the 2004–5 consolidation, critics argue that the CBN's rationale was neither soundly grounded in economic theory nor supported by any empirical evidence.

Beneath the soundness of the CBN's argument for consolidation are more fundamental questions. Is a Big Bang approach to financial sector development the best? Is larger size or scale always the endgame or main intended outcome of banking sector reform, as the Soludo reforms suggested? Was the Nigerian challenge one of creating additional absorptive capacity in the economy at all costs, or one of expenditure efficiency? In this chapter, we examine these arguments within the context of Nigerian banking, and attempt to test whether the Soludo proposition for consolidation was based on objective facts, and whether it had beneficial consequences for the market on one hand, and for the economy on the other.

4.2 Does size matter? Empirical evidence

Contrary to popular belief, the evidence about whether large banks are more efficient than small ones, or whether larger bank capitalization (a proxy of size) mitigates bank failure, is inconclusive. In simple terms, the basic argument suggests that larger financial institutions achieve lower costs, either through economies of scale or through economies of scope. Most of the studies, however, yield varying results depending on the time period, the average size of the financial institutions studied and the jurisdiction involved (Santomero and Eckles 2000, Berger 2000). Interestingly, some studies suggest that there are 'higher expectations' of economies of scale than those reported in most of the academic studies conducted. This variance in outcomes is attributed to the difficulty in accurately estimating and comparing economies of scale across banks. It is expected that the outcome of any research into the size–efficiency hypothesis would vary across jurisdictions based on the level of barriers to entry, including regulatory barriers, on the one hand, and on the rigidity of the market structure on the other.

According to Dymski (1999), at any rate, since economies of scale in banking are achieved at relatively low asset volumes 'as low as $100 million', larger banks may not achieve significant or material cost efficiencies beyond those enjoyed by mid-sized ones. Many studies also seem to suggest that some of the cost economies are lost as the bank or financial services organization grows too large and complex, creating a lot of governance overheads and potential managerial dispersion.

Overall, the most convincing argument for large banks in developing countries like Nigeria is the correlation of a bank's lending capacity with its capital base or shareholders' funds, which implies that larger banks can finance larger scale transactions to propel economic development. However, this positive advantage of capital financing capacity has its risks, with a direct negative correlation between the size of the bank and the extent of the systemic threat it poses.

In Africa, as in Western countries, available evidence is inconclusive. First, the larger banks, according to shareholder capital or assets, do not necessarily enjoy higher returns on assets (ROA) or returns on equity (ROE). Secondly, while capital size and asset size (in addition to the extent of ownership concentration) may be significant company-level determinants of bank profitability in Nigeria, the relationship between bank risk and bank profitability, and hence bank size, is inconclusive (Aburime 2008). An earlier study by Cronje (2003) applied the data envelope analysis method to 16 South African banks and concluded that inefficiency can be ascribed primarily to size inefficiency. The seven large banks that were classified as inefficient were found to be operating at decreasing returns to scale. This research suggested that the efficiency of the large, inefficient, banks worsens as their scale of operations increases. On the other hand, the smaller banks that were classified as inefficient were found to be operating at increasing returns to scale, suggesting that increased size would confer efficiency advantages on them.

Using a smaller set of four large and four small South African-based banks for the period 2000–5, Nokuthala Siyaka examined the cost efficiency of South African banks relative to profit efficiencies. Overall, Siyaka's findings are that the correlation between the cost and profit efficiency of South African banks is low but statistically significant. On the other hand, the results suggest a significant negative correlation between cost efficiency and bank size. However, interpreted in line with other studies such as Isik and Hassan's (2002) survey of Turkish banks, and Berger *et al.* (1993), possible conclusions are that smaller banks may not enjoy size or scale economies until they reach a certain size or scale of operations. Even after reaching that minimum scale of operations, there is no linear relationship between size and cost efficiency, even though there may be between size and revenue efficiency.

A similar statistical study was conducted for African banks in general. Focusing on the relative efficiency of the Top 100 African banks, Mohamed (2008) suggests that, while the performance of several banks is suboptimal, there is no evidence of a clear correlation over time between the size of the bank and its relative efficiency.

Beyond banking, the available evidence also questions whether size as a primary objective or as a means of defining a company's strategic intent may seem appealing to the ego of managers and intimidating to competitors but hardly guarantees sustainability. Among several examples, in October 2009, Akio Toyoda, president of the Toyota Motor Corporation (Akio 2009), described the company's policy of securing 15 per cent of the global market by 2010, and chasing volume at almost any price, as creating a sustainability problem for itself after it attained size leadership.

Findings on the inconclusiveness of the size–efficiency hypothesis are similar whether a sample set of African banks or subsets for South African banks and Nigerian banks are used. South African banks represent, approximately, over 70 per cent of the aggregated Tier 1 capital and aggregate pre-tax profits of the Top 100 African banks, and over 80 per cent of aggregate assets (*The Banker* annual publications 2005, 2006 and 2007), while several Nigerian banks appear in the Top 50 African banks.

Given this inconclusive relationship between size and cost efficiency and revenue efficiency, what then was the rationale for the regional ambitions of several Nigerian banks, and the foray into European financial capitals? Based on interviews with Nigerian bankers, three possible reasons can be proffered. First is the self-aggrandisement of the new generation of CEOs, who wanted a regional status rather than a domestic Nigerian status. Second was a follow-your-customer or follow-the-money strategy for some banks, which had transnational corporate clients and wanted to be able to serve those customers across their entire value chain, as well as trap all aspects of their import trade flows. Third was a risk diversification motive for a few of the banks, which realized that it was strategically valuable to have a portfolio of geographically diverse businesses whose income patterns could smooth the inevitable variability of the normal business cycle in individual business economies.

4.3 African regional banks: the Nigeria versus South Africa rivalry

The rivalry between Nigerian and South African banks had come to a head by early 2006. Ever since the demise of official apartheid in 1994, after which much Nigerian talent had moved to South Africa as either immigrants or expatriates, many South Africans had come to view Nigerians as "aggressive" people who wanted to take their jobs.

On the other hand, the South Africans exported their businesses in response to Nigerians exporting their talent. The fast growth of South African companies in the fast-food restaurants and retail supermarket/megastore/department store sectors was gradually becoming a source of threat to local companies. The classic case of South African ambition to dominate Nigeria, and the counter-response, is best illustrated in the satellite cable television market. For a long time, the South Africans had dominated the Nigerian satellite television communications market. But in early August 2006, Nigeria liberalized subscription broadcasting in Nigeria, ending the monopoly which the South African company had enjoyed in Nigeria since the early 1990s (Famakinwa 2006).

As part of its strategy to remain the only profitable satellite subscription company in Africa (with annual subscriptions of ₦15 billion, approximately US$120 million at that time), DSTV had up until that year leveraged its first-mover advantage to negotiate with foreign channels and content providers, bundling Africa as a continent. Its related company, Multichoice, had used the tool of exclusive acquisition of channels and content to dominate the Nigerian and other markets, and entrench South Africa's role in African broadcasting.

Even though South African banks did not operate under the same notion of exclusivity, the ultimate intent was the same: to achieve market dominance across Africa, and treat the African market as a single enclave.

By 2005, after the consolidation, Nigerian banks had acquired substantial capital beyond their immediate needs, and probably beyond the availability of bankable projects, given the capacity of the banks to assess and manage the risks. In fact, by the end of the consolidation exercise, the Nigerian banking industry had one of the highest equity to asset ratios in the world. It continued to worsen, such that by 2008, with similar equity bases, the South African banking system had about three times the asset base of the Nigerian system.

Even though the whole consolidation exercise had been successful in raising additional capital, the additional managerial skills needed to manage the risks associated with the extra capital were not forthcoming, and a logical outlet for that capital was geographic diversification.

Empirically, rapidly expanding corporations often outpace the internal capacity of their managers to manage and absorb the impact of the change they create (Penrose 1995). The rapid growth of Nigerian banks and their metamorphosis into regional banks was therefore not without its own consequences.

Jim Collins (2009) in his book *How the Mighty Fall* describes the stages through which many successful corporations pass. They were typical of the Nigerian banks. First is *hubris*, euphoria or overconfidence born of success. Second, is the era of undisciplined growth or 'undisciplined pursuit of more'. Third, is 'the denial of risk and peril', fourth, is 'grasping for salvation' and fifth is 'capitulation to irrelevance or death'. For many Nigerian banks, the five-year period from 2002 to 2007 was one of unbridled, undisciplined growth made worse by the inaction of sleeping regulators.

Professor Charles Soludo, as governor of the Central Bank, said in a speech on 6 July 2004 :

> As at end of June 2004, there were 89 deposit money banks operating in the country, comprising institutions of various sizes and degrees of soundness. The ten largest banks account for about 50 per cent of the industry's total assets/liabilities. Most banks in Nigeria have a capitalization of less than $10 million. Even the largest bank in Nigeria has a capital base of about US$240 million compared to US$526 million for the smallest bank in Malaysia. The small size of most of our banks, each with expensive headquarters, separate investment in software and hardware, heavy fixed costs and operating expenses, and with bunching of branches in few commercial centres lead to very high average cost for the industry. This in turn has implica-

tions for the cost of intermediation, the spread between deposit and lending rates, and puts undue pressure on banks to engage in sharp practices as [a] means of survival.

Based on these two rationales of small inefficient banks relative to Nigeria's comparator countries, Malaysia and South Africa, and the internal cost inefficiency of these banks, the governor of the Central Bank's hypothesis was that increasing the statutory capitalization of the banks would improve their efficiency and make them financially stronger, in order to fund Nigeria's large-scale infrastructure problems. From the governor's speech, there also was a third rationale, a hedonistic desire to have Nigeria's banks play in the global league, even if only for temporal motives such as self-aggrandisement or national pride.

Other countries had detailed blueprints for their banks on how to meet their revised capital requirements and be more relevant to the domestic economy. But, the Nigerian experience was not only hasty but also a regional play with the overall intent of creating transnational megabanks.

In Egypt, the banking consolidation of 2002–4 had witnessed a similar pattern. Interestingly, there were several parallels between Nigeria and Egypt. In July 2003, the Central Bank of Egypt, under its governor, Farouk El-Okdah, had announced Law No. 88 of 2003, requiring all banks to raise their paid-in capital to a minimum of £E500 million in the case of Egyptian banks and US$50 million in the case of local branches of international banks. Out over 60 banks in Egypt, many had a paid-in capital of only about £E10 million when the Unified Banking Law was announced in 2003, giving the banks an initial period of one year to increase their paid-in capital, though this was later extended by another year to July 2005. As the 14 July 2005 deadline approached – with 11 Egyptian banks and three international bank branches seemingly unable to meet the capital requirement – optimists predicted that the Egyptian banking sector regulators would extend the period of grace further. However, the central bank was firm on its deadline, with only 27 local banks meeting the new capital requirements. Eleven banks were not compliant with the new capital requirements. Seven of the 11 foreign banks operating in Egypt met the stipulated regulatory increase, while three of the domestic banks that could not comply were scheduled for a government-led merger, the expenses of which were to be subsidized or undertaken entirely by the government.

As in the Malaysian example, the consolidation was not without legal challenge. Investors in the Islamic International Bank for Investment &

Development (IIBID) challenged the powers of the Central Bank of Egypt and the constitutionality of the capital requirement. Though that case was lost on the technical grounds of filing a petition past the allowable period, there were still further challenges, including operational integration and obtaining buy-in from the entire investment community.

As in many other countries, the foreign bank chief executives played safe. In a manner typical of the posturing by CEOs of multinational institutions, a foreign bank CEO was quoted as saying: 'The enforcement of the capital requirement will ultimately make the banking sector stronger. This is part of an international trend that has been unfolding since the 1990s where small banks are either bought out by bigger ones or banks merge to consolidate their assets and improve their services. It's healthier for the market and for all banks to have a relatively high and comparable paid-in capital'.

Banks in operation in the country at the time of the announcement of the Unified Banking Law 88/2003 were given four options by the Central Bank of Egypt:

1. **Strategic Partnerships/Foreign Investors.** Banks were allowed to seek a strategic partner or partners to acquire shares in the bank. The additional equity was then added to the capital of the bank, to bring the total paid-in capital above the minimum.
2. **Public Offerings.** Banks were allowed to raise additional capital from the public by issuing new shares to investors via an initial public offering (IPO) on the Cairo and Alexandria Stock Exchanges.
3. **Liquidation.** Banks unable to raise or unwilling to meet the capital requirements were allowed to liquidate their assets and wind down operations. Several international banks went this route and adopted this option by closing their branches in Egypt. A few others, such as Citibank, increased capital and maintained their presence.
4. **Merger and/or Acquisition.** Under-capitalized banks were allowed to merge with other banks to bring their combined assets above the minimum capital requirement. Although this was one of the preferred approaches by the Central Bank of Egypt (CBE), very few banks voluntarily pursued this option.

By early 2009, five years after Soludo's global ambitions, when the impact of the global economic squeeze had withered some of the market attractiveness of countries into which the Nigerian banks had expanded, many of these banks had effectively passed through the first three stages of corporate decline – excitement, undisciplined growth, and denial of risk and peril. A couple more banks were in Jim Collins' fourth stage of grasping for salvation.

With the benefit of hindsight, the managing director of the Nigerian Deposit Insurance Corporation (NDIC), Ganiyu Ogunleye, has pointed out that the rapid expansion of Nigerian banks without the capacity to manage had been one of their greatest banes, 'placing as priority competition for size rather than focusing on asset quality and risk management' (Aderinokun 2009). According to Jim Collins, fourth-stage companies that react frantically to their situations and adopt revolutionary change may end up hastening their own demise. Rather, what is needed is calmness, market focus and deliberate action/strong execution capabilities.

This craving for global bank status eventually ruined many of these banks, and was partly responsible for ruin in the system, with many of the banks spreading their resources very thin, unmatched by any corresponding income.

On top of the challenges created by global expansion, and the setting up of branches or full fledged banks in countries where they had little business and few synergies, there was the additional burden many of these banks assumed due to mergers with banks with which they had nothing in common. For instance, 8 months ahead of the 31 December 2005 deadline for banks to meet the ₦25 billion capitalization requirement, 55 of the 89 banks had fused into 15 groups. Thirteen banks with ₦25 billion opted to stand alone whilst five banks sought ₦10 billion debt relief from the Central Bank (see, for instance, the front page of the *Guardian*, Monday 2 May 2005, vol. 21, no. 5673).

The Central Bank policies of 2004 and 2005, which encouraged mergers in the Nigerian banking system even though these created a few large, regional banks like the United Bank for Africa (UBA), ended up being more counterproductive than beneficial to the banking system: there were more victims than merger successes. One of the greatest challenges of mergers is the switch of managerial focus from the core business and markets to operational integration issues.

Many of these banks commenced their regional expansion without either securing their positions in the local market or assuring their efficiency levels. The increased governance and management requirements for many of these fast-expanding banks created challenges to their capacity to run larger and more complex financial conglomerates, an increased risk base, and multi-currency transactions efficiently. They went global without addressing basic issues.

Predictably, many of the mergers had major issues from the start. While some of the mergers eventually consumed their participants, other mergers eventually resulted in stronger entities. For the larger mergers such as that between the UBA and the Standard Trust Bank (STB), key issues included wide differences in corporate culture and different IT platforms. For instance, the cultural diversity between the STB and UBA was very stark, as the STB had relatively young employees compared with the older, more conservative staff profile of the UBA. While this combination of the operational conservatism of the old UBA with the market dynamism and entrepreneurial spirit of the former STB was a potential area of synergy, and it was fairly well managed in the UBA–STB merger, this was not the case with all of the mergers. For the UBA, there was a reshuffling of staff across the board that eventually resulted in improved customer satisfaction, if only minimally.

As was legacy practice, the merging banks maintained their separate identities until the IT platforms were merged and customers could access their accounts irrespective of which legacy bank they belonged to. By mid-2005 (July 2005), the CBN had agreed the UBA–STB deal by granting an approval in principle. Equally, other statutory or regulatory bodies, such as the NDIC and Securities and Exchange Commission (SEC), had given their concurrence or approval, and the Nigerian Stock Exchange (NSE) had been notified. This came with the assurance that there would be no forced employee attrition or job losses in the first year of the merger. A few banks, such as the UBA, adopted a talent-accumulation approach to fund their aggressive growth and diversification in the quest to attain the by-line of 'Africa's global bank'. To do this meant adopting a Mourinho-style talent strategy: signing up and retaining a talent in the squad, even if he did not play regularly, instead of allowing him to play against him in another team's colours. This was a sound strategy, at least in the short run, in a country where there was not enough skilled talent to go round.

According to economic opponents, such as Ayo Teriba, Nigeria's banking consolidation policies were not evidence- or fact-based: evidence based from a historical viewpoint or fact based from an empirical viewpoint. Moreover, the lessons from international experience were not inculcated in Nigeria's banking reforms, either wilfully, due to the desire of the governor of the CBN to push through a predetermined, though sincere, consolidation agenda, or inadvertently, due to the limited modelling capabilities in the central bank. Other critics in the banking industry, such as Mr Peterside, joined academics such as Teriba in their attacks on Soludo's consolidation, sparking off a vigorous media debate. While the Central Bank of Nigeria likened the consolidation process in Nigeria to the Malaysian model, albeit incorrectly, one of the leading investment bankers, Atedo Peterside, embarked on a unexpected media campaign asking why the Lebanese model was not followed. This campaign was quite oblivious to the fact that any comparison to Lebanon was certainly not politically correct for any country trying to lose its pariah status. Lebanon was not only a much smaller country but, worse, had been one of the 12 countries on the US Anti-boycott law's list of boycotting countries.

Overall, the lessons from the UK, India and Malaysia suggested that the Big Bang approach adopted by Soludo in 2004, while epoch making, sensational and revolutionary sounding, was fraught with more long-term difficulties than the short-term victories which its proponents celebrated. Banking history was replete with lessons from several countries on the danger of having ambitions about size as promoted by Soludo, on one hand, and his Big Bang approach on the other. The CBN seemed not to have had the benefit of these lessons from economic history.

In the 1980s, London had launched a radical set of industry reforms, which became known as the 'Big Bang'. During the regime of former Prime Minister Margaret Thatcher, the Big Bang financial revolution had fostered the emergence of a buckling global financial system with huge global banks whose influence extended beyond any one regulator, from both a country perspective and a market standpoint. Revising decades-old regulations at the stock exchange and other financial institutions, the Thatcher advisors believed the Big Bang would put London at a relative size and performance advantage in catching up with rapidly globalizing markets. Indeed, these 1980s reforms triggered short-term economic growth, which strengthened London's position as one of the world's prime financial hubs.

However, like the Nigerian experience of 2004–9, the relaxed regulations in the City of London had encouraged size, and fostered the emergence of banks that grew too big (See Table 4.1) for both regulators and their boards of directors. Corporate control and ethical corporate governance were the first twin casualties. Managerial capacity and executive integrity were simply incapable of keeping pace with the unbridled growth. The irony of the London megabank conundrum was that the greatest critics of the unbridled size hypothesis were one-time Secretary of State for Trade and Industry, Cecil Parkinson, and Chancellor of the Exchequer Nigel Lawson, who had played a role in Thatcher's Big Bang reforms in the 1980s.

From the UK experience, it seems that simple changes in regulations always trigger unforeseen opportunities for market operators, who often ignore the cumulative or ratchet effect of their actions. Predictably, regulators neither fully anticipate these changes nor are they properly

Table 4.1 Nigerian banks, bank branches and operations

S No.	Name	Total number of branch operations in 2005	Total number of branch operations in 2009	Total number of country operations in 2009
1	Access Bank	35	130	10
2	Afribank	147	250	
3	Bank PHB	95	216	2
4	Citibank Nigeria	12	13	98
5	Diamond Bank	128	100	2
6	Ecobank	29	600	29
7	Equitorial Trust Bank	62	100	
8	FCMB	59	150	1
9	Fidelity Bank	79	154	
10	FinBank	144	182	
11	First Bank	404	536	6
12	GTB	73	160	6
13	Intercontinental Bank	174	342	3
14	Oceanic Bank	135	435	5
15	Spring Bank	188	120	1
16	Skye Bank	142	250	9
17	Stanbic IBTC	67	60	19
18	Standard Chartered	6	19	69
19	Sterling Bank	71	100	1
20	Union Bank	384	405	
21	UBA	456	750	19
22	Unity Bank	200	221	1
23	Wema Bank	134	151	1
24	Zenith Bank	114	400	5

Source: Bank websites and annual reports.

skilled in managing the uncertainties created by their actions, often responding with belated risk controls. In London, the undercurrent had been the abolition of fixed commissions at the London Stock Exchange, which until the 1980s had been an exclusive association of small financial houses that dominated the UK trade in stocks and bonds. In Nigeria, it was the abolition of the small banks. The deregulation of commissions set in motion intense competition that encouraged brokers to veer into jobbing, and vice versa, and encouraged mergers. Eventually, the process broke down the barrier between brokerage firms, which executed client trades, and "jobbers" or securities firms, which took proprietary positions and risked their own capital by taking asset positions in stocks and bonds. Beyond the benefit of ensuring that brokers were not betting against their clients, the distinction between brokers and jobbers also, in some indirect way, prevented firms from getting big enough to become a systemic threat or 'too big to fail'.

The Big Bang reforms eroded all of those inherent safeguards in the UK's financial system without considering the risk. The Nigerian banks' approach to growth, either through cross-country diversification, local mergers or 'purchase and assumptions', was going to have the same risk effects as the UK reforms – phenomenal growth in the short term, unmanageable risks in the medium term, and a financial crisis in the long term.

4.4 Mergers and apprehensions

Most of the mergers and acquisitions (or business combinations) in Nigeria were accompanied by apprehension, hence the term 'mergers and apprehensions'.

By the end of the consolidation exercise, 13 of the 89 banks that had liquidity problems and had not found any banks with which to merge were subsequently declared failed banks by the NDIC. The 13 failed banks were African Express Bank, Allstates Trust Bank, Bond Bank, City Express Bank Limited (formerly Industrial Bank), Eagle Bank, Fortune Bank, Gulf Bank, Hallmark Bank, Lead Bank, Liberty Bank plc, Metropolitan Bank, Trade Bank and Triumph Bank.

However, the real measure of the success or otherwise of the hasty consolidation exercise of 2005 was not necessarily the banks that failed to meet the requirement, but the disastrous impact of those that made the minimum capital requirement superficially but had so many complex unresolved underlying issues. It made them economic time bombs waiting to explode.

With little consultation between the Central Bank of Nigeria and the Securities and Exchange Commission, the regulator for the Nigerian capital markets, and the Nigerian Stock Exchange, which traded all equity stocks of public companies in the country, several lapses and abuses occurred in both capital raising and capital trading by the banks. The abuses in the capital raising process of Nigerian banks will be dealt with in Chapter 5.

Union Bank and Spring Bank were prime examples of banks whose mergers had created severe apprehension for the entire system – shareholders, staff, and regulator alike.

Spring Bank was a classic case of a mismanaged merger created by the hasty banking consolidation process. It was a coalition of six banks: ACB International Bank; Citizens Bank; Fountain Trust Bank; Guardian Express Bank; Omega Bank; and Trans International Bank. Most of them were weak institutions with differing corporate cultures. A six-way merger of anaemic banks, many of which were on financial life-support systems, was the ultimate recipe for a merger disaster. More fundamental were allegations of distorted or illegal shareholding, proved by the joint investigation report of the Central Bank of Nigeria/NDIC released in October 2007, and confirmed by another report of the Nigeria Police Special Fraud Unit released in July 2008.

To beat the 31 December 2005 deadline for banks in Nigeria to meet the ₦25 billion minimum capital base, the six banks had executed a legal document, called a Heads of Agreement, which was a legal but non-binding document outlining the main aspects of their commercial agreement.[1] The Heads of Agreement had provided for two necessary activities to complete the transaction – a post 2005 due diligence and capital verification, and a post-merger adjustment (PMA) to adjust the capital allocated to each of the merging parties. However, with the continued poor performance of the bank after the merger, a post-merger adjustment yet to be finalized by June 2007, and several legal tussles yet to be resolved by June 2007, the regulators appointed an interim management board. Central to the legal issue was the discovery of "toxic" or "bubble" shares, which some of the shareholders alleged had been created in favour of some Guardian Express Bank directors, contrary to CBN rules that forbade banks to grant loans to their own directors for the acquisition of their own capital.

Ultimately this hasty merger created problems for the successor banks, and it was therefore not surprising that one of the country's top ten largest banks, which technically acquired Spring Bank, ultimately ran into a near-liquidity crisis, or that the members of its executive board were sacked by the Central Bank in 2009. With several unresolved petitions to the regulators – the CBN and SEC – and several legal suits in the courts, the acquisition of Spring Bank was concluded by Bank PHB in December 2008 under curious circumstances. By October 2009, the Central Bank had removed the managing directors of both Spring Bank and Bank PHB.

The citation of these two banks is not intended to demonstrate the culpability or otherwise of the key players in either bank but it does demonstrate the consequences of the hasty regulator-induced mergers of 2005 that the Central Bank's consolidation process created. The failure of many of these mergers to result in creating positive shareholder value only three to five years after the consolidation also lends credence to the need for central banks in volatile developing markets to promote fact-based policies rather than grandiose untested normative policies.

5

Policy on the Run: Currency Re-denomination and Bank Manipulation

5.1 Introduction: a new policy thrust

By 2006, the Nigerian economy had finally taken off on a path of near-sustainable growth, even adjusting for the spurious growth in the banking sector. With the average annual growth rate of the Nigerian economy shooting from less than 3 per cent in the period 1994–9 to nearly 4 per cent between 1999 and 2003 and up to 6 per cent in the period 2003–7, there were several indications that the economy might finally have entered a recovery phase. Driven by the non-oil sector, with the average growth rate doubling in the five years up to 2007, industries such as telecommunications had become the fastest growing.

The key growth drivers were mainly twofold. First was an external driver – the international oil price, which occasioned the phenomenal increase in the nation's total revenues, on the one hand, and the democratic reforms on the other. With the fiscal and revenue allocation reforms, the sub-national governments were collecting over half of the nation's revenue, and this was creating multiplier effects across the economy. However, overall policy coordination remained rather weak.

The disconnected positions of the three main regulators in the financial services system (the National Insurance Commission (NAICOM) for insurance companies, the Central Bank of Nigeria (CBN) for banks, and the Securities and Exchange Commission (SEC) for capital market operators) was one major factor that continued to show that the nation's policy on fixing the financial system was a policy on the run.

The Central Bank of Nigeria had apparently been successful in completing the recapitalization and consolidation of the Nigerian banking industry from 89 banks to 25 in 18 months by December 2005, despite resistance from influential power brokers, mainly from the northern part of the country. This had created a wave of recapitalization across many other sectors of the economy. For instance, as early as December 2005, the IFC (the World Bank's private sector lending arm), demonstrating support for the ongoing financial sector reforms in Nigeria, had launched a new project called the Nigerian Banking Reform Strategy aimed at addressing the scarcity of term finance in Nigeria. The strategy provided lines of credit to Nigerian banks and supplemented the country's low foreign direct investment. It resulted in loans to banks such as Diamond Bank, with a seven year facility of up to US$20 million to increase the banks' medium- to long-term funding for local small and medium enterprises (SMEs). That same year, the minister of finance, Dr Ngozi Okonjo-Iwealla, was given an award as the Best Finance Minister of the Year 2005 by Euromoney at an impressive awards ceremony in Washington DC, USA. Prior to her ministerial career in Nigeria, Okonjo-Iweala had worked for decades at the World Bank rising to the position of vice-president and corporate secretary of the World Bank. In 2003, she was appointed to President Obasanjo's cabinet and in October 2005, as Finance Minister, she led the Nigerian team that negotiated a deal with the government or bilateral creditors, to pay a portion of Nigeria's external debt in return for an $18 billion debt write-off, with gains expected to translate to increased funding of Millennium Development Goals and poverty-alleviation projects in Nigeria.

Other support, acclaim and awards came to the governor of the Central Bank, who won *The Banker* magazine's African Award and Global Central Banker of the Year award (announced in December 2005), which has been described as the pinnacle of achievement to which the governor of any emerging market central bank could aspire. A subsidiary of the *Financial Times* Group, *The Banker* magazine had based its process on selecting five central bank governors, one each from Europe, Asia, Africa, the Middle East and the Americas, after which a panel of judges selected one of the five as the Global Central Banker of the Year.

It was the first occasion that the governor of any African central bank had been so honoured. It was ostensibly to reward Soludo for his,

> fundamental restructuring and reorientation of the banking sector as a result of the on-going consolidation which is expected to hit $3 billion mark by the end of this month. About $500 million of this came from abroad. No policy has raked in so much investment into Nigeria's non-oil sector within a period of one year in the

> country's entire history. As at the commencement of the banking consolidation in July 2004, the share of the banking sector in the market capitalization of the Nigerian Stock Exchange (NSE) was about 24 per cent, but by September, 2005, it had risen to almost 50 per cent, making banking sector stocks the preferred stocks on the exchange. The Soludo-inspired and driven consolidation programme is also reputed to be the least-cost industry-wide restructuring of the banking system anywhere in the world, having cost as at the beginning of December 2005 a paltry one per cent of Gross Domestic Product (GDP). The Malaysian experience until now held the world record of 4 per cent of GDP. (Speech/citation read at The Banker Magazine Awards in London)

It is true that the apparent success of the consolidation exercise in the banking sector had led to similar consolidation exercises in several other sectors of the economy, including the insurance sector. However, the results were sometimes disappointing.

For instance, as part of the insurance industry's recapitalization exercise, which ended in 2007, the federal government had promised, or at least indicated, a possible tax concession for insurance companies, similar to that extended to the banks. But the absence of a well thought through policy, and the involvement of the tax authorities before the announcement was made, meant that the tax concession was not realized in time to be useful to the operators. In addition, while the insurance industry's capital base rose from ₦200 billion in 2005 to over ₦670 billion in 2008, and met the new stipulated capital bases, little else changed in the industry. The consolidation did happen, and reduced the number of insurance companies from 104 to 49 and reinsurance companies from four to two, but the long-run survivability of many of these companies was in question. Nonetheless, recapitalization and consolidation became buzzwords in the Nigerian economy. Accordingly, not long afterwards, minimum capital requirements were being recommended for divergent industries ranging from stock broking, to registrarship, and even for airlines. All of a sudden, recapitalization had become a magic wand to solve the myriad problems being faced by various industries.

5.2 Consolidation: the morning after

On Tuesday 3 January 2006, the Central Bank of Nigeria issued a press release announcing the outcome of the bank consolidation exercise.

> On July 6, 2004 the central bank of Nigeria announced to the nation a major reform program that would transform the banking landscape of the country. The main thrust of the 13-point reform agenda was the prescription of minimum shareholders' funds of ₦25 billion for a Nigerian deposit money bank not later than December 31, 2005. The banks were expected to shore up their capital through the injection of fresh funds where applicable, but were most importantly encouraged to enter into merger/ arrangements with other relatively smaller banks thus taking the advantage of economies of scale to reduce cost of doing business and enhance their competitiveness locally and internationally.
>
> The program has resulted in the shrinkage of the number of banks from 89 to 25 through merger/acquisition involving 76/70 banks which altogether accounted for 93.5% of the deposit share of the market. The Capital Market has also received a boost with a total of ₦406 billion raised so far and ₦360 billion accepted by the CBN in foreign capital including foreign capital inflow of US$654 million and £161,993 GBP. The general banking public is therefore advised to henceforth transact their banking business with only these 25 banks as listed below.

The fall-out of the consolidation was that 13 of the 89 banks, accounting for 6.5 per cent of the deposit share of the industry, according to the CBN report, were not able to make the required level, even though the Central Bank assured the safety of customer deposits trapped in the 13 banks.

The 25 banks that met the ₦25 billion mark, according to the CBN release, were:

Access Bank
Afribank
Diamond Bank
Ecobank
Equitorial Trust Bank
First City Monument Bank
Fidelity Bank
First Bank plc
First Inland Bank
Guaranty Trust Bank
IBTC-Chartered Bank
Intercontinental Bank

Nigeria International Bank
Oceanic Bank
Platinum Bank
Skye Bank
Spring Bank
Stanbic Bank
Standard Chartered Bank
United Bank for Africa
Sterling Bank
Union Bank
Unity Bank
Wema Bank
Zenith Bank plc

According to the front-page report of *ThisDay*, Tuesday 3 January 2006, titled 'CBN Hammer Falls, 13 Banks to be Liquidated', and the *Guardian* of the same day, the 13 banks that did not meet the new capital requirements were ACB International, Afex Bank, Allstates Bank, Assurance Bank, City Express Bank, Eagle Bank, Fortune Bank, Gulf Bank, Hallmark Bank, Liberty Bank, Metropolitan Bank, Trade Bank and Triumph Bank. Later, Lead Bank became the fourteenth bank in this group.

Predictably, the consolidation game brought with it the revelation of the underbelly of many banks, and accordingly sowed the seeds of their destruction. Interestingly, one of the characteristics or major distinguishing factors between mid-sized banks that easily met the ₦25 billion mark and those that did not was the concentration of ownership and management in a core set of a few individuals. Banks that had a diffusion of ownership and control simply could not survive, for two main reasons. First, banking institutions in which the leadership team, in particular the managing director and his deputy, were not the principal investors often created in the executive directors a greedy desire to amass enough wealth either to set up their own banks or to store up reserves for the rainy day when they were kicked out of their positions, or had to leave. On the other hand, bank owners who were also the managing executives knew that any proceeds from insider trading, insider loans and racketeering must still be kept in the 'family' and flowed back into the bank. Secondly, owners of owner-managed banks, who were also professional bankers, knew that their reputations as well as their investments were at stake, unlike the hired managers, who knew they had a limitless upside but a limited downside – a damaged reputation – if they ran their banks into the ground and were blacklisted. In a country where investigations into financial crimes were not always followed through, the judiciary was limited in its effectiveness and there was no system for credit referencing, most daring bankers knew that the only risk involved in looting a bank, in so far as you did it intelligently and didn't leave too many footprints or audit trails behind, was a damaged reputation. Moreover, in a country where three-quarters of the population live below the poverty line, people have short memories, and their preoccupation with survival creates a spiritual mental attitude, making them forgiving and tolerant of incompetence even when it raises issues of integrity.

Assurance Bank was one of the banks for whom the bells first tolled. Created by a merger between Almond Bank which had yet to receive a banking licence, and the under-capitalized Assurance Bank (formerly the Nigerian-Arab Bank), the new Assurance Bank (see the *Guardian*, Saturday 7 January 2006, page 9, and several *ThisDay* reports) was a forced marriage of dissimilar partners. Parmex Gensec Consortium had bought the distressed Assurance Bank from the Bureau for Public Enterprises (BPE) and was requested to recapitalize it. Around that period, a new bank by the name of Almond Bank, which had commenced setting up its operations, was denied a banking licence by the regulators due to the CBN's new restrictive licensing policy. Almond and Assurance banks therefore had needs in common. The agreement signed by the BPE and the purchasers of Assurance Bank allegedly provided for a five-year turnaround plan. In addition, the old Assurance Bank had loans of almost ₦4 billion when capitalized with interest, which had been approved for individuals and corporate bodies when the bank, as the Nigerian–Arab Bank, belonged partly to the government. This high debt overhang and the marriage of convenience between the unlicensed Almond Bank and the distressed Assurance Bank eventually began the destruction of the new Assurance Bank. The bank's former chairman admitted in interviews syndicated in two national newspapers (the *Guardian*) on Saturday 7 January 2006, that the bank also had significant problems with its executive management, problems so bizarre that the chairman described them as something '...better packaged in a home movie to be appreciated.' Summarizing his views on the integrity and capacity of some of the directors of his own bank, a view that applied to many other banks that didn't meet the regulatory requirements, the chairman, Chief Leo Stan Ekeh, who had been humorously described as Nigeria's own Bill Gates, opined:

> ...It was a tough one managing the MD/CEO and the DMD due to their personal differences, and again we hadn't the luxury of time to sack them and recruit new ones looking at the terminal date of

> the consolidation. Sincerely I didn't want to inflame a fast growing but negative impression that Igbos fight dirty in every business partnership. The only mistake we made was investing in these chaps and I sleep and wake up depressed everyday because what it reminds me of is that we still have a long way to go in this country. This is why I continue to shout everyday that until the educational system starts impacting the right culture on our people there is no way this country can move beyond the present level. All we have today is a culture of greed, mafia, selfishness, deceit and disrespect. The system is producing a lot of confident trick stars [sic] and this is very dangerous when you consider the fact that they have age on their side... Definitely, these can not take the country to the next level no matter the earnings of the country. (See *ThisDay* 2006).

In April 2007, the federal government approved new minimum capital requirements for all categories of players in the capital markets, which included the need to strengthen the financial base of the market operators. By August 2007, the Securities and Exchange Commission had issued recapitalization guidelines for stock broking firms, with the expectation that all qualifying stock broking firms would have increased their minimum shareholders' funds to ₦1 billion naira (US$8.5 million). Even though this recapitalization was either supported or endorsed by the director general of the Nigerian Stock Exchange, the director general of the Securities and Exchange Commission and the minister of finance, there was a policy reversal by August 2008, when the SEC issued a press release suspending the recapitalization of the stock broking firms. While the official line was that the suspension was a response to protests by the stock broking firms themselves, or to instructions from the Senate Committee on Capital Markets, inside market speculation was that the suspension was ordered by the SEC partly to protect the stock market from a further crash. The explanation was that the SEC policy reversal was made in order to pre-empt the diversion of funds from the stock market to the private placement market. An enforcement of the ₦1 billion recapitalization for stock-broking firms would inevitably have depressed prices on the stock exchange, especially at a time when the share index on the NSE had started to crash.

While many of the proposed recapitalizations of various operators in the financial services and aviation industries did not come to fruition, despite the Central Bank's successes in the banking sector and the parallel, not-so-successful, attempt in the insurance sector, several other institutional and political changes were happening in the background. First, elections had been held in early 2007, which had led to the emergence of a new regime and a new president and commander-in-chief, with a new cabinet of federal ministers and different policy biases. Secondly, the power base of the governor of the Central Bank had shrunk with the exit of Chief Olusegun Obasanjo. The sustainability of the banking reforms had also been put into question, not least because the governor of the Central Bank was yet to develop his own independent power network and personal circle of influence at the seat of power, but also due in part to the fundamental question of whether the reforms were systematic and evidence-based enough to stand the tests of time and rigour.

5.3 Currency re-denomination or revaluation

In August 2007, barely 18 months after the banking consolidation exercise had been concluded and with few, if any, evidence-based measures of the success of that major CBN campaign, the Central Bank announced another hastily designed policy: the re-denomination of the *naira*, optimistically tagged the Strategic Agenda for the Naira, which was aimed at making the Nigerian *naira* the reference currency in Africa.

The CBN's currency reforms were devoid of any understanding of the 'political economy' of the Nigerian *naira*, the sensitive politics of currency issues in Nigeria's political evolution or the historical antecedents of currency reforms in Nigeria. Though obviously well intentioned, Mr Soludo's strategic agenda for the *naira* ended up being the final act that ended his romance with the ruling class and brought him into disfavour with the power brokers in the federal cabinet.

The Nigerian currency game was one that had in the past transcended banking, becoming involved in politics and in the traditional rulers' power circles, eventually triggering a series of events that led to the deposition of two powerful emirs, including a former sultan and chairman of the Bank of Credit and Commerce International (BCCI) in Nigeria. In the late 1960s and early 1970s, a re-denomination of the Nigerian currency had been made to alter the regional economic power balance during the civil war, and in the mid-1980s a similar one had been used by the military regime to checkmate its political enemies.

For instance, in 1984, shortly after the December 1983 military coup in Nigeria, the *naira* had lost value not only due to an official devaluation resulting from worsening terms of trade, but also due to large-scale counterfeiting, cash-based corruption driven by kickbacks paid in cash, reckless printing of the currency and massive cash withdrawals from the central bank. Accordingly, the naira was all over the place, with little possibility of differentiating genuine from counterfeit currency notes. The monetary authorities had no reliable estimates or control over cash in circulation, and hence little control over key macroeconomic levers. Regaining control of the economic levers required the currency to be changed within a short timeframe and the nation's borders closed temporarily to avoid massive cash repatriation from neighbouring countries and other offshore sources. Though the currency change of 1984 was fairly successful, several powerful interest groups clashed in the process, sowing the seeds of vendetta among some power brokers. That same year, BCCI Nigeria had been investigated, following allegations of money-laundering, by a special panel headed by a top Nigerian secret service agent, who later became the national security adviser in Abacha's regime (see, for instance, Ashaka 2006).

Subsequently, the parent company of BCCI ran into critical issues globally and went into liquidation but a lot of confidential information on the wealth of some influential Nigerians had been obtained by the local intelligence authorities from the detailed investigations. With the volatile tenure of power in Nigeria during the military regime and the voracious appetite of soldiers to pursue vendettas against old enemies, most wealthy soldiers who had no visible sources for their untold wealth often created blind trusts for their money or simply gave it to trusted relatives or business associates to hold for them as proxies until they left office. Ten years later, by 1994, the power equation had changed in the country, and a new military head of state emerged, who used the intelligence reports on the currency change of 1984 to destroy the political strength of some of his opponents. For many politicians, who understood the real economic power circles, any discussion of the Nigerian currency needed to be understood in all its ramifications before even being mooted in public.

Looking at the public announcements of the governor of the Central Bank of Nigeria on 14 August 2007, and information releases on the CBN's website, the 2008 currency re-denomination was a multidimensional policy whose ramifications had not been fully analysed. Stakeholders were not carried along, and much of the enlightenment that followed subsequently was reactionary. The new policy, which entailed the introduction of new currency denominations, implied a total currency exchange and phasing-out of all the denominations in existence in Nigeria in 2007 from 1 August 2008. By dropping two zeroes from the existing denominations, the re-denomination exercise implied, at the then prevailing exchange rate of ₦125 naira to the US dollar that ₦1.25 would exchange for US$1.00. In addition, the plan under the new currency structure was to issue new 1 *kobo*, 5 *kobo*, 10 *kobo* and 20 *kobo* coins, most of which had faded out of use due to their hitherto low values. The governor of the CBN cited countries that had undergone similar exercises in the past, such as: Afghanistan (2002); Germany (1923, 1948); Argentina (1970, 1983, 1985, 1992); Bolivia (1963, 1987); Brazil (1967, 1970, 1986, 1989); China (1955); Mexico (1993, 1996); Israel (1948, 1960, 1980, 1985); Ghana (2007); and Angola (1995, 1999). He said that the ultimate objective was to '... restore the value of the Naira close to what it was in 1985 before the commencement of the Structural Adjustment Programme (SAP) in 1986'.

With several anticipated benefits, such as strengthening public confidence in the *naira*, reversing the tendency for currency substitution and reducing the cost of the production, distribution and processing of currency, the *naira* re-denomination exercise was expected to lay the foundation for the convertibility of the *naira* as well as to make it the 'reference currency' in Africa, when the African common currency came into existence, especially with the privilege given by the African Union to Nigeria of hosting the headquarters of the African Central Bank.

On the CBN's website (Central Bank of Nigeria 2007) the four elements of the agenda to make the *naira* the 'reference currency in Africa' were given as:

- currency re-denomination;
- adoption of an inflation-targeting framework for the conduct of monetary policy;
- sharing part of the federation account funds in US dollars to deepen the forex market and for liquidity management;
- current account liberalization/convertibility and accession to Article VIII of the IMF.

The benefits were said to centre on four points: better anchoring of inflation expectations; enhancing pricing and payments efficiency; assisting convertibility of the *naira;* and reversing the tendency for currency substitution. The re-denomination was to continue in a market-determined exchange rate system, with the new currency notes scheduled to come into effect on 1 August 2008.

However, no sooner was the re-denomination announced than the proposed policy ran into trouble. There were two main reasons. The first was the theoretical and conceptual underpinning of the re-denomination from a purely economic perspective. The absence of an evidently objective reason for advocating the re-denomination, apart from the vainglorious ambition of making the *naira* the reference currency, had created a school of forceful opponents – eminent economists who had taken the opposite position to the governor of the Central Bank (Okwe 2007). Among several arguments raised by the CBN's critics was that re-denomination was not the appropriate solution to any of Nigeria's economic problems, from either a theoretical or an historical point of view. Most countries that had undertaken a re-denomination exercise had had macroeconomic fundamentals which were different from Nigeria's and showed symptoms of hyperinflation – an argument which the Central Bank conveniently chose to ignore. Rather, in the 'frequently asked questions' on its website, the CBN's position was: '... Re-denomination is most successful when a country has achieved a measure of price stability and restored confidence in the national currency. It then proceeds to remove the 'zeroes of shame' to get the currency properly aligned. This is the condition now in Nigeria' (Central Bank of Nigeria website, 2007). As usual with the CBN, no objective time series data were provided to support its assertion that Nigeria had attained that desired position of price stability. The second reason why the policy ran into trouble was the lack of consultation with other governmental agencies, including the National Economic Management Team. Critics observed that these had been the two major mistakes of the Central Bank of Nigeria under Professor Soludo, and that the same mistakes were being repeated with the re-denomination, suggesting that the CBN had learnt nothing in the preceding two years. According to some critics, the ostensible autonomy granted to the CBN by its enabling act was obviously subject to abuse at the discretion of the incumbent governor.

Surprisingly, neither the federal Ministry of Finance, which had responsibility for administering the government's revenue and fiscal policy, nor the Federal Executive Council – the nation's cabinet ministers – had been consulted on the policy issue before its public announcement. Even the accountant general of the federation, who sat on the CBN's board, did not appear to be fully briefed on the ramifications of the new *naira* policy. As critics later observed, it was a naïve interpretation by the governor of the autonomy enshrined in the Central Bank Act of 2007 (Laws of the Federation of Nigeria 2007).

Immediately after the briefing of the Federal Executive Council (FEC) by the governor of the CBN, members of the FEC expressed a veiled displeasure at his condescending statement that he was telling the cabinet ministers for information purposes only, and not for approval, as the CBN had the autonomy to take currency decisions. Subsequently, the FEC directed the National Economic Management Team, which reported to the president and commander-in-chief, to examine the CBN's strategic agenda for the *naira* and 'advise it accordingly'.

Acting on behalf of the National Economic Management Team, the minister of finance, Dr Shamsuddeen Usman, gave assurances that the right signals had been sent to the local and international financial markets. He had been a deputy governor at the Central Bank between 1999 and 2007, reporting to Professor Soludo, but was now, by a twist of fate, technically the cabinet minister with oversight over the now autonomous CBN, Even the accountant general, who was a member of the CBN's board, was very diplomatic in his comments to the public on the parallel initiative of paying state government allocations in foreign currency, another initiative that had been sponsored by the governor of the CBN.

The abrupt manner in which the currency reform announcement was made, without any bilateral consultations with relevant agencies, pre-syndication or exhaustive policy debate, even if only in restricted institutional circles, had weakened support for the policy among domestic stakeholders. The Central Bank responded to the initial resistance from other high-level government functionaries and independent academics by launching a public communication and awareness programme through its website and the national media but the battle had already been lost. The CBN's aim of setting up a Steering Committee and an Advisory Technical Committee, as stated on its website, was only a late reaction to events: the 'unintended effects' of the re-denomination which the CBN had wanted to avoid could have been better avoided if consultations had been undertaken with the relevant agencies, especially the Ministry of Finance.

The new *naira* policy, again like many other policies, was well intentioned but hastily conceived and rushed into implementation, making it dead on arrival. The rationale for the new *naira* policy was articulated but its positive economic impact was never fleshed out to make its benefits obvious to its critics.

Some industry operators, such as the managing director of the United Bank for Africa, applauded the new *naira* policy but other business economists, including Folarin Alayande (Kuforiji 2006), believed that the case for the *naira* policy, though well intentioned, was not compelling enough, given the scant evidence presented by the Central Bank.

According to Folarin Alayande: 'First and foremost, I think, as a business economist, it is premature for anybody to commence a holistic dissection of the multi-faceted ramifications of the CBN's new *naira* policy. This is because the policy announcement only dealt with the monetary angle and we need to understand the fiscal complementarities as there could be heterogeneous fiscal policy responses'.

In addition, the aspects of the new *naira* policy that required input from the Ministry of Finance – revenue management and accounting, domestic tax collection and budget management – were never factored in by the CBN. The CBN appeared to be moving towards what economists call a 'Ricardian regime' in which fiscal authorities act prudently and government debt does not constitute a significant element of net wealth. That would enable monetary policy to target inflation, with the ultimate goal of attaining 'external current account convertibility' and IMF Article VIII status. However, Folarin Alayande, who was a regular commentator on financial economic issues in the Nigerian press, succinctly captured the mood of the conservative macroeconomists in a radio interview shortly after the announcement of the new *naira* policy. According to Alayande, the policy had to be examined on three levels, even if the net impact was going to be zero:

1. **The domestic level** – impact on wages and domestic prices of consumer goods;
2. **The regional level** – impact the re-denominated *naira* would have on Nigeria's competitiveness in the West African community, and possible timelines for convertibility of the *naira*;
3. **The international/global impact** – how the policy could impact on Nigeria's balance of trade and competitive positioning vis-a-vis other nations.

None of these analyses had been provided by the Central Bank in its justification for the currency reforms. The Central Bank itself had said that the major challenge, or key success factor, for the new *naira* policy was the execution of other macroeconomic reforms that would underpin price stability and maintain continuing confidence in the economy.

The key question, according to Alayande, was really whether the *naira* in its current form and denominations was still performing the key functions of money: as a unit of account; a medium of exchange; a store of value; and finally as a standard for deferred payment – the liquidity function. For Nigeria, the complicating factor was that the US dollar had been a variable standard in the preceding 18 months before the announcement of the re-denomination proposal, which in itself had undermined the value and claim of the dollar to being a standard. By definition, a standard had to be something that was reliable. If the US dollar was not a stable reference, then anchoring the *naira* currency to it would become an instrument of instability in itself. Yet the instability of a reference currency was never a substantiating basis for justifying the re-denomination of a currency.

Other commentators, such as Ayo Teriba (Ojowu 2007), who had been an arch-critic of Soludo's policies, compared the *naira's* US dollar exchange rate of ₦127 to the Japanese yen at ¥120 to the dollar, opposing the claim that the exchange rate was what made the *naira* weak. Beyond economists, private sector operators and foreign investors such as Simon Harford of the private equity company Actis took a more practical view of the proposed re-denomination, describing the cost implications of the reprinting of invoices, receipts and price lists as very high and preferably to be avoided.

From a taxpayer perspective, economists such as Adedipe also highlighted the absence of any coherent policy formulation on currency management by the Central Bank of Nigeria, given that a new ₦1000 bill had only been introduced in 2006 and other currency notes had been redesigned in the preceding two years. The new *naira* re-denomination policy announced by the CBN, which meant the phasing out of higher denominations, was in effect a sheer waste of the taxpayers' money spent on the earlier effort of 2005 to 2006. Above all, on top of the policy somersault was the absence of clear thinking on whether this effectively meant a subtle shift from a floating exchange rate system to a fixed exchange rate, as economists such as Professor Sam Aluko interpreted the new policy.

The other fundamental issue was that, if the new *naira* policy was part of the Financial Systems Strategy 2020 (FSS 2020), for which documentation had just been completed, were the links to the overall policy clear? If they were not, were the CBN's *naira* re-denomination and the so-called strategic agenda for the *naira* a credible policy alternative or another policy made on the run? Objective evidence suggested the latter.

While the World Bank expressed its preliminary support for the policy through its acting country director, Sorotiva Galine, and promised technical support for its implementation if formally approached by the Nigerian government (Okwe 2007), other notable economists, including Professor Ode Ojowu and Osita Ogbu, both previous economic advisors to the president and chief executives of the National Planning Commission, expressed either caution or reservation about the policy. Amidst the intellectual discourse on the objectivity of the rationale for the policy, barely one-and-a-half weeks after the governor of the CBN triumphantly announced his decision, the *naira* re-denomination move was suspended by the attorney general on the orders of the president (Lohor 2007) on the basis of the very Act on which the governor of the CBN had relied. Section 19(2) of the CBN Act required that 'the standard weights and composition of coins issued by the Bank and the amount of remedy and variation shall be determined by the president on the recommendation of the Board'. In the absence of any written request by the Board of the Central Bank for presidential approval, and the lack of such approval, the attorney general affirmed that the CBN action lacked any legal basis and as such could not be valid.

The dispute between the governor of the Central Bank and the attorney general on a technical point of law heralded the diminution of the influence of the governor on the country's economic management team. It was only the climax of the effects of a lack of consultative teamwork at the Central Bank itself, and the tendency of some of the governors appointed from outside the institution not to carry influential stakeholders with them in their policy formulation. Within his first three years at the apex bank, Professor Soludo had seen the departure of two out of his four deputy governors in circumstances which media reports suggested could have been better handled. The sudden exits of both Mrs Wahir Mshelia, who resigned in May 2005, and Dr Obadiah Mailafia, a former chief economist at the African Development Bank, who left in 2007, were initial signs of cracks in the executive leadership team. (See, for instance, Owete 2009). The two deputy governors subsequently took their protest about their treatment to the Central Bank and then to the House of Representatives, but without any real outcome.

In November 2005, the influence of the governor of the Central Bank had become so prominent, according to media reports, that he still remained an influential economic adviser, if not the *de facto* chief economic adviser, to the president, at least 18 months after assuming the governorship of the Central Bank. This was maintained after the *de jure* substantive chief economic adviser to the president, and head of the National Planning Commission, Professor Ode Ojowu, retired suddenly. (See *ThisDay* 2005.) Described as resolute and determined, Chukwuma Charles Soludo had fought and won many quiet people-related battles, even though he always maintained a calm demeanour, appearing unruffled, cool, calm and collected at Bankers Committee meetings with bank CEOs, while still being resolute in pursuing the economic agenda he argued for and implemented. Internal power playing and politics at the Central Bank and in the National Economic Management

Team had suggested a divided leadership team, dominated by an influential governor, who was very close to and had the ear of the president. However, the events of August 2007 confirmed that the power base was shifting – this was going to change the overall direction of the government's policy thrusts.

In the week of the currency reform cancellation, in a separate statement, the minister of finance, Dr Shamsuddeen Usman, revealed another major policy reversal. Acting on a presidential directive, he announced that the issue of waivers – exemptions from taxes, duties and tariffs to individuals, companies or organizations – would be suspended with immediate effect. The objective was to plug a number of revenue leakages through which corruption had been perpetuated in the last three years of the Obasanjo administration.

Meanwhile, the lack of policy coordination among various arms of government and government agencies responsible for financial sector stability had become most evident in the nation's capital market, which to all intents and purposes was synonymous with the stock market, of which the Nigerian Stock Exchange had gained a virtual monopoly. With banking stocks contributing about two-thirds of the capitalization of Nigeria's stock market, the banking industry dominated the capital market. The effectiveness or otherwise of the banking sector reforms would definitely have an impact on the capital market.

5.4 Market manipulations and the banking industry

The Nigerian economy recorded growth rates above 6 per cent per annum, with the banking sector recording some of the fastest growth rates in emerging markets, and there were impressive returns on the stock exchange. The governor of the Central Bank continued to receive accolades from within and without the country. However, this headline growth of the banking industry masked some looming fundamental issues as to the sources of this growth and the transparency of bank reporting. Most importantly, the sustainability of the growth figures posted by the banks was an issue, given the alleged connection of a number of banks with the proceeds of money-laundering – a source that was not long-lasting.

After, the bubble burst on the foreign exchange scam in the Nigerian banking sector in 2001, the newer generation of bankers had continuously been devising more ingenious ways to avoid being caught by the regulators. But, with the trio of finance minister Ngozi Okonjo-Iwealla, Central Bank governor Charles Chukwuma Soludo and Economic and

Financial Crimes Commission (EFCC) police chief Nuhu Ribadu determined to clean up the nation's financial system, there was little hiding place for the miscreants.

Following the arrest of the governor of one of Nigeria's 36 states in England in 2004, and the implication of one of the banks, Allstates Trust Bank, in aiding the diversion of a cheque meant for the state's ecological fund to the governor's personal use, the nation's banks had again come under serious scrutiny. In the period up to 2001, the nation's banks had become so morally bereft, so awash with cheap liquidity from money-laundering, and the surveillance capacity of the regulators had been so weak and toothless, that political appointees did not learn any lessons from the arrest of the influential governor.

On 13 September 2005, another state governor of an oil-rich state in Nigeria, Diepreye Alamieyesiegha, was arrested for illegally holding about £1 million in his house. It was that arrest, and the following interrogation, that confirmed that Allstates Trust Bank had been a recurring feature in the money-laundering racket and in the diversion of public funds to private accounts. Interestingly, the relationship between the Allstates Trust Bank and the Bayelsa State government had been an incestuous one. Upon the return to democratic rule in 1999 and the accession of the new civilian administration, Allstates Trust Bank had been the only universal bank in Nigeria owned by a Bayelsa State indigene. Over time, Bayelsa State's share of the federal revenue allocation, which was a monthly subvention from the federal government, went to the Allstates Trust Bank.

Barely one month later, a shareholder of a mid-sized bank, who had been a federal cabinet minister, was arrested by the agents of the Economic and Financial Crimes Commission based on recommendations by the Central Bank. The principal charge against the man known as the Godfather was the allegation that he used his position as a bank director to facilitate insider loans to himself, worth about ₦12 billion at a time, which violated the single obligor limit. (See, for instance, *The Week* 2005). The single obligor limit, or what was called the maximum lending limit, had been a feature of the Banks and Other Financial Institutions Decree (BOFID), later BOFIA, of 1991. It provides that no bank may advance a loan to any single client in excess of one-third, approximately 35 per cent, of the shareholders' funds in the bank, and maximum facilities to any single client must not exceed this. In a globalized world, the idea of a single obligor limit was indeed of limited use to the international banks, most of whom arranged their loans using offshore booking units supported by parent guarantees, which justified their treatment as advances secured against the parent company and not the subsidiary in the emerging market. However, the violation here of this simple rule of banking by a number of banks revealed the audacious attitude of some bank boards.

That same week an executive director of a large bank was relieved of his appointment and a former director of the United Bank for Africa was appointed to lead the interim board of the bank. Earlier, in August 2005, the Central Bank had dismissed the board of the Citizens Bank when a big hole in its finances and grave malpractices were allegedly discovered in the bank's accounts. Specifically, the Central Bank accused one of the directors of the bank of 'gross misconduct and abuse of office'. The bank was also accused of unsafe and unsound banking practices, inimical to depositors' funds. The investigation by the Central Bank had revealed the interlocking directorships of different generations of failed banks in Nigeria, after the distress of one of these banks was linked to another that had failed in the 1990s – the notorious Alpha Merchant Bank. This had become evident when a director of one of the 13 banks that were failed during the 2005 recapitalization fled the country to Cotonou in the neighbouring Republic of Benin. Ridiculously enough, he often sneaked back into the country to attend parties and other social functions and left again through the nation's porous borders before the security operatives could arrest him for interrogation. He was trying to escape his alleged role in the crash of Alpha Merchant Bank – a bank that had been liquidated by the National Deposit Insurance Corporation (NDIC) in the 1990s, and some of its directors convicted for abusing their fiduciary duties. Its failure had been linked to the crash of another bank in Nigeria in the 1980s.

The verdict of the Failed Banks Tribunal, established during the military regime of General Abacha in the 1990s to try promoters and directors of banks alleged to have contravened their duties, was eventually set aside and declared 'null and void' by the Federal High Court in 2005. But, the facts presented to the courts opened up a can of worms, revealing the incestuous interlocking relationships between three generations of failed banks in Nigeria.

Alpha Merchant Bank had been a peculiar case, using one of its investment vehicles to buy 40 per cent of the equity of Afribank Nigeria plc in 1991, an equity stake originally owned by the Banque Internationale pour l'Afrique Occidentale (BIAO). After Alpha Merchant Bank was liquidated, the Court of Appeal ruled that the NDIC should sell one of its veiled properties, a 400-room select hotel in an exclusive part of Lagos Island, belonging to a sister company in Lagos. However, this apparent resolution to pay the depositors of Alpha Merchant Bank, created another tussle between two agencies of government – the Bureau for Public Enterprises (BPE) and the NDIC. The NDIC, as liquidator of Alpha Merchant Bank, asserted its claim to an equitable interest in the shares formerly held by Alpha, while the BPE, the agency responsible for privatizing government enterprises, sought declaratory relief from the court that the disputed BIAO shares in Afribank Nigeria plc, which Alpha Merchant Bank had ostensibly bought, belonged to the federal government. The BPE's proposal was that the disputed BIAO shares in Afribank should revert to the government. In 2000, directors of the liquidated Alpha Merchant Bank accepted a proposal to relinquish their interest in disputed shares of Afribank Nigeria plc, according to the BPE. Effectively this meant that the directors agreed to be paid back their US$6.3 million, or half of the 33.96 per cent or 375 million Afribank shares that had originally belonged to BIAO, out of which a former executive director got 20 per cent, a former non-executive director and key promoter 43 per cent, and Alpha Merchant Bank 37 per cent of the refund. On conclusion of the legal case, a settlement was reached: the BPE finally obtained the BIAO shares and paid off all interested parties, as well as some legal fees. NDIC, as receivers of Alpha Merchant Bank, had received more than US$10 million, depositors were fully repaid and the outstanding amount was used to settle with shareholders.

However, the interlocking directorships of Alpha Merchant Bank and other institutions eventually sowed the seeds of destruction for any bank which had dealings with it. Citizens Bank, which held some remains of Alpha Merchant Bank, fell under the CBN hammer in 2006 and was liquidated. Afribank also ran into major liquidity challenges in 1999 and needed a massive injection of funds to save it from distress and eventual collapse. Needless to say, the eventual sale of the 30 per cent of warehoused Afribank shares, which the directors of Alpha Merchant Bank agreed to surrender, and the pricing of those shares, subsequently created additional issues for Afribank.

The discovery of links between another mid-sized bank, and a corrupt top government official led to an extensive probe by the CBN and the withdrawal overnight of about ₦2.1 billion (approximately US$16 million) by the state-owned national oil company, Nigerian National Petroleum Corporation (NNPC). The bank's liquidity was squeezed, with its branches unable to honour customer cash obligations.

In addition to the gross abuses allegedly discovered by the Central Bank in these banks, several other high-profile indictments of bank executives continued to suggest that the CBN consolidation agenda could not be effective if the other 12 points in Mr Soludo's 13-point agenda were not tackled with the same vigour.

By October 2005, a CEO of a relatively upscale bank on a prominent high street on Victoria Island, in the capital city of Lagos, was being investigated on charges of concealment and diversion of about ₦1.6 billion (approximately US$13 million), traceable to a former inspector general of police, and he was arrested by the EFCC. The ex-police chief had been arrested earlier, in March 2005, and was facing a 50-count charge of corrupt enrichment, despite several denials and assertive press releases.

An extensive investigation led to the discovery of an intricate network of money-laundering involving other banks. An executive director of the Fountain Trust Bank, the principal bankers of the corrupt police chief who was indicted in the sleaze, fled almost immediately to the United States. Industry sources alleged that the former police chief had intended to layer the diverted police pension funds into the capital market by acquiring a significant chunk of the shares of a regional bank in Western Nigeria, Wema Bank plc, which had its main foothold in the south-west. The police chief's personal banker, together with the stockbrokers, assured him that, even though the closing date of the public offer had passed, it was still possible to inject the funds that the bank needed to meet the ₦25 billion consolidation target set by the CBN. It was at that stage that the whistle was blown and the intricate link between the proceeds of money-laundering, bank deposits and the capital being raised to meet the ₦25 billion target became firmly established.

As with most money-launderers on the west coast of Africa, a good portion of the stolen funds were spent patronizing traditional rulers and public officials to win their support whilst the majority of the funds were spent by the looters on securing their economic future. For one of the uniformed officers under investigation, who was already approaching retirement age, the final game plan was to get a seat on the board of directors of one of the largest banks in the country and later enjoy a luxurious life in retirement as one of the king-makers of the south-western part of the country. In a way, it was reminiscent of the approach of a lot of the ex-military generals in their heyday during the 1990s. They looted the nation's treasury and layered the money through proxies and in-laws into oil and gas, construction, telecommunications and hospitality (but rarely manufacturing). Then they sat back and remote controlled their underlings, who were acting as trustees for their stolen wealth and as their proxy directors of newly quoted companies on the

Nigerian Stock Exchange. The multiplicity of the layers, and the complexity of layering of funds into the nation's commercial sector, were so intricately woven that it was extremely difficult, if not impossible, to indict any of the military generals for this ingenious privatization of public wealth.

For one police chief, his egoistical desire was to be the first uniformed but non-military officer to play in the big league. His downfall was that he stole the wrong funds. In Nigeria most public officials stole funds either at the source of origin or at the point of disbursement. That way it was easy to cover their tracks and claim there were irregularities in the due process, which had little to do with them. Alternatively, some public officials simply manipulated the process of either tendering for government contracts, or issuing new licences in a deregulated industry, or privatizing government companies. This was done by several sequences of activities, including using proxies, who acted as a front, and feeding them with classified 'insider' information, while inflating the costs along the way.

The new forms of corruption and money-laundering of the 2000s were, however, slightly different from the techniques of the 1980s and 1990s. The new generation of uniformed chiefs appeared too brazen when they diverted funds mid-stream, even more so when they diverted pension funds. In most African societies, where spiritual forces are still believed to hold sway, it was believed that the outright diversion of funds from pensioners, most of whom were old, sick and wretched, would bring down the ancestral curses of the pensioners – no matter how far-fetched this might sound.

Altogether, the indictment of some of these new generation banks was only symptomatic of a more fundamental problem characteristic of the newer banks, most of which were suffering from a rushed transition from their owner–founders. They had made a remarkable fortune from industry and commerce in the 1970s and 1980s, before investing in banking, and now in old age they were handing over the management of the banks to their under-experienced sons and nephews. Some of them had just returned from MBA schools in America but had little first-hand understanding of the rigorous sophisticated controls and the street savvy which were needed in a market such as Nigeria. On the other hand, the close link between malpractices in banking and the capital market also confirmed a separate, but interrelated, problem. Despite all the apparent reforms in the banking sector, the nation's capital market was still under-regulated and devoid of any active surveillance, making it the easy target for smart money-launderers. For instance, the know-your-customer (KYC) policy, which had been commonplace among the banks, was still non-existent among stockbrokers and other capital market operators. Section 16 of the Money Laundering Decree of 1995 required banks to verify the identity and address of their prospective customers before they could open an account. Section 15 (2) of the same decree, as amended by the Tribunal (Certain Consequential Amendments etc.) Decree of 1999, stipulated the penalties for the violation of customer due diligence. However, many of these legal provisions were not fully adhered to, either by some banks or by the stockbrokers, so that many hundreds of millions of dollars found their way into the capital market to fund the banks' recapitalization, creating a huge demand and resulting upswing in stock prices.

By December 2007, exactly 24 months after the completion of the forced consolidation of banks in Nigeria, capital market performance had improved significantly due to heightened domestic retail and institutional participation in the public offers of the banks that had come to the Nigerian Stock Exchange. Predictably, the huge demand for banking industry stocks had driven up the prices of bank stocks favourably relative to other stocks. Sixty-five per cent of total market capitalization and 70 per cent of the total market value of the Top 50 stocks was contributed by banking stocks. Of the Top 50 stocks on the Nigerian Stock Exchange, as of December 2007, 22 of those stocks were banking stocks and 25 of them were financial services institutions.

The banking sector had therefore become the centre of gravity of the Nigerian economy. Accordingly, if the banking sector collapsed, or if the prices of bank stocks collapsed, the whole stock market would collapse. The same purported achievement that had won Soludo the Global Central Banker of the Year Award for 2005 had now become the albatross of the nation's financial system.

Nigerian banks had been able to grow their earnings rapidly, largely from increasing fees, commissions and interest rates on letters of credit, and from other trade-related and loan transactions, which were required to finance economic activity in the fast-growing economy. However, there began to be speculation that some of the banks' stock market performance was due to price manipulation rather than to an increase in the banks' intrinsic value. For the period January–December 2007, the price of banking stocks had gone up by 167 per cent relative to the Nigerian stock market average of 75 per cent and the 31–35 per cent average for emerging markets (Afrinvest Nigeria (2007 and 2008) 2007 Review, 2008 Market Outlook).

Similarly, banking stocks provided the greatest amount of liquidity on the exchange, much higher than the exchange market liquidity of 20.4 per cent. Alongside other contributory factors to the supernormal performance of the banking stocks, such as the increased inflows from foreign portfolio managers, a relatively stable *naira* exchange rate and low money market interest rates, anecdotal evidence of price manipulation by banks persisted in the marketplace.

By April 2008, the alarm bells had started ringing deafeningly, even though the banks continued to ignore the warnings. That month, one of the three largest banks in the country, which had earlier been penalized by American regulators, was again fined US$15 million for ignoring money-laundering regulations yet again. The previous year, the 24 banks in the country had declared combined profits before tax of nearly US$10 billion. An independent report by J. P. Morgan had suggested that many of the leading Nigerian banks were overvalued by as much as 50 per cent. Meanwhile, the exceptional period of abnormal and supernormal growth continued. Between 2005 and mid-2008, driven by the capital-raising activities of the Nigerian banks in a liquid global economy, overall leverage increased in the economy. Banks lent money among themselves and to their subsidiaries to trade in their own shares. This artificially increased demand, supplemented by the demand created by increased awareness of capital market opportunities, and it created an era of 'irrational exuberance'.

Three key sharp practices were alleged by some banks against others, and the prevalence of those tales gave some legitimacy to the allegations. Moreover, the cultural attitudes of Nigerians, which incline them to talk a lot and discuss confidential matters openly, revealed that these practices were not isolated events but a regular occurrence that had become the order of the day. First, was the practice of trading in their own stocks through employees, second was insider trading in their own stocks through third party stock broking companies and, third, was the practice of warehousing and dumping other banks' stocks to damage their price. The Central Bank of Nigeria had instituted a process of 'capital verification', which meant that it tried to verify that banks actually had the unimpaired value of the capital which they claimed to have raised, and that the additional capital was raised from the stock market without violating local laws, such as the one prohibiting the granting of loans to purchase their own stocks. Nonetheless, the banks still found several ways to violate the rules. Typical practice was for some of the more unethical banks, such as one of the nine banks later suspended by the Central Bank for having impaired capital, to give loans to staff to purchase the bank's own shares under fictitious names, and then sell the shares immediately after the CBN capital verification. The Central Bank had instituted a process of capital verification at the beginning of consolidation to avoid 'bubble' or temporary capital but the frequency of these capital verifications declined and then stopped soon after the consolidation in 2005.

According to the current governor of the CBN (Sanusi 2010), many of these banks used special purpose vehicles to lend money to their own companies for stock price manipulation. For a few of them, nearly half of their entire capital base had been funded through depositors' funds and insider-related loans to buy bank stocks! The net effect was a whirlpool of bubble capital. While some banks set up shell companies to circumvent the CBN's single obligor limit and evade audit trails, other banks used depositors' funds to purchase their own public offerings. According to the governor, Afribank used depositors' funds to purchase 80 per cent of its initial public offer (IPO), buying its own shares at over double the market price – paying ₦25 per share when the shares were trading at ₦11 on the exchange – and finding itself exposed when the shares later collapsed to less than ₦3. A CEO of one of the top ten banks was reported to have controlled over 35 per cent of the bank through special purpose vehicles.

By 25 October (*ThisDay* 2009b), the EFCC had hired foreign forensic analysts to trace an estimated ₦1 trillion allegedly looted from various Nigerian banks by bank executives, or in connivance with bank senior executives, with some of the funds allegedly being traced to Dubai. At a bank conference in Abuja, this comment was attributed to the governor of the CBN: 'As far as I know, the so called key shareholders and bank executives that ruined these banks do not deserve a place again in these institutions, but should find their place in jail or even [be] shot dead' (*ThisDay* 2009a).

Part of the issue was that Nigeria's minimum financial reporting standards only demanded the quarterly publication of gross earnings, pre-tax profit and net profit. It was difficult for investors to verify the consistency of a bank's income statement or estimate future cash performance, and easy for bank CEOs to window-dress their books.

Another practice, as was later proven in the case against the Union Bank, was the granting of substantial loans, sometimes close to half of the bank's single obligor limit, to a selected stockbroker to make serial purchases as a market-maker in the bank's stock. This was a means of driving up the stock price for one of three objectives: so as to be able to raise more capital at inflated offer prices during an impending public offer; to allow the executives to make abnormal profits by insider trading on their own account; or to enable the company to 'beat' the stock market and reap abnormal 'extraordinary' profits through its subsidiaries.

Margin loans are loans secured against the portfolio of shares the loan is used to purchase, with the borrower providing a little deposit margin on the total loan to serve as a buffer against stock price fluctuations. By 2007, they had become the order of the day in the Nigerian banking system. In a stock market where most liquid stocks more than doubled their prices every year, compared with a maximum of 16–18 per cent on a money market interest-bearing deposit, the widespread rush to the stock market soon led to irrational exuberance. This was worsened by the high level of financial illiteracy in the country, which made many investors follow a herd instinct. It was a doubly cataclysmic effect that inadvertently legitimized the high stock prices by applying excessive demand to a manipulated limited supply, and led to a self-fulfilling prophecy. In a country with a poor electricity supply, and hence a weak real sector, and little or no manufacturing, many banks found it safer to grant loans to stock market speculators through the notorious margin loans rather than lend money to the unstable real sector. Cumulatively, the overall impact was an artificially high stock market index, worsened by arbitrary pricing of initial public offers, which created unrealistically high benchmarks for many of the listed shares.

By April–May 2008, when the NSE issued new guidelines to check the arbitrary pricing of shares in the nation's capital markets, the worst of the damage had already been done. Most banks had perfected the act of share price manipulation, so that the checks and balances announced by the director-general of the NSE on the minimum volume of shares to be traded to effect a price movement had little impact.

Before April 2008, the rules on the NSE were that the price of a stock was allowed a maximum 5 per cent movement, either up or down in any single trading session. Such price movements had to be based on a minimum volume of 50,000 shares. But, on 23 April 2008, the rules were changed to a minimum of 100,000 shares. From that date, the NSE directed that any company seeking to be listed by introduction on the NSE should make 10 per cent of its outstanding shares available on the day of listing for trading. The primary considerations cited for the new directive were to promote liquidity and obviate undue price appreciation arising from interference in trading by owners of listing companies and their brokers. In the preceding 12 months, the average stock that was listed had risen by close to 100 per cent in share price within a month of listing, which supported the NSE's position on price manipulation and abnormal price gain, irrespective of the fundamentals of the company.

The abnormal price appreciation was worsened by the concentration of the stocks in the hands of a narrow circle of a few individual and institutional investors, especially companies that had recently completed a private placement. Even though price manipulation had been made relatively more difficult by the new rules, irregularities persisted.

Price manipulation was, indeed, not a new phenomenon on the Nigerian stock exchange. Its real origins lay in the 1990s, when stockbrokers began the reckless practice of selling short stocks of companies they did not have, thereby creating artificial demand. Due to the 'open outcry' system of trading on the stock exchange floor, which was not automated and allowed a lot of manual recording, manual settlement of shares crossed and, hence, there was a lot of human intervention and manipulation, so stockbrokers began the practice of collusion and insider trading. By 1997, when the Automated Trading System was introduced, together with a new settlement system, the market had a temporary reprieve. However, by the early 2000s, the management of some large companies began employing the services of unethical stockbrokers and manipulating the prices of stocks that were either completely unavailable or had minimal volumes in the market. Similarly, owners of newly listed companies formally listed their companies without making a critical mass of shares available for trading, thereby creating artificial scarcity and driving up share prices. This practice was compounded by the twin evils of delayed releases of certificates to investors after the completion of a public offer, and delayed verification or delayed dematerialization of those certificates for secondary market trades. Through such a delay in the issue or verification of the shares, ordinary investors were denied access to trade their shares, creating a low supply. Selected brokers working for the listed companies then created an artificial, unmet demand, continuously driving up the pent-up demand and aggressively moving share prices up to allow the directors dump their shares at phenomenally high prices.

Many banks obviously funded these share racketeering and price manipulation games for their own stock accounts, and also for other non-banking stocks in which their subsidiaries traded. However, the last straw, and the climax, was when the share price manipulation moved to dormant companies. This was the SEC case of Afroil plc, which had been wound up by a Federal High Court Lagos Order dated 30 March 2001, following its inability to pay its debts. Nonetheless, it continued to trade its shares on the floor of the NSE. The price increases that were recorded gave clear evidence of the rot and decadence in the Nigerian capital market. Predictably, neither the SEC nor the NSE was formally notified of the high court ruling. Needless to say, the Afroil instance was also a major indictment of the surveillance and market intelligence capabilities of both the exchange and the regulators. Another case in point was Capital Oil plc, with similar antecedents to Afroil plc: there was no evidence to show it had gone into liquidation but the company was not proven to be in active operation, and only occupied obscure office accommodation in Ikeja, Lagos (*ThisDay*, 7 May 2008).

In the case of the banks, it was difficult to secure any conclusive evidence, or follow through with a prosecution of any of them for share price manipulation, especially as this was done through an intricate and well-disguised layer of subsidiary and associated companies, including third-party stock broking firms, with the regulators often turning a blind eye.

Barely six months after the first major media publicity over the multiple infractions on the Nigerian Stock Exchange, and the rampant cases of price manipulation, the SEC, Nigeria's capital market regulator, formed a 15-member committee to assess the capital market's current state and make recommendations for its future direction. It was led by Adedotun Sulaiman, then chairman of global consulting firm Accenture's business in Nigeria, and leading insurance underwriter, Cornerstone Insurance. The committee submitted its report, 'Nigeria's Capital Market: Making World-class Potential a Reality – The Report of the SEC Committee on the Nigerian Capital Market' in February 2009.

The committee observed on page 37 of its report that the Nigerian capital market, as it was then functioning, had a 'high capacity for insider dealing and market manipulation by market operators'. Specifically, this capacity for severe abuses was described thus:

> Current standards for identifying, terminating and correcting market manipulation in trades are inadequate. Some market operators, regulators, ... and company officials have access to privileged and price sensitive information before the information is disclosed to the public, giving room for imperfect information availability and insider trading. Indeed, the NSE requires that listed companies must file with it all reports and planned corporate actions before release to the public. Stock market operators, especially stockbrokers, are also able to utilize privileged and confidential client information to 'front run' and execute proprietary deals in advance of client trades.

Shortly after the banking and insurance industry consolidation exercises, an attempt was also been made to increase the minimum capital requirements for stock brokers and registrars. Even though the mandatory recapitalization of stock broking firms was later suspended by the SEC, the craze for 'bigger is better' had started a capital-raising binge which made three of the nation's largest stock broking firms attempt to raise their share capital to over ₦25 billion, which was the minimum required for universal banks. At the then exchange rate of US$1.00 to approximately ₦118, this translated into about US$212 million. Predictably, the mechanism for this was the use of ubiquitous private placements to raise money from upper middle-class employees in blue-chip companies and from a few undiscerning high net worth individuals. In the most sensational of the capital-raising efforts, a Lagos-based stock broking firm had approached some employees of the Shell Petroleum Development Company in 2007 to invest at least ₦7 million (US$59,322) each in its private placement, assuring them that the shares would be listed on the stock exchange by the end of 2008. Subsequently, some other employees of a leading oil exploration company in Nigeria had used a leading investment vehicle to take a margin loan, guaranteed by the stock broking firm, from a commercial bank to enable employees to subscribe to the private placement. Yet, by mid-2008, the Nigerian Stock Exchange had still to approve the procedures for listing publicly quoted stock brokers on an exchange in which they traded, due to the inherent conflict of interest in which such a position would put publicly quoted stock broking firms. Effectively, the stock broking firm could neither list its shares on any exchange nor reap the artificial windfall profits, such a trading window would have provided for it. On the other hand, the investors held shares in a private company whose market value could not be ascertained and which could not be traded or exchanged. This debacle, and the gradual crash of stock prices in Nigeria, eventually led to a class action suit by the investors, the nation's first class action suit in the margin loan crisis. (See, for instance, Nkanga 2010.)

Between an all-time price peak in March 2008, when the irregularities were widely publicized, and the end of 2008, the market recorded a dramatic tumble, crashing by about 45 per cent. Effectively, by January 2009, the price index on the Nigerian Stock Exchange had dropped back to the level it was in 2004, just before the banking industry consolidation. Among several other possible drivers of the capital market spike and bust, one key factor stood out – the manipulation of banking sector share prices. In another case of hurried policymaking, the Securities and Exchange Commission issued a directive to registrars to increase their share capital. This directive was later faulted and reversed by the Senate for alleged non-compliance with the due process in respect of recapitalization.

Predictably, the Sulaiman Committee report acknowledged that, although the Nigerian stock market crash coincided with the global financial crisis, some of the Nigerian problems were not only endogenous but self-inflicted. These included, among other tactical causes, two fundamental issues – ineffective market regulation and supervision on the one hand, and a lack of regulatory proactivity and cohesion, on the other. This was most evident in the lack of partnership between the Central Bank and the Securities and Exchange Commission, and by implication the day-to-day management of the country's monopolistic stock exchange, the NSE.

Beyond the evident issue of the intricate interpersonal dynamics between the leaders of the various institutions, the absence of an effective formal coordination structure, or formal forum for interaction between the regulatory chiefs, fostered an atmosphere in which decisions were made in silos, and the interdependencies were never factored in at the start. Despite the existence of a Financial Services Regulation Coordinating Committee (FSRCC), originally set up in April 1994, its impact was hardly felt in the first 14 years of its life.

Originally set up as the Financial Services Coordinating Committee (FSCC), the name of the inter-agency committee was subsequently changed to the Financial Services Regulation Coordinating Committee, and accorded legal status by the 1998 amendment to Section 38 of the CBN Act 1991.

The committee comprised the three key financial services regulatory bodies in Nigeria (the CBN, SEC and NAICOM). The Corporate Affairs Commission, and other institutions, such as the Nigerian Deposit Insurance Corporation, the Nigerian Stock Exchange, and the National Board for Community Banks were co-opted as observers. By 2008, 9 years after being established, the FRSCC had still not been able to fulfil its key objective: the 'reduction of arbitrage opportunities usually created by differing regulatory and supervisory standards among supervisory authorities in the country'. Its second key objective was to 'Eliminate any information gap encountered by any regulatory agency in its relationship with any group of financial institutions, and that was also not achieved, since many of the 25 banking groups conducted disguised back-to-back inter-subsidiary transactions.

Indeed, for several months before and after the prolonged Nigerian stock market crisis, there were serious allegations that the FRSCC had not been holding meetings (Ajibade 2010). This absence of regular information sharing among the regulators was also worsened by the balance of power between the Nigerian Stock Exchange, a self-regulating organization and monopoly stock exchange in Nigeria, on the one hand, and the SEC, the securities market regulator, on the other. The weakness that made the SEC ineffective in regulating the NSE for several years had three main causes. First, the NSE had been in existence for longer than the SEC and had a relatively more stable and better qualified leadership on paper (factors that collectively made it sometimes more visible to the public). It also enjoyed better access to the media and the nation's politicians and decision makers. For several reasons, the former Lagos Stock Exchange had changed its status, in curious circumstances, to become the Nigerian Stock Exchange. It became a virtual monopoly with a director general who became a formidable institution in her own right. The proposed alternative stock exchange in Nigeria had never seen the light of day. The Abuja Securities and Commodities Exchange (ASCE) was initially set up as the Abuja Stock Exchange (ASE), to trade in securities, just like the Nigerian Stock Exchange. However, intense lobbying by some vested interests compelled the government to revoke the operating licence of the ASE in 2001, shortly after it was opened with some state-of-the-art trading equipment. In 2003, the licence to trade in both securities and commodities was restored, leaving the exchange with only the option to trade in commodities, even though it was yet to acquire new equipment or reconfigure existing equipment to suit large-scale trading in them.

Second, was the compromised position of the then SEC director general, who had been a stock broker on the floors of the NSE, and whose lack of assertiveness had been raised by several commentators, including the nation's leading business daily, *BusinessDay*. Third was the absence of transparency in the operations of the NSE, a company limited by guarantee, whose operations had become more opaque over the years, coupled with the presence of an intimidating personality at its helm.

Accordingly, with this kind of dictatorship at the NSE, and a compromised SEC as policeman, it was not surprising that the Sulaiman Committee concluded that:

> The frequent non-compliance by many listed companies with NSE's rules, especially in relation to the completeness and frequency of

> interim and full-year financial reports, appears to go unpunished by either SEC or NSE....
>
> Several companies, including Transcorp, which is chaired by the Chief Executive of NSE, are culpable in this regard.... The lack of clarity of the ownership and governance structure [rule making, nomination and selection of Council members, management authority, etc.] of NSE, even to market operators, is quite apparent and raises questions about transparency and accountability.... It would appear that the principal stakeholders cannot properly exercise their rights of participation in the governance of NSE.... The verification of transfer certificates by registrars sometimes frustrates the process of transferring securities, especially in view of the wide availability of certificated shareholdings.... Several abuses also abound in relation to delays in the issuance and despatch of share certificates for primary issues and verification of shares bound for the secondary market.... It is believed that some companies use the Registrar's office, especially for in-house Registrars, to regulate the supply of their securities to the market

Meanwhile, the governor of the Central Bank, Professor Chukwuma Soludo, continued to maintain the propaganda that the nation's banking system was immune to the global economic crisis in different forums, including a lecture to the Chartered Institute of Bankers in Lagos in September 2008, according to newspaper reports. This was, however, later refuted by the governor of the Central Bank (Kolapo 2009).

However, towards the end of the first quarter of 2009, nearly five years into the era of banking reforms driven by the Central Bank under Soludo, both the nation's capital markets and banking system were in a near shambles. Coincidentally, the five-year tenure of both the governor of the CBN and the director general of the SEC expired that same year, and there was mass lobbying by concerned parties to ensure that neither Soludo nor Musa Al-Faki, the director general of the Securities and Exchange Commission, were given another term.

Soludo was both chairman and chief executive of the Central Bank, and answerable, by virtue of the CBN Act, to no one except the president and commander-in-chief of the Federal Republic of Nigeria. But the director general of the SEC not only reported to the chairman of his board, but was also under the supervision of the federal Ministry of Finance. By January 2009, market failures were obvious and there was a perceived inability to bring the NSE leadership to book for its failures. When a dramatic power play developed between Al-Faki, and the board chairman, the former was pressurized into resigning three months before the expiry of his tenure.

In January 2009, also, the Central Bank began deploying resident examiners in banks in response to fears that some large banks were facing severe liquidity pressures and risked not meeting their obligations. This also followed the worrying pleas by many banks to the Central Bank not to implement the December 2008 uniform year end for all banks. That same month the *naira* suffered an almost 30 per cent major devaluation to ₦153 against the US dollar from the earlier exchange rate of ₦118. Following these moves, the whole of the first half of 2009 was a time of panic moves by the regulators, with the three chief executives of the CBN, NSE and SEC under media pressure to resign. In February, the CBN reversed its earlier liberal stance on exchange controls by introducing what amounted to stronger ones – the Wholesale Dutch Auction System (DAS) was replaced by the Retail DAS, and, with a lack of clarity on the reasons for this policy, speculation against the *naira* intensified.

In early February 2009, there were increased calls for the Securities and Exchange Commission to be entirely overhauled because of its obvious failures. *BusinessDay* had commenced a series of articles exposing the weaknesses in both the Nigerian Stock Exchange and the regulator, the SEC. In an article in one of the leading business dailies (*BusinessDay*) in the country, Ogho Okiti, chief economist of *BusinessDay*, criticized the director general of the SEC for weak, incoherent leadership, including not being able to take firm positions against the Nigerian Stock Exchange, on which he had once been an operator (Okiti 2009).

By March 2009, 12 months after the first major slide of March 2008 on the Nigeria Stock Exchange, the capital market in Nigeria became one of the worst performing in the world, based on its capital losses. April 2009 saw the minimum policy rate (MPR) reduced in the face of exchange rate speculations and worries about inflation. Policy analysts were uncertain as to whether the incumbent governor of the CBN wanted a second term, as his first five-year term expired in May 2009, but the actions of the CBN were increasingly less decisive and more short-term oriented, as if to appease the politicians. According to newspaper columnists such as Okey Iheduru:

> [Soludo's] tenure was a breath of fresh air, coinciding with Nigeria's biggest economic expansion since the oil boom years of the 1970s. Soludo's CBN however self-destructed by allowing his controversial consolidations to degenerate into a casino, where operators went on a borrowing binge on the global markets to feed a rising 'easy

> money' culture.... Soludo's CBN made matters worse by becoming too chummy with bank executives and denied the existence of a bubble just a few months before it burst. (See, for instance, Iheduru 2010)

Despite invitations by the Senate to the governor of the Central Bank during the early days of the banking crisis, he had assured the Senate that the situation was under control and would not affect the country. (See, for instance, the comment attributed to Senate President David Mark in Olawuni and Akintola 2010)

At around the same time, three people had been short-listed for consideration for the office of governor of the Central Bank of Nigeria, and some had already commenced security screening. Due to the nation's federal character, which in simple terms implies that political office holders have to be evenly distributed or rotated between the nation's 36 states or three major tribes, the fact that the immediate past two governors of the CBN had been from the West and the East tended to suggest that the president might be inclined to appoint a northerner.

By May 2009, when it was clear that the incumbent would not be retained, it became apparent that the president, as early as April 2009, had chosen Sanusi Lamido Sanusi, the group managing director of First Bank of Nigeria plc,. On Wednesday 3 June 2009, Mallam Sanusi Lamido Sanusi took his place at the Central Bank as its tenth indigenous governor.

Curiously enough, for a stock market that was in disarray, no substantive successor was appointed director general of the Securities and Exchange Commission until several months later.

6
Politics of Banking Reforms

'I cannot point to any banker of my generation who became a rich man'

Gamaliel Onosode, Chairman and Chief Executive NAL Bank, now Sterling Bank (1973–1979), and Member Board of Fellows, Chartered Institute of Bankers of Nigeria.

(Quoted in an interview with *The Guardian*)

6.1 Financial terrorism and the games banks play

In his first official speech, on 7 July 2009, the new governor of the Central Bank of Nigeria (CBN) Sanusi Lamido Sanusi remarked that the banking sector did not face a systemic risk: 'The CBN surveillance activities will receive new impetus to ensure efficient management and good corporate governance... Our view is that there are stress points in banks' balance sheets (margin loans, proprietary positions, oil marketing names, unsecured large exposures) and these are being dimensioned.' (based on various newspaper reports between 7 July and 9 July 2009)

Early in the same month, a Paris-based bi-monthly publication, *The Africa Report*, released a damning analysis, questioning the health of most Nigerian banks (Norbrook and Lawal 2009).

In Sanusi's four-point agenda (*Leadership* newspaper, 17 August 2009), 'the need to strengthen regulation and supervision through enhanced disclosures by financial institutions' stood out clearly. The stated objective was to have in place a full disclosure regime that would put the nation's banking industry on a par with best practice and international standards such as BASEL II and the International Financial Reporting Standards (IFRS).

Accordingly, Sanusi's first move was a major stress testing of the system and a widespread media campaign on full disclosure of accounts by all banks. By mid July 2009, it was clear that many banks were permanently dependent on the expanded discount window (EDW) in an economy whose fiscal revenue had declined by 40.7 per cent in the first half of the year. The CBN introduced an interest rate corridor and reduced the minimum policy rate (MPR) further to stimulate lending. Furthermore, the CBN closed the notorious EDW, which had been a lifeline for some of the nation's larger banks. The governor of the CBN announced the restoration of a managed floating exchange rate for the nation's currency, the Nigerian *naira*.

The results of the subsequent CBN audit of the 21 local banks and the three foreign-owned banks in the nation's financial industry provided incontrovertible evidence that many of these banks had been window dressing their account books and playing games with their financial reports. The CBN public disclosures of 14 August 2009 disciplined five of the ten banks – Afribank, Finbank, Intercontinental Bank, Oceanic Bank and Union Bank – which were referred to by the media as 'the famous five' or 'the *in*famous five'.

Of the 21 local banks, 11 passed the CBN audit, eight failed, and two were put on a watch list and given until June 2010 to recapitalize. The five troubled banks were claimed to have accumulated margin facilities of ₦456.28 billion and an exposure of ₦487.02 billion to the oil and gas sector, totalling ₦943 billion or US$6.4 billion. These five banks and a few others had overshot their single obligor limits and taken unrestricted advantage of the expanded discount window offered by the CBN to the tune of ₦127.85 billion. Overall, the joint examination of banks had revealed concentrations of credit to a few not very liquid corporations and undue exposure to margin lending. When Sanusi closed the EDW, the same banks went to the inter-bank market to increase their unsecured bank borrowings to ₦253.3 billion (US$1.7 billion), which confirmed the distressed liquidity signal noticed with the EDW. To inject liquidity into the five ailing banks, the CBN released a total bail out of ₦620 billion to these banks, which had a total loan portfolio of ₦2.9 trillion.

In mid-August 2009, the president also strengthened the leadership of the CBN with the appointment of the revolutionary head of the federation's civil service, Mr Steve Oronsaye, to the board of the CBN in a personal capacity. In addition, the president and commander-in-chief approved the nominations of Dr Adedoyin Salami, Mr John Oshilaja,

Prof. Chibuike Ugochukwu Uche, Dr Shehu Yahaya, and Mr Abdul-Ganiyu Garba as members of the CBN's Monetary Policy Committee.

In Figure 6.1 the banks in the right quadrants are the ones that passed the CBN audit while the ones in the left quadrants failed it. Wema Bank and Unity Bank had been given waivers in order to recapitalize because the regulators claimed there was insufficient evidence to discipline their managements and boards. The board and management team of Wema Bank had assumed control less than six months before the audit and the regulators granted them some breathing space.

With an investigation by the Economic and Financial Crimes Commission (EFCC) ongoing into financial malpractice by the executive boards of the eight banks that failed the audit, and with the other two banks watch listed, additional evidence of financial recklessness became increasingly obvious. Without prejudice to the outcome of the court cases instituted by the CBN against the CEOs of the banks for allegedly misappropriating depositors' funds, and the counter claims by the owners for violation of their fundamental human rights, the CBN audit revealed the extent of insider abuse by bank directors and the dangerous games banks had played with depositors' funds.

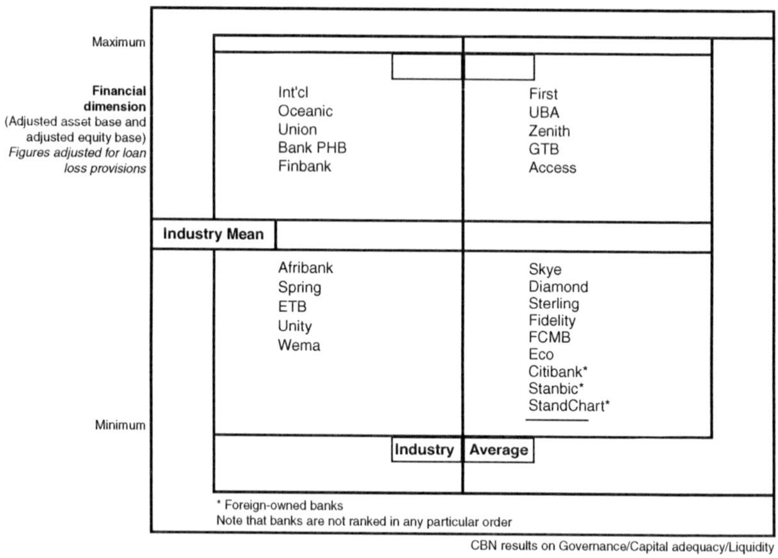

Figure 6.1 The Nigerian banking industry landscape October 2009

Source: Various banking data supplemented with Renaissance Capital Banking Industry Update of October 30 2009, '*Nigerian Banks After the Audit*'.

According to the governor of the CBN in an inaugural lecture at Bayero University in February 2010 (Sanusi 2010), some of the banks created special purpose vehicles to lend money to themselves to drive up their stock prices and make artificial profits, purchase private jets and set up fake companies (in one case up to 100 fake companies) to layer money. Worse still, the CBN findings suggested that the banking recapitalization of the Soludo years had been a major sham since much of the capital raised by the so-called mega banks had been financed by round-tripping depositors' funds. Two of the eight banks rescued by the CBN were alleged to have purchased at least 30 per cent of their enhanced share capital with customers' deposits. In the words of the new governor of the CBN: 'In many cases, consolidation was a sham and the banks never raised the capital they claimed they did.'

This was confirmed by a Securities and Exchange Commission (SEC) disclosure on Thursday 29 July 2010, alleging that Afribank senior executives had perpetrated a fraud in connection with the purchase and sales of Afribank shares in a 'false trading' scheme involving several of its executive and non-executive directors. The false trading and illegal share buy-back scheme was alleged to have involved entities financed by Afribank and Union Bank plc buying shares in the names of 1258 subscribers, which accounted for 66.4 per cent of the public offer. All the shares held by these 1258 subscribers were later consolidated to reflect the beneficial ownership of nine companies owned by Afribank and its directors (see, for instance, a front-page article entitled 'SEC Says Afribank Executives Manipulated 2007 Public Offer' in *BusinessDay*, Friday 30 July–Sunday 1 August 2010.) The corollary of this fictitious capital-raising and stock price manipulation was that many bank CEOs and directors had vast fortunes. Essentially, the stereotype of the conservative banker of the 1970s had given way to the hustler banker of the 1990s and the wildly manipulative bankers of the early 2000s.

Given the fears of the Central Bank of Nigeria that the banks were understating loan loss provisions and cross-classifying 'lost loans' as 'substandard' and 'doubtful', the regulators required that interest charges be suspended on all non-performing loans, and the level of specific provisioning increased. The cumulative effect of this was the declaration of losses of the magnitude of about US$2 billion by some of the nation's largest banks, as shown in Table 6.1.

Prudential guidelines by the Central Bank (1979, as amended in 1990) stipulated a 1 per cent general provision on all performing loans, a 10 per cent provision for 90-day defaults, a 50 per cent provision for 180 day defaults and a 100 per cent provision for 360-day defaults, which

Table 6.1 Interim financial performance of selected banks as at September 2009

	Oceanic Bank (US$ million)		**Intercontinental (Nm)**		**Union (Nm)**	
	Sep '08	Sep '09	Sep '08	Sep '09	Sep '08	Sep '09
Gross Earnings	943	312	161,822	119,770	59,715	97,506
Provision for Losses	–10	–2101	–1,780	–436,686	–36	–252,896
Prior Year Adjustment		–92				
Profit Before Taxation	307	–2673	33,033	–447,451	14,193	–222,858
Taxation	–63	766			4,372	4,633
Profit After Taxation	244	–1907				
Net Assets	2,138	–461	221,079	258,694	136,722	146,154

were considered 'lost'. With the increasing pressure from the Central Bank for banks to comply with the directives on full disclosure of loans and toxic assets, directors and executive management were now challenged to take all legal avenues to recover their debts before the 31 December 2009 deadline for a uniform financial year-end for Nigerian banks. Many of these debts were in one of four categories: loans to oil companies which had been made when crude oil was trading at about US$160 per barrel; margin loans to speculative investors in the capital and property markets; loans to large local corporations who were facing decreased liquidity due to the global economic crisis; and debts from syndicated loan arrangements for the purchase of federal government companies. Estimates were that the federal government owed the Nigerian banks about ₦3.2 trillion (something over US$2.2 billion), and critics argued that these outstanding government debts compounded the illiquidity of the banks.

The CBN and National Deposit Insurance Corporation (NDIC) joint investigation generated a lot of pressure on the banks to recover their bad debts, a classic case being that of a quoted downstream oil company which had an outstanding debt of ₦2.9 billion (*Next on Sunday*, 9 August 2009). In the celebrated case of Access Bank, the bank had filed a winding-up application in the Federal High Court in early August 2009 over an alleged default on the payment of a US$35 million loan facility. The issues concerned the legal tussle between the bank and the oil company over disagreements over mechanisms for the payment of the loan, which had been used to import refined petroleum products into Nigeria in July 2008. While the loan was a regular transaction loan, as opposed to a corporate finance deal, with a 12 month repayment period, the obligor had been unable to honour the repayment terms due to the devaluation of the dollar by over 30 per cent, which meant an unforeseen 30 per cent increase in the amount of *naira* to be repaid.

The case went to arbitration, after a hearing in the Federal High Court. A ₦2.9 billion payment was agreed in an out-of-court settlement 'without prejudice to all outstanding issues such as the underwriter commitment claim'. The oil company then demanded ₦4.8 billion from the bank 'being your underwriter commitment for our last hybrid offer'. The grey areas arising from the underwriting aspect of the offer for subscription by the oil company, underwritten by several banks, had once again revealed the poor regulatory oversight in Nigeria's banking and capital market sectors.

A similar case was the legal case filed at the Federal High Court in Lagos by Guaranty Trust Bank for the nation's national air carrier, Virgin Nigeria Airways, to pay its outstanding debts of about US$9.2 million (₦1.3 billion) or be wound up. The matter was later resolved, but underscored the intense drive by banks to recover their debts after the Central Bank audit.

The publication of the list of bad debtors with non-performing loans predictably generated a lot of controversy, with several large local corporations disputing the veracity of the amounts owed and the status of their companies. The CBN had to admit to potential errors, as the list was dated from 31 May 2009, the cut-off date for the special examination of the first ten banks.

Also included were inter-bank loans, with the CBN claiming that a loan via a special purpose vehicle by Intercontinental Bank to a company in which the owner-directors of a mid-sized bank had interests, had not been serviced on time (*ThisDay* 20 August 2009). The management of Intercontinental Bank later corrected that position in a letter dated 19 August, confirming that the ₦211 billion outstanding for the special purpose vehicle had been significantly paid down, and the company was 'up to date on both principal and accrued interest due on the account as at today'.

As well as the inter-company loans, the loans to oil companies and the margin loans, there was the unbridled inflation of mortgage loans and other property development loans (see, for instance, the article, 'How Property Valuers, Bankers Aided Financial Sector Crisis' by John Omachonu and Chuka Uroko, on page 4 of *BusinessDay*, Thursday 7 January 2010). For the real estate and mortgage loans, bank loan seekers had connived with estate valuers to inflate the value of properties used as collateral for mortgage loans – a practice called 'dictated valuation'. Consequently, banks could never realize the full sum of their loans in the event of a sale. Market values of properties were at variance with figures quoted on valuation papers, and, according to the *BusinessDay* report (Omachonu and Uroku 2010), approximately one-quarter of the ₦1.83 trillion (US$12 billion) loan losses arising from provisioning by banks resulted from insider dealings between banks and valuers.

The final report of the CBN audit (otherwise known as the special joint examination by the CBN and the NDIC), released on Friday 2 October 2009, took place without the fanfare and threats that had accompanied the release of the first report in August. The release of the second CBN audit report, later in September 2009, had revealed another three stressed banks, bringing the total non-performing loans of the eight stressed banks to ₦1.524 trillion or US$100 billion, or 60.75 per cent of industry's total non-performing loans (NPLs), compared with a total deposit liability of ₦3.019 trillion (US$201.3 billion). With a joint proportion of 35.6 per cent of the banking industry assets and 36.11 per cent of loans, the stated rationale of the CBN's action was to intervene in the weaker banks, whose collective market share could interfere with the normal functioning of the market.

The CBN appointed interim replacements for the managing directors and the executive teams of Bank PHB, Equitorial Trust Bank (ETB) and Spring Bank. G.O. Folayan replaced Ike Oraekwuotu at ETB. Cyril Chukwumah replaced Francis Atuche of Bank PHB and Sola Ayodele replaced Charles Ojo of Spring Bank plc. While maintaining that the overall banking system was safe and secure, the governor of the Central Bank continued to justify his intervention in the eight institutions because 'the banks were in grave condition'. The governor of the CBN addressed a joint press conference with the minister of finance, Mansur Muhtar, at the annual meeting of the World Bank and IMF on the banking sector quagmire. This was a move quite unlike the dramatic announcement of the results of the first audit, and the brazen manner of the takeover with the Central Bank unilaterally appointing new managing directors and chief executives. They had arrived at their designated banks accompanied by policemen and the governor or the CBN appeared to presume that all the accused managing directors of the eight rescued banks were criminals.

The presidency took steps to temper the actions of the governor of the Central Bank and avoid the wild controversy and threats engendered by the sensational approach to announcing the results of the first phase of the joint CBN/NDIC audit in August 2009, (*The Guardian*, 4 October 2009, page 1). Authentic reports suggested that the presidency had briefed the finance minister, the Chief Economic Adviser (CEA), and the director general of one of the internal security organizations to ensure that the governor of the CBN, and the chairman of the EFCC, Farida Waziri, were more civil and temperate in handling the ongoing reforms in the banking sector. Overall, a more subtle approach to changing the leadership in the second set of banks that failed the CBN audit was promoted by senior government officials, who pleaded that discretion was a better tool than valour, notwithstanding the veracity of the CBN's claims. Unswayed by the criticisms, the new governor of the CBN continued to maintain his hard line against the banks' options, stressing that the key objective of the clean-up effort was to return the banks to good health; otherwise, the banks could be sold off to foreign investors or liquidated. The first option was controlled liquidation, in which the banks would be managed until they were gradually no longer systemically important to Nigeria. Under this option 'all the depositors are paid back their money until the bank is wound up.' The second option would be for the government to convert its loan stake to equity until it found a buyer. Whichever option the CBN adopted would have created significant issues for bank valuation in addition to ownership transfer issues, as some of the distressed banks had issues not only with asset quality but also with ownership.

For Bank PHB, the US$521 million (₦62 billion) it had committed to buying a majority interest in Spring Bank had created a big accounting 'hole' in its own capital base. This subsequently impacted adversely on its liquidity base. The weakened liquidity base and the legal tussle over ownership of Spring Bank were factors identified by industry analysts as operational obstacles which would put off a buyer. More fundamental was the issue whether the Central Bank itself had exercised good judgement by ever approving the Bank PHB and Spring Bank merger, given the history of both banks. Spring Bank itself was a classic case of a mismanaged merger created by the hasty banking consolidation process: a coalition of six banks – ACB International Bank, Citizens Bank, Fountain Trust Bank, Guardian Express Bank, Omega Bank and Trans International Bank – most of which were weak institutions with differing corporate cultures. Worse, there were allegations of distorted or illegal shareholding, proved by the joint investigation report of the Central Bank of Nigeria and the NDIC, released in October 2007, and confirmed by another report of the Nigeria Police Special Fraud Unit, released in July 2008. Simply put, Spring Bank was a polygamous and incestuous marriage of convenience between terminally sick partners. To beat the 31 December 2005 timeline for banks in Nigeria to meet the ₦25 billion minimum capital base, the six banks had executed a Heads of Agreement, which was a legal but non-binding document outlining the main points of their commercial agreement. The Heads of Agreement had provided for two necessary activities to consummate the transaction: a post-2005 due diligence and capital verification and a post-merger adjustment, to adjust the capital allocated to each of the merging parties.

However, because of the continued poor performance of the bank post-merger, and the failure to finalize an adjustment by June 2007, as well as several legal tussles at the same time, the regulators appointed an interim management board. Central to the legal issue was the discovery of 'toxic' or 'bubble' shares, which some of the shareholders alleged had been created in favour of some Guardian Express Bank directors, contrary to CBN rules that forbade banks to grant loans to their own directors for the acquisition of their own capital. With several unresolved petitions to the regulators, the CBN and SEC, and several lawsuits in the courts, the acquisition of Spring Bank by Bank PHB was approved in December 2008 in curious circumstances. Like the Citibank and Travelers Group merger in April 1998, which had been abandoned by 2008 (a 'flawed conception' according to the *Financial Times*, quoted in *BusinessDay* Nigeria, 20 January 2009), the Bank PHB/Spring Bank merger was never consummated.

If Spring Bank was a classic case of a mismanaged merger, Wema Bank was a case study in over trading and poor corporate governance. A report, on 30 April 2007, of a routine examination conducted into Wema Bank by the NDIC in 2007 raised serious questions about the conduct of one of its directors, blaming him for running it into the ground with a net shareholders' fund of ₦1.14 billion (*ThisDay*, 9 March 2008 'Wema Bank: NDIC Report Indicts ex-MD').

An important infraction, according to the NDIC, was the alleged lack of transparency with which the shares of the previous majority shareholder, the Odu'a Group, a company owned by five South Western states, had been disposed of. Even though the recommendation for the government-owned firm to sell its shares was made by NDIC in its previous report, and was said to have been done by 2 April 2007, the bank could not produce evidence of how the shares were sold, except that Odu'a Group had appointed a financial adviser – Greenwich Trust – to carry out structural sales of its shares to indegenes of Odu'a states, which were large South-Western states in Nigeria.

Other issues were the board not reflecting the ownership structure, having only two executive directors, and the remuneration of the managing director. The committee that decided the managing director's remuneration had him as a member, with one assistant general manager and two non-executive directors. The chairman of the board establishment committee recommended that,

> The current accommodation of the GMD/CEO of the bank could not be said to be befitting of the size of the bank, and the anticipated position in the industry. The residential accommodations of the Chief Executive officers of banks are meeting/ marketing places to meet [the] top echelon in the society. A survey carried out [of] some banks of our peers in the industry shows that the [a] house in Ikoyi worth between ₦950 million and ₦1.5 billion, to be written off in five years, were [was] provided for their Chief Executive officers.

Effectively, the bank had increased the cash remuneration of the CEO from about ₦38 million (US $322,000 at $/₦ 118), inclusive of a ₦7 million housing allowance, to ₦135 million (US$1.14 million), inclusive of a ₦45 million an up-front housing allowance.

More fundamentally, the board and managing director were accused of manipulating the bank's records, repackaging the bank's loans as commercial papers and treating them as off-balance sheet items, to improve the bank's leverage. A classic example that was quoted was a loan in favour of a leading indigenous conglomerate for the acquisition of Le Meridien Hotel from the Bureau of Public Enterprises (BPE), which was repackaged as a 180-day commercial paper against the original tenure of 42 months, without recourse to the Board. Many of these were loans which were deemed by the examiners not to qualify as commercial papers. In all, a total of ₦11.78 billion was extracted from the contingent obligations of the bank and reported as loans and advances by the bank examiners. These had previously been wrongly classified as contingent obligations, largely as commercial papers, by the bank to conceal the bank's excessive lending and violation of the single obligor and legal lending limits.

Similarly, it was established that several non-performing loans had been reclassified as equity investments. This was in addition to disbursing loans above the single obligor limit, in spite of a CBN refusal to waive the limit. Finally, the bank's total exposure to its subsidiaries was suspected to be 'not unconnected with the bank funding the trading in its shares'. Overall, the bank's capital-resultant adjusted shareholders' funds were reported to be ₦15.95 billion, which had already been used up in investments in subsidiaries of ₦10.44 billion and an outstanding goodwill of ₦2.27 billion, leaving a paltry sum of ₦1.14 billion as qualifying and available capital, as of the examination date of 30 April 2007.

Like most of the other stressed banks, Wema Bank had had a remarkable turnover of leadership, at both senior management and board levels. The bank had witnessed at least eight chief executives in a space of 10 years, putting the bank under pressures which few, if any, institutions could have survived without an adverse impact on their viability. Not surprisingly, many of the five distressed banks had high board turnovers and/or a substantial propensity to mergers.

For Union Bank (*The Nation*, 14 November 2007), the challenges were not unconnected with the bank's acquisition of Broad Bank. According to shareholder claims, using an interest group called the Integrity Group, Union Bank acquired Broad Bank plc with a debt burden of about ₦15 billion and paid-up capital of ₦3.3 billion. This translated into 1.67 billion share capital, and 85 per cent of the shares being owned by only five of about 50 shareholders.

From the banks' pre-merger agreement, it was claimed that the directors of Broad Bank were obliged to recover the debt or ensure that the loan became performing as a condition of handing over the proportion of shares accruable to the directors, as agreed for every unit of Union Bank shares which was released. The agreed exchange ratio was one Union Bank share for every 43 Broad Bank shares, if the loan were recovered or made performing. Alternatively, Union Bank was to release only the portion of its shares commensurate with the amount recovered from the outstanding Broad Bank loan.

However, as of October 2007, when the bank held an extraordinary general meeting to write off the goodwill of about ₦15.72 billion expenditure associated with the acquisition of Broad Bank of Nigeria Limited, the Universal Trust Bank plc and Union Merchant Bank Limited, the bad debt of ₦15 billion was yet to be recovered, and the Integrity Group claimed that '[the board] had gone ahead to release Union Bank shares to Broad Bank shareholders when the debt had not been recovered'.

Only about ₦2.5 billion of the ₦15 billion loan was said to have been recovered, effectively creating a hole in the bank's books.

Similar cases of abuse of corporate governance, of accounting irregularities and sheer abuse of office were the reasons the Central Bank justified its intervention. However, several fundamental issues remained. First, was whether the governor of the CBN had the *de jure* powers to take over the eight banks, which he did without presenting the owners of the banks with the audit report findings, and, even if he had the powers, whether he had exercised those powers in utmost good faith as expected of a governor of a central bank.

Second, was whether his unilateral injection of ₦620 billion was the optimal means of injecting funds into the banks, with several recapitulations and a lack of clarity over whether the injection was equity or debt. Third, was whether the actions of the governor, whether legal or not, were in the overall interest of the economy, and/or whether the Central Bank was not itself externalizing its own failures. The CBN's actions had sent shock waves through the system, freezing further liquidity, and the lack of consultation by the governor of the CBN with other agencies of government had resulted in different agencies taking different positions. Since the banking reform had begun, according to the minister of national planning, commercial banks had been finding it difficult to lend money, thereby creating a credit squeeze resulting in a contraction in the real economy. Reassurances from both the minister of finance and the deputy governor of the CBN, Tunde Lemo, were slow to heal the liquidity problem Sanusi's policy decisions had created. The nation's minister of finance, Mansur Muhtar, had said in Istanbul, Turkey, that the nation was facing 'serious challenges in the economy' with respect to liquidity, while Lemo volunteered that the federal government had agreed to pay contractors 'the money it owes them so that they can, in turn, repay their bank loans', suggesting that the CBN itself could have planned its so-called reforms better.

6.2 Regulatory capture, regulatory failure and corporate governance

Even though the former governor of the CBN had asserted that the banking system in Nigeria was secure, the joint CBN–NDIC audit results of August 2009 had signalled to everyone that there was a banking crisis of some sort in the country. Whether or not Professor Soludo, the former governor of the CBN agreed, 'It's a crisis if everybody calls it a crisis,' to quote Morgan Downey, a managing director of LaSalle

Global Fund Services in Europe. (quoted in the *Financial Times*, 11/12 August 2007).

Based on personal interviews and submissions by both former CBN directors[1, 2]and some of the nation's most respected bankers, the conclusion is that 'regulatory capture' and regulatory deficit were two key long-standing contributors to the Nigerian banking crisis that eventually crystallized in 2008–9. Regulatory capture is defined as a situation where either the regulatory agency, as a monolithic body, or individual principal officers in the regulatory agency, are inefficient or totally compromised either as a result of financial incentives, inferior intellectual or technical skills, or through political hijack. It results in regulators exhibiting impaired judgment and hence not being able to make and enforce firm decisions with market operators.

Regulatory capture has been defined as a situation where '...the regulated institutions exercise excessive influence on the regulator. A captured regulator acts primarily in the interests of the regulatees, rather than in accordance with their putative mandate to promote the common good' (Hardy 2006). Economic theory (Stigler 1971) suggests that regulators are often subject to intense and effective pressure from operators to modify regulations and their implementation to suit the narrow interests of the latter. This may include lobbying politicians with one-sided evidence supporting their narrow positions, and attempting to gain their allegiance through direct financial incentives or indirect gifts and favours in kind (Stigler 1971; Laffont and Tirole 1991).

Regulatory capture is of two types, direct and indirect. The Nigerian situation was one of a complex regulatory capture. Anecdotal evidence from the interviews mentioned above suggests that there was not only a high degree of compromise or capture of the banking regulator but also some covert capture of the political authority that provided remote oversight to the regulator.

In a presentation by the chairman of the board of directors of one of the three foreign-owned banks in Nigeria at the London School of Economics Alumni Association public lecture entitled 'Financial Risks, Financial Crises, and Public Policy With Special Reference to Africa', ten key areas of failure that led to the Nigerian crisis were identified.

1. Failure of 'gatekeepers' (both regulators and bank CEOs) to fully understand the specific risks of some products, and demonstrate such an understanding before being licensed to conduct the business.
2. Excessive optimism or poor judgement about risks: losses incurred from unhedged positions in petroleum products; losses incurred on

margin loans given to speculators, and on proprietary positions; losses incurred on unhedged dollar loans to speculators with *naira* income.

3. A deliberate tendency to ignore early warning market signals, with poor market discipline, and regulators having weak market intelligence capabilities, which made regulators shut down or suspend activity, at times freezing important price signals.
4. Regulatory capture, which weakened interventions to check compliance failures.
5. Poorly skilled management teams, who in some cases usurped the powers of the board and disenfranchised minority shareholders.
6. Outdated or one-size-fits-all corporate governance codes, which did not take cognizance of the unique set of risks facing each institution.
7. Misuse of the CBN's expanded discount window, which led to a moral hazard problem for weak banks that delayed taking cost-optimization measures.
8. Issues with remedial asset management – the asset management company may create further moral hazard problems without a transparent policy.
9. A dysfunctional legal system with obsolete laws and slow administrative machinery.
10. Lack of accountability or remorse by bankers, making it difficult for some sections of the banking community to regain trust ('Exploiting crisis to build new banking structure' *BusinessDay* Monday 14 December 2009).

Some retired directors of the CBN, including a retired governor, agreed with the intent and mission of the CBN action against the banks, but maintained that the CBN could have acted differently to achieve the same results. Ola Vincent, governor of the CBN from 1977 to 1982, was one strong voice from the opposing school of thought. In an interview with Marcel Mbamalu in *The Guardian* in September 2009 (Mbamalu 2009), Mr Vincent, an octogenarian, articulated a fourfold thesis.

First, banks needed to be given a fair hearing before being sanctioned. According to the former governor of the CBN, the basic rule that a bank examiner or regulatory official should discuss his findings with those involved under a democratic, or any other modern system of government, was not adhered to by the CBN.

Secondly, the lopsided overemphasis of the incumbent governor of the CBN on the fact that many banks gave loans without collateral, even though the sufficiency of collateral is not necessarily a cardinal principle in risk management. The weakness of the CBN's governor's argument was later highlighted when public evidence became available suggesting that, at the commercial bank of which he had been executive director, risk management officers had consented to an ₦89 billion loan to a start-up oil company during his tenure, which was allegedly over 20 per cent of the bank's shareholders' funds. Even though these claims were not fully proven, a few used the ₦89 billion as additional ammunition in their criticisms of the CBN's actions.

Thirdly, the CBN decision was hasty and resorted to questionable means of loan recovery, including the early involvement of the Economic and Financial Crimes Commission. The apparent rashness of the CBN decision and the rough, unpolished manner in which the shake-up and loan recovery were carried out were identified as responsible for disrupting the climate of trust in the Nigerian banking system.

Fourthly, the issue of capital injection to boost the liquidity of the affected banks was not necessarily invidious but the premature determination by the governor of the CBN to sell the banks raised questions whether the CBN was acting *ultra vires* the Companies and Allied Matters Act, which dictated how ownership in a public company could be changed, notwithstanding any other powers in the CBN Act.

The legality of the CBN action was subject to the interpretation of the Bank and Other Financial Institutions Act and the CBN Act. Among other things, section 55(1) of the CBN Act, on which the CBN appeared to be relying, states that 'the Governor may make regulations, published in the Gazette, to give full effect to the objects and objectives of this Decree [sic].' Section 55(2) states that 'without prejudice to the provisions of subsection (I) of this section, the Governor may make rules and regulations for the operation and control of all institutions under the supervision of the Bank' (Anaro 2010).

Industry critics such as Sonny Nwosu, the coordinator of the Independent Shareholders Association of Nigeria, however, continued to suggest that the governor of the CBN had acted beyond his powers (Anaro 2010). Other stakeholders questioned the culpability of the CBN itself in creating the crisis. These were some of the accusations.

- The Central Bank did not do what it ought to have done (which is to proactively strengthen supervision of the banking system) after the consolidation, and hence the Central Bank was almost as culpable as the commercial banks.
- A number of issues surrounded the Central Bank itself, for instance an issue around the allegation of bribery regarding the new polymer notes issued by the Central Bank, in a transaction which appeared not very transparent according to critics.

- The integrity of the regulators was questioned, and their passive connivance, which led to the banking crisis.
- There was a tendency towards parochialism, showmanship and personal aggrandisement on the part of regulators, which inclined CBN governors to take headline-making actions that appeared dramatic in the short term, without considering the long-term implications for all the stakeholders.
- A conflict between short-term pressures to demonstrate action and long-term imperatives, often resulting in short-termism, which could cause a far-reaching decline or depression in the economy.
- A plan for boosting consumer spending and consumer confidence was needed alongside any risk-management agenda the CBN Governor was pursuing.
- Many of the banks parked their debts in their subsidiaries, including some of the banks that passed the audit. Some critics felt that the regulators could not pretend that they were unaware of this absence of a level playing field, which was caused by the different levels of financial reporting by banking institutions, as some reported as single bank entities while others reported as consolidated banking groups. This failure of the Central Bank to plan adequately and regulate banks' subsidiaries was conceded by the CBN's director of banking supervision at the 6th Annual Corporate Financing Report Summit, organized by the Nigerian Accounting Standards Boards.
- The nation is over-centralized and so is the central bank.

It is worth saying that in 2004, the then governor of the CBN, Mr Soludo, had cited the problems of many Nigerian banks including 'weak corporate governance evidenced by high turnover in the Board and management...' as the reason for his intervention and reforms. In 2009, the new governor of the CBN also quoted '[the] excessively high-level of non-performing loans in the five banks, attributable to poor corporate governance' as part of the reason for the banking crisis. Evidently, if the statements of successive governors of the CBN were anything to go by, the Central Bank of Nigeria had made little or no progress in five years with respect to the impact of its supervisory capabilities.

6.3. Managing the bail out versus managing the economy

'The problem with having cockroaches under the kitchen sink is that there is little way of knowing how many are left to come out' (Howard Wheeldon, senior strategist at BGC Partners, quoted in 'Banks Leap In to Add Liquidity', *Financial Times*, 11–12 August 2007, p. 3).

According to several leading government officials, including the minister of state for finance and the national security adviser, the banking reforms of 2009 were far from balanced. In the words of the minister for finance, the central bank reforms were being driven 'as the spirit leads', suggesting that there was no identifiable structure or methodology to the reforms, but that they were being left to the whims of the CBN leadership. After seven months of frenzied policymaking by the new Central Bank leadership, the federal government asked the CBN to provide a detailed blueprint of the banking reforms, to allow objective policy assessment and align the CBN programme with the government's overall long-term economic programme. According to the minister of state for finance, 'We want a blueprint of the reforms to know where the CBN is headed and more importantly be sure that actions are not just taken "as the spirit directs"'. While the government was fully in support of the CBN reforms, this was only to the extent that the actions of the CBN did not jeopardize confidence in the economy (see, for instance, the article, 'FG [Federal Government] Demands CBN's Blueprint on Bank Reforms' by Emele Onu on the front page of *ThisDay*, Friday 12 February 2010). By some twist of serendipity, that same week, the governor of the CBN, in a keynote address at a conference in Lagos, publicly presented, possibly for the first time, an overview of the banking sector reform programme. Two months later, concerns about the integrity of the Sanusi-led reforms were increased by another very senior government officer, the national security advisor. He had concluded that 'The Central Bank of Nigeria (CBN) intervention in the banking crisis seems to have damaged economic activities in the banking sector to the detriment of the larger society [sic]' (*ThisDay* 20 April 2010). This appraisal by a politically savvy national security adviser to the president, who was a retired army general, a former presidential aspirant in Nigeria, and a likely nominee to the then vacant position of vice president, rang alarm bells in domestic and international communities, also sending a subtle warning to the new governor of the CBN, who subsequently became more guarded in his utterances.

One central argument about the CBN's overall policy focus in the first year of Sanusi's tenure was whether the new CBN leadership had concentrated on the drivers of economic growth, as opposed to micro-factors in the banking sector. Banking reform was no doubt critical to sound economic management, but the media attention the CBN had generated due to its cowboy approach to the banks, and its shock therapy, along with several controversial statements by the governor of the CBN, had diverted attention from the larger macroeconomic issues for which the

Central Bank was responsible. After Sanusi's raid on the banks between August and September 2009, macroeconomic indicators wavered considerably, not solely due to the loss of confidence in the banking system but also because of the increased regulatory volatility and the threat of an illiquidity shock. As an immediate reaction, many Nigerian banks had witnessed a temporary freezing of their credit lines from foreign international banks. Subsequently, foreign trade partners also became concerned about the appropriateness and implications, if not legality, of the CBN's actions, especially institutional shareholders in banks such as Intercontinental Bank, who felt that it was a violation of their ownership rights. In addition to the fright that Sanusi's shock approach had brought to the system was a concern that there was little if any evidence of planned fiscal and monetary counter measures to restore confidence in the system. The crisis of confidence in the credit market also worsened as the CBN did not offer any clear position on the prospects of a short-term lubrication of the economy. Nor was a long-term policy agenda set out that factored in the interaction between the lending freeze that the bank scare would potentially trigger and the nation's economic growth targets. Many decisions appeared reactionary, and critics opined that Sanusi's background as a bank risk manager tended to make him focus so much on reflecting the true asset quality of banks that he almost forgot that his primary job was not banking regulation, important though this was, but macroeconomic growth and stability. Several analysts and industry chieftains were also concerned that the new governor of the CBN, rather than working on a holistic approach to economic reform, in conjunction with his colleagues in the finance ministry and the national economic management team, seemed to enjoy being in the limelight, granting interviews to foreign business journalists when he travelled abroad rather than actively engaging local stakeholders.

Many of the CBN's pronouncements were made in the absence of detailed circulars or policy guidelines. Though the governor of the CBN (Sanusi 2010), in a convocation lecture to a federal university in February 2010, debunked the widely held opinion and narrative that 'the Central Bank really has no strategy' and that 'there is no roadmap to the reforms,' many commentators still maintained these cynical, even if incorrect, views. Other views which the governor of the CBN had to combat included 'assertions that the actions taken by the Central Bank are part of a grandiose "Northern" agenda', and that they were part of 'an Islamic agenda pushed by a Muslim fundamentalist' (Sanusi 2010, page 2). Overall, the multiplicity of diversionary claims and counterclaims over the integrity of the CBN reform agenda was reflective of the poor consultation and stakeholder management by the Central Bank. The absence of any structured policy communication to provide clear guidance to operators was one area on which several critics, including the chairman of the Nigeria Economic Summit Group (NESG), the nation's private sector economic think tank, continued to fault the CBN. Instances of these vague or one-off CBN pronouncements without detailed guidelines included the funding of the CBN bail out and limiting the tenure of bank managing directors to 10 years.

In August 2009, for example, when the CBN announced that five banks were in a grave situation, the specifics of the ₦420 billion bail out (approximately US$2.8 billion)[3] and the nature of the loan granted by the CBN to the banks, were not defined upfront. It was only several weeks after the announcement that some clarity was provided about the terms and tenure of the bail out funds. This had raised issues about whether the CBN could appropriate that money without recourse to the executive, given section 80(3)–(4) of the Constitution of the Federal Republic of Nigeria:

> No moneys shall be withdrawn from any public fund of the Federation, other than the Consolidated Revenue Fund of the Federation, unless the issue of those moneys has been authorised by an Act of the National Assembly. No moneys shall be withdrawn from the Consolidated Revenue Fund or any other public fund of the Federation except in the manner prescribed by the National Assembly.

Technically, the two key criteria for funding a government bail out had been met in Nigeria. First, there was clear evidence of possible systemic risk, meaning that the failure of those institutions could pose significant risk to the entire financial system. Secondly, the institutions, according to the CBN, were technically insolvent, meaning that the capitalization of the banks had been materially eroded. What was in contention was the funding of the bail out, and whether it was the most efficient use of public funds, regardless of the legality or authority of the Central Bank to authorize the release of the funds to the banks.

While the CBN contended that the relevant sections of the constitution could not be applicable to the ₦420 billion, as the bail out money was not sourced from the consolidated revenue fund, the lack of disclosure on the terms of the 'loan' created some grey areas.

When asked how he sourced the bail out money, the governor replied that the Central Bank printed money. Eventually, the Vice-Chairman of the Senate Committee on Banking, Insurance and Other Financial Institutions, Senator Felix Kolawole, said that the ₦420 billion with which the Central Bank of Nigeria had bailed out the five banks in distress did not require appropriation by the National Assembly (Ojeifo 2009). This was several weeks after the chairman of the Senate Committee had publicly challenged the legality of the CBN action (Onwuka 2009).

Several alleged procedural lapses in the Central Bank's actions on top of the release of the bail out funds had also indicated the absence of any concerted approach in the CBN's rescue solution.

First, the CBN's actions reflected a one-dimensional view, focused only on improving the risk profile of the banking sector. According to some critics, the other aspects of a Central Bank's functions, which included stimulating growth and employment, seemed overlooked or downplayed by the new leadership. While inflation and the exchange rate were under control, public policy analysts and watchers of the CBN were not certain that keeping inflation and exchange rate stable was a major achievement, as they had been fairly stable for over a year. Secondly, by removing only the executive directors of some of the rescued banks and leaving the non-executive directors, the CBN had created a grey area between the powers of the executive management it was appointing and the non-executive board, who represented the shareholders. Unlike previous bank management takeovers by the CBN, in which the entire board had been removed, Sanusi's actions suggested that some of the CBN's actions had not received the expert legal advice needed to iron out grey areas and potential areas of ambiguity for operators. Even though the CBN, in previous instances of sacking an entire board and appointing an interim leadership, had often not consulted the shareholders, the August 2009 situation of changing only the executive directors of some banks while retaining some non-executive directors reflected a gross violation of applicable laws and a hasty plan of action by the CBN. There were also reported lapses managing directors appointed by the CBN, for example in taking statutory actions such as releasing the bank's annual accounts without seeking the consent and approval of the board or seeking to rectify any grey areas (Pat Utomi versus CBN, Federal High Court suit number FHC/L/C/1403/09 of December 2009).

Thirdly, the absence of any articulated strategy document or policy paper on either the banking reforms of the new governor, or the episodic June–October joint CBN/NDIC joint audit, also raised some fundamental questions. Several leaders of opinion, such as the chairman of the NESG (*The Guardian*, 6 September 2009), criticized the hastiness and double-speak of the CBN on issues such as foreign investors, whom the governor had initially stated would be the preferred buyers, before changing his tune to admit that it would be left to the banks to find buyers, whether local or foreign.

As well as the technical lapses of the Sanusi reforms alleged by some stakeholders were a few actions which gave rise to concerns about whether the new CBN chief had an ethnic agenda (*ThisDay*, 6 September 2009).

For instance, between August and September 2009, the governor gave a lengthy interview to the Hausa Service of the BBC, which critics claimed had touched some ethnic nerves: 'Given his Islamic studies background and the Northern agenda rumour about his banking reforms, that interview was ill-advised. The CBN Governor is a public servant and not a politician so does not need the Hausa Service of the BBC or the target audience of that service to justify his actions as the nation's banker. It was a costly extravagant action that does the image of the CBN governor no good.' (*ThisDay*, 6 September 2009)

In another controversial statement quoted in an article by Dipo Onabanjo titled 'Banking on Sharia', on page 28 of *TELL* Magazine of 14 September 2009, the governor was quoted as saying at a reception held for him in Kano that 'the economy of Nigeria is now in the hands of Kano. Once we do our work, there is nothing anybody can do.' The reference to Kano indigenes controlling the economy was an apparent reference to the fact that most of the sensitive positions in the economy, including the minister of finance, the minister of national planning and the governor of the Central Bank, were then occupied by indigenes of Kano State.

Several media campaigns by informed insiders of the banking system also provided a balanced view of the reforms beyond the CBN's agitated explanation for its actions. Critics of the new governor included an interest group called 'Renaissance Professionals' (RP), which ran advertorials in leading newspapers from August 2009 until 2010. An anonymous group of financially savvy professionals, they had insinuated themselves into the privileged space of being the only industry (as distinct from media) source of alternative information about the facts and motives behind the 2009 overhaul of the nation's banking industry.

Questioning the rationale behind the 'banking sanitization' and the *modus operandi* of the CBN, the Renaissance Professionals, from as early as August 2009 through to the following December, raised some compelling arguments as to the logic and sincerity of the CBN action. Even though public opinion was divided, and some of their arguments were sometimes jaundiced, the Renaissance Professionals' position could be analysed as hinging on five points

1. The legality of the CBN's actions and the rule of law.
2. The economic disruption caused by the governor of the CBN's activities.
3. Consistency of policies. Of several instances cited, the most notable was the removal of the chairman of Equitorial Trust Bank, an influential Nigerian billionaire who owned one of the nation's third largest telecoms networks, and the sudden reversal of that decision, leading to his reinstatement, ostensibly because he had offered to inject fresh capital into the bank. Another instance was the discretionary concessions given to Unity Bank, a bank largely owned by Northerners, and indeed the only Northern bank to survive the 2005 consolidation, even though its finances were weak and the bank had not published audited accounts in at least two years (Abubakar 2009; Ogunwale 2009; Osae-Brown 2010). This argument did not however take into cognizance the fact that a south-western bank, Wema Bank, had also been given some concessions. Third, was the allegation made by the interest group that one of the big three banks, for which the governor of the CBN had been a director, had violated the CBN's prudential guidelines and basic credit risk principles by awarding a loan to a start-up over the bank's single obligor limit. For these and some other actions of the CBN, though defensible by the regulators and justifiable within the CBN Act, the argument was that Central Bank could be seen not to be applying a consistent yardstick for sanctions.
4. The discretion and ethical conduct of public officers. On 23 October at the NESG Policy Dialogue, the governor of the CBN was alleged to have said that the bank chiefs – who were already being tried – deserved to be tied to the stake and shot. According to the interest group, this showed an utter lack of discretion in a public officer who was beginning to descend to personal and vindictive emotions, over a matter that was already in court.
5. Consistency of utterances. Statements by the governor of the CBN on 31 August that the government did not intend to own the banks and that the bail out funds were temporary capitalization for the banks were contradicted by a 2 November statement, attributed to the governor, that the CBN was only being charitable to shareholders because the shareholders had lost all their money (*Business News*

and Articles 2009). Given that the shareholders had not been given an option to recapitalize and no capital market valuation analysis results were released, the Renaissance Professionals questioned the motives of the governor.

By December 2009, the cumulative impact of the CBN's reforms was beginning to emerge. In the last six months of 2009, an estimated 6,000–8,000 employees in the banking industry (*The Guardian*, 14 November 2009) had been relieved of their jobs. While the Central Bank denied any responsibility for directing the banks to initiate the layoffs, the Renaissance Professionals on page 26 of *The Guardian* of 1 December 2009, in 'CBN's Reforms – Economic Sabotage or Bank Sanitisation', quoted a CBN letter dated 28 October 2009 (reference number BSD/PAT/ICB/CON/01/57) to the managing director of Intercontinental Bank, which 'directed him to immediately reduce executive and other staff emoluments by at least 30 per cent and submit an action plan for branch and staff rationalisation ... and forward the above information not later than Friday November 6 2009'. According to the Renaissance Professionals, this was also reinforced by the deputy governor of the CBN, Dr Kingsley Moghalu, at an NTA public lecture.

By Wednesday 16 December 2009, in a full-page advertorial in *ThisDay* newspaper titled 'THE NEW CBN: Transparent Regulators or Crafty Manipulators', the Renaissance Professionals ('RP') again quoted an item on page 20 of *The Punch*, Friday 11 December 2009 in which the deputy director, Banking Supervision, CBN was quoted as denying giving banks in the country any directive to reduce their workforce. According to RP, this was also reinforced by the deputy governor of the CBN, Dr Kingsley Moghalu, at an NTA public lecture.

However, a letter on CBN headed paper (which was never refuted or denied), reference BSD/PAT/ICB/CON/01/57, was published, in which the CBN-appointed managing director/ CEO of Intercontinental Bank was requested to take 'the following steps immediately', including 'reducing executive and other staff emoluments', and 'submit an action plan for branch and staff rationalisation'.

Predictably, the Central Bank response was that the media assault by Renaissance Professionals was being sponsored by faceless agencies funded by former wealthy bankers with a budget of ₦300 million (US$2 million). It only helped slightly to strengthen the CBN's argument. Notwithstanding the responses from the Central Bank, these and other vacillations or somersaults in the CBN's actions appeared to damage the credibility of some of the Central Bank's reform efforts.

Meanwhile, other media reports continued to question the apparent radicalism of the new governor of the CBN. In an article that summed up most of the media comments on the new governor, Jideofor Adibe in 'Sanusi: Radical in a Conservative Job' (*BusinessDay*, Friday 4 – Sunday 6 December 2009) stated that '...Central Bank governors are barometers of the direction of the country's economy so every utterance they make is laden with meaning by investors'. He likened Sanusi to Willem Frederik Duisenberg, first president of the European Central Bank (1998–2003), who was considered not to have been a success because he did not have the appropriate temperament for the job. Adibe quoted the *Financial Times* ('The Wrong Man for an Impossible Mission', 8 February 2002), which described Duisenberg's weakness as his style of presentation: 'The biggest criticism of Duisenberg is not over the substance of his decision, but over his presentation. His willingness to talk off the cuff and his often vivid turn of phrase have frequently raised eyebrows among other policymakers.' In summary, Adibe's comments were that the governor of the CBN had not been 'as meticulous as he ought to be in his utterances and actions'. Most of the initial policy moves under Sanusi, including the appointment of auditors and rescue-cum-turnaround managers and CEOs, and the publication of the list of bank debtors, had been dogged by controversy. Quoting Alan Greenspan ('We will never have a perfect model of risk' *Financial Times*, 17 March 2008), Adibe's opinion was that '... it is important ... that in any reforms, ... regulation not inhibit our most reliable and effective safeguards against cumulative economic failure: market flexibility and open competition'. This view was reflective of most media comments and was elucidated further by Chike Orjiako in *ThisDay* on 14 September 2009. According to Orjiako, 'The business of banking by its very nature is ultra-conservative; a profession that affords little or no showmanship or grandstanding. Confidence building without sacrificing prudence is the singular distinguishing characteristic of reserve bank governors the world over. When the Fed chairmen speak, people make forward-looking judgements and decisions, which is why they often speak discreetly.' According to Elombah (2009), the governor of the CBN's approach '... tends to be simplistic. One example of such is the contradictory signals. It seems he could not separate outrage over alleged infractions by the bank chiefs from the requirements to follow through with[in] the dictates of the law. Sanusi also suffered [*sic*] accusation[s] of dictatorship and that could undermine risk-taking, which is at the heart of entrepreneurship; again, it is being suggested that the reforms being pursued could undermine the autonomy of the banks'.

The media onslaught against the governor of the CBN generated by his provocative comments was a regular aspect of the first six months of his tenure, and distracted both the CBN itself and other investors from the central issue of managing the economy.

6.4. Managing the banking system versus managing the economy

Sanusi's first major test was protecting the value of the *naira*, even in a free-floating system. By the last week in July 2009, the *naira* had declined to its weakest level in at least 15 years. With a 19 per cent slump in the country's foreign reserves to US$43.2 billion on 3 July, compared with US$53 billion as of December 2009. In June 2009, when Sanusi took over, the Central Bank of Nigeria began to limit its supply of dollars at the weekly auction. The *naira* had slipped to ₦156.85 to the dollar by 31 July 2009 – its weakest level since 1994.

While the official exchange rate of the *naira* fell, the gap between the official and the parallel market rate apparently shrank from over 20 per cent to less than 5 per cent, and the CBN focused on this index rather than on the devaluation in the *naira*. The CBN's second explanation for the devaluation was that the low exchange rate of the *naira* had made the currency the target of speculative attacks, based on the volatile oil price and the varying foreign exchange reserves. The other rationale for the devaluation of the *naira*, according to the new CBN administration, was that the gap between the official and parallel exchange rates led to a lot of round-tripping by the banks. Overall, the theoretical underpinning of the Sanusi-led policies at the Central Bank between 2009 and 2010, either on bank reforms or on balanced economic growth, remained unpopular, and in some cases problematic. Contrary to the policies of the CBN under Charles Soludo, Sanusi Lamido Sanusi's policies were a major departure from the previous era. For instance, Sanusi had a 'fundamental disagreement with inflation targeting' (see, for instance, pages 9–12 and 53 of *The Guardian*, Friday 19 March 2010).

In an interview with *The Guardian* published on 19 March 2010, the CBN governor criticized the inflation-targeting policy, stating that it was different from the general policy of seeking price stability, and citing the examples of several African countries that had low single-digit inflation but little or no economic growth.

Apart from the ideological underpinnings of the CBN's actions and the inevitable criticisms that the Central Bank faced, the strengthened

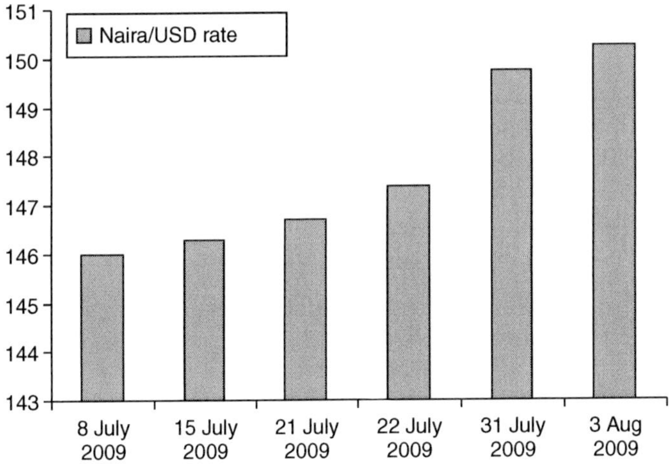

Figure 6.2 Exchange rate of the Nigerian Naira to the US dollar in July–August 2009

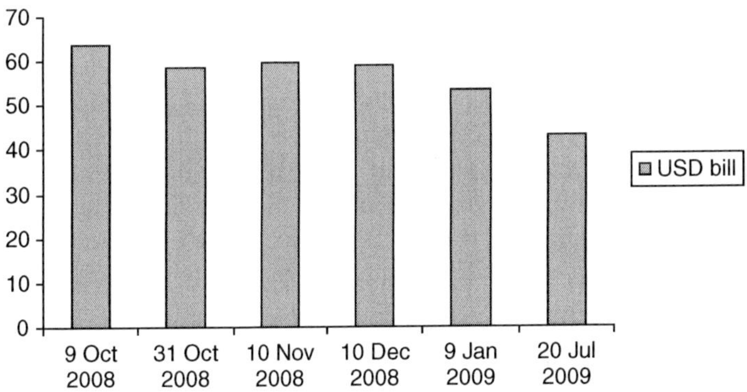

Figure 6.3 Nigeria's foreign exchange reserves October 2008–July 2009

leadership of the Central Bank's Monetary Policy Committee ensured that the economy remained on track. With low external debts (below US$5 billion in 2010, US$3.6 billion in March 2009) owed to the multilateral group of creditors, virtually no increase in Paris Club debts from 2006 levels, ongoing reforms in the form of the Fiscal Responsibility Act, public procurement laws and a National Debt Management Framework (2008–12), the Nigerian economy remained within the global safety net from a debt management perspective. Relative to peer countries such as Brazil, Egypt, and Ghana, and even developed countries such as the UK and the USA, Nigeria's external debt to GDP ratio remained sound. In conjunction with the Central Bank of Nigeria, the Ministry of Finance and the Securities and Exchange Commission, and working with several capital market operators, the Debt Management Office (DMO) had also worked to transform the nation's domestic debt market from its short-term orientation to a longer-term structure. The tenure of FGN debt instruments had been progressively increased from 91 days to 20 years within the period 2005 to 2009, and several other initiatives were underway to deepen the nation's financial markets. The only missing link appeared to be about driving the reform of the banking sector in a way that was complementary to the other reform efforts in the nation.

One of the stated rationales for the banking reforms of 2004 was that Nigerian banks were rent-seekers who were not contributing optimally to economic development (see, for instance, Alayande 2004 and Soludo 2004).

Ultimately, the expectation was that any banking reforms would demonstrably have an impact on the capability of the financial sector to support the real sector of the economy. In the absence of that, the banking reforms would be deemed to have been of limited success. Evidently, the continued rent-seeking orientation of the banks to earn income by exploiting the inefficiencies in the economy, and the ineffectiveness of the regulator, served as anecdotal evidence that the 2004–5 banking reforms under Soludo had limited or no impact. The absence of any apparent linkage between the Sanusi reform effort and the overall government agenda also made it difficult for independent observers to find the nexus between banking sector reform and tangible economic development, even though the basis for criticizing the Central Bank was often weak.

Even though there were several other initiatives to stimulate the economy and to drive growth in the real sector, the theatrical and sensational banking battle stirred up by the CBN distracted both industry captains and investors alike from working energetically with government on the other initiatives. In mid-July 2009, for instance, the federal government announced a ₦500 billion (US$3.33 billion) bail out fund for manufacturing, but, sadly, this was not well received by cynical manufacturers, nor did it receive the level of interest and public discourse that the banking bail out was to generate. This was exacerbated by the fact that it was not clear what form the bail out would take: tax holidays; tariff waivers; duty waivers on machineries and raw materials;

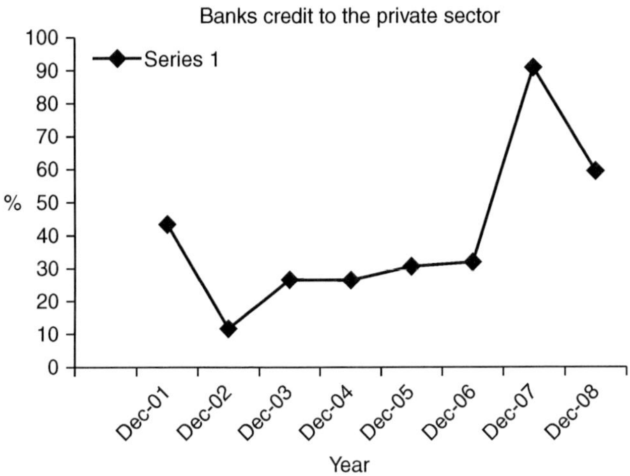

Figure 6.4 Banking sector credit to the private sector in Nigeria 2001–8

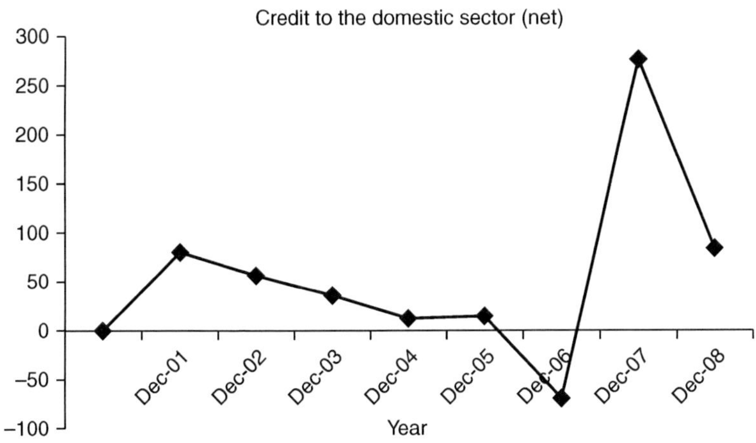

Figure 6.5 Banking sector credit to the domestic sector 2001–8

subsidy on power and electricity; or credit. As with many other bail outs announced by previous administrations, such as the Export Expansion Grant and the ₦70 billion relief for textile manufacturers, execution of the policy was delayed.

Six months before the uniform year-end of December 2009, most Nigerian banks had begun to reduce lending to customers and started resorting to the inter-bank market, as a result, inter-bank rates shot up. This was partly due to the Central Bank's policy clarification that the 15 per cent interest rate cap on deposits did not apply to inter-bank rates, the effect of which was to stimulate inter-bank lending to the detriment of customer lending. The reluctance of banks to lend to the real sector led to an inadvertent concentration of liquid assets at the short end of the inter-bank market. This happened despite the increased liquidity resulting from the additional Federal Account Allocation Committee (FAAC) disbursement for the month of December 2009. Overall, most banks wanted liquid balance sheets by the December 2009 year-end given their competitive mindsets. Some of the banks withdrew their funds from the system but were reluctant to trade in the inter-bank market. Earlier, in 2008, after observing an interest rate spike in both lending and deposit rates, and a steep decline in lending activities by banks, the Central Bank had announced a U-turn by proposing a deferment of the common year-end from 2008 to 2009.

By September 2009, the CBN had also agreed in principle to remove the 10 per cent cap earlier placed on banks' participation in sub-national and corporate bond offers to boost investment in bonds. Simultaneously the SEC was working on getting approvals for obtaining tax holidays on bonds.

Meanwhile, the nation's capital markets continued to flounder, with a lot of market volatility and anxiety over the road map for change. As regards the SEC, the House of Representatives Committee on Capital Markets and Institutions had posed a subtle, if veiled, question as to the experience of the candidate proposed by the president as the new director general of the SEC, quoting Section 3, sub-section 2 (A and B) of the Investment & Securities Act 2007(ISA), which states: 'In the case of the chairman or director-general of the Commission, he/she must be a university degree holder or its equivalent with not less than 15 years cognate experience in capital market operations.' The politics involved in confirming the appointment of the new director general of the SEC and the delay before he assumed office created an unintended hold up in cleaning up the capital markets – a procedure without which the banking reforms could be only partly successful.

While a few attempts were made to hold individuals personally responsible for their fiduciary responsibilities as bank directors, there were no major convictions or landmark successes in prosecuting for capital market violations or insider trading. The obvious conclusion was that the nation's investment laws and the machinery for enforcing them were weak.

In December 2009 (in an advert in *Leadership*, Monday 7 December 2009), the SEC's Administrative Proceedings Committee began the process of investigating allegations of violations levelled against some of the banks and in respect of supposed securities market manipulations and other violations of the Investment and Securities Act 2007, SEC Rules and Regulations 2000 as amended, the Code of Conduct for Capital Market Operators and their Employees, and the Code of Corporate Governance. In the Union Bank case (Case No. APC/3/3009), 23 respondents, mainly former directors of the Union Bank between 2007 and 2009, and selected subsidiaries (Union Registrars) and agents (Falcon Securities), were invited to respond to such allegations. In a public notice, the SEC invited 17 persons to do the same in respect of securities market manipulations in the affairs of Afribank plc. It was not in dispute, based on several cases, that share manipulation, share price manipulation, and trading in the banks' own securities were rife (contrary to Nigerian law, which typically did not permit buy-back of own shares). Share buy-back is ordinarily the purchase of outstanding shares of a company's stocks that are in the possession of the public. Even though Nigerian company law – the Companies and Allied Matters Act (CAMA) – provided for share buy-back, this was only under specific conditions, which included at least three requirements. First, the share buy-back must be authorized by a special resolution of the shareholders of the company. Secondly, the notice of the general meeting authorizing the buy-back must be published in at least two national daily newspapers. Thirdly, the shares can only be repurchased out of the share premium account and/or accumulated profit of the company available for distribution as dividends. In a widely publicized case (see, for instance, a letter dated 5 August 2009 and published in the *The Guardian* newspaper of Wednesday 12 August by Intercontinental Bank – 'Open letter to His Excellency, President Umaru Yar'adua: a Case for Presidential Intervention'), a Lagos-based oil and gas trading company had provided circumstantial and unrefuted evidence that one of the five banks that failed the first round of the CBN audit had extended to it a share purchase facility of ₦700 million *naira* in 2007 to acquire the Bank's shares, contrary to law. In certain instances, even when the facility relating to the shares had long been liquidated, the shares were still kept in the bank's custody.

In the few cases that came close to securing a clear judgement against reported violators, operational issues and ineptitude on the part of the regulators were often used as a reason for not securing any sanctions. In one of the major cases of share price manipulation, for instance, the

Investment and Securities Tribunal held on Wednesday 9 September 2009 that the chief executive of a stock broking firm and his company were not given fair hearing, as no adequate notice and fair opportunity had been given to them to defend themselves before serious sanctions were imposed on them by SEC with regard to the alleged manipulation of the shares of a publicly quoted petroleum trading company. The tribunal then overturned the SEC's decision in its letter of 15 April 2009.

Policy on the run ... Again?

By 4 November 2009, barely five months after assuming office as governor of the CBN, Sanusi had started to flinch, making positional, if not policy, somersaults. After much criticism of the Equitorial Trust Bank (ETB), the CBN, in a press release, restored the largest shareholder and business mogul, Dr Mike Adenuga Jr to the board of the ETB, effectively returning the bank to the business mogul. In spite of plausible explanations by the CBN that the return of the bank to this influential tycoon was based on an undertaking by the core investor to recapitalize and comply with corporate governance agreements, this reversal of its own decision by the CBN suggested hasty decision making on the part of the regulator.

All in all, about 6,000–6,500 workers were dismissed from the banking sector in the last half of 2009 in preparation for a stricter operating environment under the Central Bank of Nigeria in 2010. Meanwhile, in the second half of December 2009, due either to factors internal to the banks, such as drastic cost-cutting and employee rationalization, or to external ones such as capital-raising and some banks' enthusiasm for the potential of bond options, share prices of a few of the banks, including Intercontinental Bank and Oceanic Bank, posted some rises. At a time when banks were declaring record losses due to heavy provisioning for bad debts, all but one of the bailed out banks approved the payment of bonuses to their staff. The bonuses were factored as 13th-month salaries despite losses declared in the third quarter (see article by Omachoru and Anaro, 'Bailed Out Banks Pay Bonuses with Tax Payers' Money', *BusinessDay* Monday 14 December 2009).

During the consolidation era in 2005, it was estimated that about 30 per cent of the workforce in the banking industry had been made redundant. This was partly due to the failure of 11 banks that found no buyers, several redundancies due to lack of placement during employee integration, and outright discrimination against workers who had polytechnic diplomas, which a few banks considered inferior. By 2008,the boom in 2006 and 2007 had restored the banking industry workforce to its 2005 pre consolidation level. But, the layoffs in 2009 shrank the bank workforce back to 2005 or early 2006 post-consolidation levels. The week before Christmas in 2009, the Intercontinental Bank management laid off an estimated 1,500 employees, 2 weeks after removing about 25 senior officers from positions ranging from assistant general manager to general manager. Average salaries at the bank had been reduced by about 30 per cent some months before.

That same month, one of the country's largest banks had been quoted as having released an estimated 2,000 officers from its workforce. Oceanic Bank was reported by *ThisDay* (on Sunday 27 December 2009, page 67) to have released over a thousand workers. Intercontinental Bank made 1,339 workers redundant, and 26 of its top managers including general managers. Spring Bank laid off 200 staff and Wema Bank dismissed 500 workers including 25 of its top managers. As well as the layoff of thousands of employees by the five bailed out banks, who were worst hit by the retrenchment exercise, there were large-scale embargoes on branch expansion plans, rationalization of bank branches and reductions in staff salaries, perks and other allowances by up to 30 per cent (Adebowale and Momodu 2009).

Simultaneously, the immoral undercurrents in the banking industry still ran strong under the bridge of reforms. An estimated ₦9 billion (US$60 million), due as termination benefits to 12,000 former bank employees who had been laid off from banks during the 2004–5 consolidation exercise, remained unpaid. They had been laid off by 14 of the 89 banks that failed to meet the new capitalization levels by December 2005 (see the article 'Ex-bankers Seek Intervention Over Unpaid ₦9b Benefits' by Enitar Ugwu in *The Guardian*, Wednesday 12 May 2010, page 15). Scandalously, over four years after the banks had been shut, there was still no clarity as to how the entitlement benefits of former employees, classified as 'Other Creditors', would be paid under the normal liquidation process by the National Deposit Insurance Corporation. According to a letter from the Central Bank, 'The Central Bank of Nigeria management has resolved that the terminal benefits of ex-staff of banks that failed the consolidation cannot be paid under the Purchase and Assumption Arrangement'.

The allegations of insider abuse, management recklessness and director avarice that had brought the banking sector to its knees were to be highlighted when a female employee finally sued one of the Big Ten banks in the country for alleged acts of corporate prostitution (*ThisDay*, 5 November 2009). In suit No. E/386/09 in the High Court of Enugu State of Nigeria, the plaintiff sued the bank and five of its officers, seeking

₦1 billion (US$6.67 million) in damages. The main allegation was that the bank had imposed and encouraged a policy by which women were recruited to sleep with influential and wealthy personalities in order to bring in huge current account deposits. Circumstantial evidence was also provided to prove that she had been compelled to dress in short mini-skirts and meet potential clients at questionable locations, including red-light hotels. In addition, the complainant petitioned the Human Rights Commission and the EFCC.

While several professionals denied the authenticity of the allegations, to others they were not far fetched. To many of these ladies, commercial banking (in an era of high deposit targets) was just an extension of campus prostitution, very pronounced in a country where a number of ladies made money this way. In a country rated globally as one of the top ten most dangerous in terms of HIV, such risky lifestyles, whatever the safe sex practices, only confirmed the wanton indiscretion of these professional-looking ladies (both campus girls and bank employees), who did everything from event ushering to modelling as pretend sources of income.

By the end of December 2009, there were media reports of an arm of the ASSBIFI (Association of Senior Staff of Banks, Insurance, and Financial Institutions) sponsoring a bill in the National Assembly to investigate the reported acts of corporate prostitution, sexual harassment, indecent exposure, and the violation of other labour rights and of the International Labor Organization's (ILO) decent work agenda.

After protests from several stakeholders, a summons by the House of Representatives, and the public statement by the minister of state for finance that the CBN should submit its documented programme for banking sector reform, the Central Bank eventually began to set itself deadlines. Early in December 2009, in a public lecture, the deputy governor in charge of financial systems stability, Dr Kingsley Moghalu committed the CBN to its first major documented deliverable. A harmonized code of corporate governance for all banks was scheduled for release by the first quarter of 2010. As of June 2010, this document was still to be published.

The last week in December 2009 had left the nation's economy in a mixed situation. Earlier on in 2009, the Standard & Poor's (S&P) research update had revised Nigeria's outlook from 'Stable' to 'Negative', and by the end of 2009, the economic fundamentals had not improved. Unlike most emerging markets outside Africa, such as Turkey and the Philippines, which witnessed some appreciation on their domestic capital markets in 2009, the Nigerian Stock Exchange, of which banking stocks constitute approximately half of total market capitalization, declined by 30–35 per cent. With a decline in overall fiscal revenue in the first half of 2009 of 40.7 per cent to ₦2.2 trillion, the fiscal balance moved from a surplus of 6 per cent in GDP in 2008 to an estimated deficit of about 6 per cent in 2009, largely occasioned by lower crude oil production and prices. Oil exports, which account for an estimated 90 per cent of exports, declined by about 40 per cent to US$58.9 billion, while external reserves fell from US$64 billion in 2008 to US$42 billion in 2009. Despite an additional US$2 billion dollars which was withdrawn from the nation's excess crude oil account and shared with the sub-national governments, the pick-up in the economy was yet to come. In October 2009, the Federal Government had released US$2 billion from the excess crude oil account to be shared by all tiers of government to stimulate the economy and clear debts owed to the banking system.

Earlier on in 2009, to curtail the effect of the global financial crisis on Nigeria, the government had reduced the minimum policy rate from 10.25 per cent to 9.75 per cent, and then to 8.5 per cent (see *Bottomline* magazine, June–July 2009, interview with Remi Babalola on 4 June 2009). The cash reserve requirement for banks and the liquidity ratio were also reduced, from 4 per cent to 2 per cent and from 40 per cent to 30 per cent respectively. The CBN under Soludo had also halted the periodic liquidity mop-ups and allowed the banks up to December 2009 to restructure their margin loans – decisions which Sanusi had reviewed.

As a whole, it was unclear whether some of the nation's non-oil-related indices could have been better if the banking sanitization had been handled differently. However, one thing was clear: Sanusi's banking reforms had not come without significant costs. Many jobs had been lost in the banking sector, but probably multiples more in the overall economy as a result of the drying up of credit and liquidity. Many companies that had been over-trading in the period 2005–8, and could not justify additional credit were denied loans in 2009, and some probably went bankrupt.

The suspension of credit facilities to firms in the oil and gas sector by banks, and the pressure mounting on them to pay their outstanding loans, had forced many to scale down operations, resulting in unplanned job cuts in that sector. In response, oil and gas firms started demanding up-front payments from companies, including blue chip firms, before supplying them with diesel and Low Pour Fuel Oil (LPFO) for running their plants, equipment and machinery. This cash-and-carry measure started to affect the operations of several firms, particularly those in the aviation, manufacturing and telecoms sectors. For example, there were several flight delays as airlines struggled to raise cash to pay for aviation fuel (Adebowale and Momodu 2009). Other companies started to blame the Central Bank for their problems, whether or not these were related to the CBN's policies, and the Central Bank soon became the whipping boy for everyone who suffered a credit problem. The managing director of Rockson Engineering Nigeria Limited, for instance, said that the CBN's action had affected the ability of his company to complete the National Independent Power Projects, NIPP, as banks were now rejecting letters of credit. The preferred and the reserve bidders for Skypower Aviation Handling Company Limited, SAHCOL, failed to pay at the given deadline, allegedly because they could not source finance from the banks due to the crackdown on banks by the CBN. Other unverifiable or largely unrelated issues also started to be traced to the banking crisis. For instance, the somewhat unrelated case of the unsuccessful sale of Nigerian Telecommunications Limited to a core investor was also blamed on the current crisis in the banking industry (Uffot 2009).

Small and medium enterprise (SME) operators in Abuja said in April 2010 that gaps in information sharing, and the demands from commercial banks regarding credit, had crippled micro-enterprises. The entrepreneurs of some of the SMEs said that most of their businesses were financed through small savings, family support and grants, ruling out credits from banks. Other key indicators of purchasing power, such as new car sales figures, continued to slump, with Q1 2020 car sales figures slumping by 55 per cent to fewer than 8,000 units, compared with 17,412 units in Q1 2009, during which 22 per cent of car sales had been on credit. This position was summarized by the managing director of FirstBank, Mr Stephen Olabisi Onasanya: 'Financing conditions for businesses remain difficult as banks maintain a cautious approach to credit expansion' (see, for instance, the article 'CBN Faces Challenge Stimulating Credit' from Reuters in *BusinessDay*, Monday 10 May 2010).

The slump in air traffic due to reduced consumer purchasing power, and the reduced lending to airlines by banks, also created challenges for the working capital of several domestic airlines, notably Aero Contractors, which had interlocking shareholders with Oceanic Bank, one of the banks rescued by the CBN. Oceanic Bank had, for example, frozen Aero's account over an estimated debt hangover of US $200 million (about ₦30 billion), while Union Bank had placed a *caveat emptor* on the sale of another airline over an alleged ₦3 billion debt.

The credit challenges did not exclude the agricultural sector. Even with the release of ₦200 billion by the Central Bank for lending to commercial farmers through designated banks, only ₦43 billion was released within the initial four months (All Africa Global Media 2009; Nwoji 2010).

The economy still spluttered despite the distribution of ₦4.17 trillion (or approximately US$28 billion) of funds in fiscal 2009 from the Federation Account by the Federation Account Allocation Committee, and an additional US$5.5 billion from the Foreign Excess Crude Account, totalling about US$33.5 billion, the highest injection into the system in any fiscal year since the return to democracy in 1999. (The ₦4.17 trillion comprised roughly ₦2.8 trillion as statutory revenue allocation, N0.45 trillion from value added tax, N0.735 trillion as augmentation for shortfalls in the budgeted revenue, and N0.158 trillion as exchange gain difference between the prevailing exchange rate and the budgeted exchange rate.) The faltering economy had been attributed in part by the minister of state for finance to '...extreme volatility and dysfunction in the financial system, particularly private sector credit which serves businesses and households. In the banking sector, a posture of risk aversion or at best extreme credit caution persists, thus crippling most businesses and with [an] under-developed debt capital market as well as [an] equity market in hibernation, working capital virtually disappeared'.

Three months later, in March 2010, *BusinessDay* reported the findings of a joint survey with the Lagos Chamber of Commerce and Industry (LCCI), in which 90 per cent of respondents had commented that the ongoing CBN reforms had affected their access to credit (see the article, 'Banks' Cautious Disposition, not Liquidity, Sustains Credit Squeeze' on page 4 of *BusinessDay*, Thursday 18 March 2010). The CBN continued to blame the banks, the system and itself. In June 2010, another report prepared by the Central Bank, as quoted on the front page of *BusinessDay* of 22 June 2010, sought to establish a link between the inefficiency of the electricity sector, the failure of the real sector, and the banking sector crisis. In the report, the authors were quoted as saying 'the banking sector crisis was largely caused by the inability of the real economy to absorb credit, thereby forcing banks to lend their freshly raised capital post-consolidation to the capital market, real estate and hydrocarbon sectors'. Attributing the inability of the banks to lend to the real or manufacturing economy due to the high cost of substitute electricity, the report argued that the long-term growth of the economy and the banking sector required fixing the electricity debacle in Nigeria.

As well as the infrastructural issues, there was also a question of consumer confidence and the need for banks to resume lending to revive the economy. 'Confidence' after all, according to the minister of state for finance, Remi Babalola, 'was a perplexing psychological phenomenon, and economists aren't sure what it will take to make consumers upbeat enough to propel a robust recovery' (see the article 'Minister Lists Bank Lending [to] Others as Conditions for Economic Recovery' by Chuka Uroko in *BusinessDay*, Friday 16–Sunday 18 April 2010). Overall, evidence whether the banking reforms had been beneficial to the economy was still inconclusive, and nine months was probably too limited a time horizon to assess performance.

What was the cause of the banking crisis? Several reasons existed – both endogenous and exogenous.

Was the 14 August 2009 intervention a concerted 'policy reform' with an intended benefit to the nation state, an *ad hoc* intervention by an inexperienced CBN leadership, or a set of reactive knee-jerk actions with a hidden personal agenda? Different opinion leaders subscribed to these three different schools of thought, and sharply differing opinions have continued to persist in the business press. That the banking sector had been run into the ground by a few power brokers and needed some aggressive cleansing was not in doubt. What was in doubt was the way the reforms were carried out and the unintended consequences for the overall economy that a wrong approach to bank reform could precipitate. Nonetheless, one thing was clear – stakeholder participation was weak, and, if private sector comments were anything to go by, whether the benefits of the reform as pursued would ever be beneficial to the business community in the short to medium term was debatable.

7
Corporate Governance and Restructuring

7.1 Introduction

The views of the governors of the Central Bank of Nigeria (CBN) since 2004 would suggest that weak corporate governance was the single most important factor in precipitating the banking crisis in Nigeria. Generally, this refers to the processes that lead to decision making in the financial institutions, that is, the responsibilities and accountabilities of the decision makers, and the separation of powers between decision-making authorities, in order to achieve balanced optimal outcomes for the corporation. (See, for instance, a seminar paper presented by Folarin Alayande, one of the leading experts on corporate governance in Nigeria, at the 2010 National Conference of the Institute of Chartered Secretaries and Administrators of Nigeria in Lagos, 22–23 September (Alayande 2010).) Weak corporate governance in banking, according to Alayande, is synonymous with weak processes and structures at the board level. It causes an imbalance between decision makers at that level, so that a single shareholder or interest group can initiate and execute decisions that are detrimental to the long-term interests of the corporation and society.

Following the boom years, when the Nigerian banking sector raced ahead of the Nigerian economy, the second half of 2008 began to reveal cracks, which hitherto had been known to insiders but were now becoming evident to less knowledgeable but more internationally credible organisations. In its 21 August 2008 edition, the London-based *Economist* magazine started to sound notes of caution about Nigerian banks. Weeks later, the cautionary signals from external reports became votes of no confidence. In the 2008 Standard & Poor's Bank Industry and Country assessment, which rates a country's banking system relative to other banking systems, Nigeria was rated 9 out of 10, with 10 representing the lowest rank. (See *Business in Africa 2008*). This low ranking was due in part to credit and operational risks, but the root cause appeared to be the more fundamental issue of corporate governance. The former governor of the CBN, Mr Soludo, had cited this canker in 2004 as a problem for many Nigerian banks, including 'weak corporate governance evidenced by high turnover in the Board and management...' He also gave it as the reason for his intervention and reforms. And it was the motive for the Sanusi-led reforms in 2009, with Sanusi quoting the 'excessively high-level of non-performing loans in the five banks, attributable to poor corporate governance' as part of the reason for the banking crisis.

Ironically, 12 months after the assumption of office by the new governor of the CBN, Sanusi Lamido Sanusi, no institutional policy response had been forthcoming from the Central Bank. On the contrary, the flurry of tactical knee-jerk responses by the CBN to the problem did not provide the holistic solution that such an industry-wide cankerworm deserved.

Evaluating the state of current governance in the Nigerian banking system can be done along three dimensions: the framework as set by regulators or self-regulatory organizations; the practices of market operators; and the compliance or enforcement mechanisms imposed by regulatory agencies to deter infractions.

7.2 Corporate governance: frameworks, practices and enforcement

The framework

Several published articles deal extensively with the framework of corporate governance in Nigeria, and a detailed review of this framework will not be repeated here. These detailed articles and publications include 'Corporate Governance in Nigeria: The Status Quo' by Elewechi N.M. Okike (2007) and 'Nigeria's Corporate Governance Codes: The Missing Links' by Folarin Alayande (2010). In accordance with the provisions of the Companies and Allied Matters Act 1990 (CAMA), which is the principal legislation on company matters in Nigeria, the Corporate Affairs Commission is the agency responsible for registering companies, receiving mandatory reports and maintaining public records on companies and their principal officers. In financial services, as in other regulated industries, other legislation such as the Central Bank of Nigeria (Establishment) Act 1991 and the Investment and Securities Act 1999, among several others, provide additional scope for regulating operators in the relevant areas of the financial services business. As well as the plethora of legislation, however, several attempts have been made in Nigeria since 2000 to develop codes, as distinct from laws', on corporate governance, which are more prescriptive, more detailed and more closely focused on the subject of corporate governance. Notable in this regard, though this list is not exhaustive, are the 2000 Code on Corporate Governance, the 2006 Code of Corporate Governance for Banks in Nigeria Post-Consolidation and the 2009 Securities and Exchange Commission (SEC) Code of Corporate Governance for Public Companies, issued as a circular in September 2010. The 2006 Code of Corporate Governance in Nigeria for Banks Post-Consolidation was released in response to the apparent lapses in corporate leadership in Nigeria. This code was a major advance in corporate direction setting for Nigerian banks but it did contain several grey areas, which made it difficult to enforce the most critical matters. Second, as noted by Folarin Alayande (2010), there are some grey areas in the country's codes of corporate governance, making them onerous for operators to comply with and cumbersome for regulators to enforce. Moreover, over 80 per cent of Nigerian banks issue public securities and are listed on the Nigerian Stock Exchange. In consequence, the corporate governance problem in Nigeria could not be fully resolved until there was some harmonization of corporate governance expectations for both banks and public companies. Pragmatists argue that the corporate governance issue is not about the robustness of the frameworks or codes but about will, discipline and enforcement. But, the clarity and robustness of the code is always the starting point. In spite of the claim that the SEC process had been consultative, and the fact that both the CBN and SEC were members of the Financial Services Regulation Coordinating Committee (FSRCC), the degree of variance between the 2009 SEC Code of Corporate Governance for Public Companies and the 2006 Code of Corporate Governance for Banks, still revealed poor coordination between Nigerian regulators. The CBN had still to release its new Code of Corporate Governance for Banks in Nigeria by May 2010. Many lawyers and corporate governance practitioners were of the opinion that rather than dealing with the structural and underlying issues of corporate governance in Nigeria, the CBN's raft of actions were too tactical, and aimed more at creating headline news and publicity. For instance, in an interview with *The Guardian* (2010a), the governor of the CBN noted that the maximum tenure of a governor of the CBN is 10 years and that of the president of the Federal Republic of Nigeria is 8 years, 'I don't know why a person will like to be in a place after 10 years.' This was the Central Bank's justification for limiting the tenure of bank chief executives in Nigeria to 10 years. It was done through an *ad hoc* pronouncement rather than a well-considered policy covering all areas of board structure and practice. Apart from the faulty analogy between political office holders and entrepreneurs who have majority investments and have built up equity in a bank, there was the fundamental issue of how to handle the long-term ownership rights of institutional investors in a free market economy. Resorting to simplistic solutions, like fixing tenure simply because a similar proposition was once applied in an Asian country, is hard to justify.

Nigeria's corporate governance problems, however, existed far beyond banking. In other sectors, the corporate value system was also beginning to creak, with several European multinationals appointing more non-Nigerians to the boards of their Nigerian subsidiaries. For companies such as Guinness, Nestlé and Nigerian Breweries (Heineken), the return to appointing expatriate CEOs was indicative of several factors (see Ogunkoya 2010), including corporate culture, which any holistic solution to weak enterprise governance cannot overlook.

Practices

Most of the corporate governance abuses and lapses of Nigerian banks have been covered in brief in some of the earlier chapters, and in a paper presented by the governor of the Central Bank at Bayero University in February 2010. Accordingly, the deficiencies in corporate governance practices – from governance structure to governance processes and board culture – will not be re-examined in this section. (See, for instance, Sanusi (2010), the lecture delivered at the convocation square of Bayero University, Kano, on Friday 26 February 2010 to mark the annual convocation ceremony of the university).

As in many other countries, the ultimate responsibility and authority for governance and decision making for registered limited liability companies and corporations rests with the board of directors. In Nigeria, the Companies and Allied Matters Act 1990 empowers the board of directors to sanction any officer of the corporation, including the managing director. Accordingly, a board that is focused on compliance and understands its powers can remove the managing director, even in instances when that managing director is appointed by the regulator, the Central Bank of Nigeria.

However, according to Alayande :

> The real challenge in corporate Nigeria emanated from the weakness of the board structure which implies that oftentimes board practices cannot be openly challenged hence consolidating board

> powers concentrically around the CEO or the Chairman, or both. When there are structural issues with a board, dealing with board practices, board processes and board culture can only be palliative while not providing a comprehensive remedy... In many instances, other board members are either anonymous in corporate Nigeria or ideologically paralysed at board meetings that their role of providing checks, balances and oversights to the CEO and or the Chairman oftentimes become[s] redundant.... Accordingly there are very few cases of publicly-disclosed CEO ouster in Nigeria amongst publicly quoted companies, and even when this is the case board directors are oftentimes reticent in attributing such ousters to non-performance or violation of corporate ethics.

The underlying weakness is always in poor board structures and practices but the outcome almost always results in compromised corporate financial reporting. In the most celebrated non-bank CEO ousting in Nigeria for corporate governance abuses, Cadbury Nigeria fired its CEO Bunmi Oni in 2006 for abuses ranging from 'stock buy back, cost deferrals, trade loading and false suppliers stock certificates to manipulat[ing] its financial reports that were issued to the public and filed with the commission', according to the Securities and Exchange Commission.

The malpractices had been discovered after Cadbury Schweppes increased its shareholding in the Nigerian unit from 46.4 per cent to 50.02 per cent in February 2006 and appointed a financial director from the European head office. Cadbury launched an independent investigation into the Nigerian subsidiary's accounts also as a result of concerns raised by the regulator over the 2005 annual accounts (see, for instance, Sulaiman 2007). Subsequently, the Securities and Exchange Commission imposed a fine of N 21.2 million, approximately US$180,783, on Cadbury Schweppes' Nigerian subsidiary for falsifying its accounts from 2002 to 2005. By 2007 hundreds of shareholders in Cadbury Schweppes' Nigerian subsidiary had launched a class action lawsuit over the accounting scandal and the auditors' breach of duty. The impact of this lawsuit on making corporate bodies more accountable is yet to be determined.

Following the Cadbury case in Nigeria, and the joint CBN/National Deposit Insurance Corporation (NDIC) audit of banks in Nigeria, several moves are currently underway by the regulatory and professional bodies to improve the practice of corporate governance in the country. Professional agencies such as the Chartered Institute of Bankers in Nigeria are also working on taking pre-emptive steps to hold their members more accountable. More recently, several shareholders' associations have also emerged in Nigeria with the intention of acting as pressure groups for boards of directors to be more accountable to minority and individual shareholders, and not just operate in the core investors' and directors' interests. A good summary of the current developments in the area of corporate governance in Nigeria can be found in 'Corporate Governance: Current Developments and Challenges', a paper presented by Folarin Alayande at the annual conference of the Institute of Chartered Secretaries and Administrators in Nigeria at the Sheraton Hotel in Lagos in September 2010.

Enforcement

In all registered companies, the primary role of enforcing the code of corporate governance rests with the board of directors. In regulated industries, such as banking and capital markets, the Central Bank of Nigeria and the Securities and Exchange Commission (SEC) have the oversight responsibility for setting standards and enforcing these through sanctions and penalties. From another perspective, professional institutes also have the responsibility for enforcing codes of ethics for their own professions. Enforcing corporate governance has, however, generally been perceived as weak. This was reinforced in a paper by the governor of the CBN delivered in July 2010 to Course 32 participants at the National Institute of Policy and Strategic Studies (NIPPS) Kuru, near Jos, in Plateau State, Nigeria (see *The Guardian* 2010b).

In enforcing the codes of corporate governance and sanctioning banks and bank directors for abusing their fiduciary duties, the Central Bank's traditional instrument was removing and blacklisting individual directors, or removing an entire board of directors in very grave instances. However, the 2009 action of the Central Bank, which removed only executive directors (including the managing directors) of selected banks, created a unique situation whereby the executive management appointed by the regulator was reporting to a non-executive board appointed by shareholders and, in some cases, aligned with the interests of the sacked managing directors.

One of the key questions posed by the appointment of new executive directors for the eight rescued banks was the legality of their appointments and their obligations to the non-executive board, as appointed by the shareholders. Technically, as in previous instances such as at Citizens Bank of Nigeria in 2005, an appropriate way round this would have been for the new chief executives to engage in dialogue with the board of directors, who could then call for a general meeting of shareholders where the appointment of the new chief executive could be ratified.

With the quality and integrity of the boards of the banks being questioned, there was a renewed emphasis on the need for independent directors. Several calls were made for this, but experts advised the CBN against imposing them on defaulting banks because of soft issues such as 'chemistry of the board'. With its proxies as managing directors of the five banks, the CBN began taking operational decisions for the banks. Critics argued that this was risky, as the regulator was no longer setting standards and had even moved beyond tactical matters to operational matters. Concerned shareholder and civil rights groups contributed to the discourse, but the objectivity of some of the shareholder interest groups was questioned at times due to the partisan nature of some of them.

The question of the independence of the regulators was raised again in early 2010, when some interest groups petitioned the Senate, about a possible conflict of interest for the chairman of the Securities and Exchange Commission between his role as non-executive chairman of the SEC and his chairmanship of a large publicly quoted company, UAC Nigeria plc. Several commentators, such as Opeyemi Agbaje, rose to the defence of the SEC chairman (Agbaje 2010). The main issues canvassed by those opposed to his chairmanship of the SEC were both potential and actual conflicts of interest. On one hand, some expressed the view that all the law demanded of him was to disclose his interest in any matter involving him, while the Senate and House Committees sought a higher standard. Comparing the Nigerian situation with the standards expected of persons in leadership roles in similar regulatory institutions in the USA, the UK and Malaysia created a dilemma: whether to choose a full-time executive chairman of the SEC, as exists in the US; or a non-executive board member role, as in the UK Financial Services Authority (FSA), where several of the non-executive board members of the FSA board also sit on the boards of publicly quoted companies.

Meanwhile, the SEC, under a new director general appointed from the African Development Bank, continued to make sweeping changes to the superintendence of both the Nigerian Stock Exchange (NSE) and the stock brokers. By mid-2010, the SEC had started to exert its authority fully and step up its regulatory role. Between April and May 2010, the Securities and Exchange Commission directed the Nigerian Stock Exchange to submit for its approval a detailed succession plan showing how a new chief executive and new executive directors of the exchange would be appointed. This was complied with, and a leading consulting firm, Accenture, was hired to manage the global search process for the new CEO and executive directors (see Imoyo 2010). Almost 2 years earlier, in 2008, the NSE had announced a restructuring exercise with indications that a group chief executive officer was going to replace the director general position, and a demutualization process was going to commence, with the NSE being eventually listed. But, that restructuring process had been long and tortuous (see *The Punch* 2008). Newspaper reports suggested that, in the organizational restructuring at the Nigerian Stock Exchange, the incumbent assistant director general Lance Musa Elakama, a licensed stockbroker, had been eased out of office in a power tussle.

In addition, the Securities and Exchange Commission released its new Code of Conduct for Capital Market Operators and their Employees in May 2010 (see, for instance, *BusinessDay* 2010 and Onu 2010b), which in principle was a code of ethics by which all employees in the capital market were bound.

Overall, while the various pronouncements, codes and guidelines have been described as being contributory to creating the right governance culture and board accountability for Nigerian banks, there is still a fundamental requirement to harmonize corporate governance codes in Nigeria, even if only from the point of view of clarity.

7.3 From regulation to control

Towards mid-2010, some of the decisions of the CBN had started moving from market regulation towards a regime that approximated a central command and control. The CBN announced in January 2010 that it would retroactively limit the tenure of bank CEOs to a maximum of 10 years. The following April, the CBN announced its intention to commence a screening exercise for prospective managing directors, executive directors and non-executive directors of banks, as well as for directors of financial services holding companies. This new process of direct screening, and the possibility of the CBN interviewing directors was to replace the former practice of banks forwarding the names and profiles of the appointees to the CBN for ratification and confirmation, after paper checks.

In its editorial of Sunday 24 January 2010, *Next* newspaper summarized the lack of objectivity of the Central Bank's policymaking by asserting that:

> ...It was not lost on most discerning observers that the primary targets of this new policy appeared to be two of our most prominent bank chiefs, Tony Elumelu, who engineered a takeover of UBA by the much smaller Standard Trust Bank...; and Jim Ovia, who built Zenith Bank from scratch and made it a ubiquitous presence...The

legality of the CBN decision is hardly in question ... But the question still needs to be asked: should the Central Bank be assuming the roles of board directors to dictate how long a chief executive may serve? Heavily regulated though they were,... setting limits, as a general principle works well in politics and government ... This may, of course, not necessarily work in private enterprise.

... The CBN, by making such a sweeping rule regarding tenure, is inadvertently admitting its own failure to regulate and supervise the banking system. Were the CBN competent in the discharge of its duties, it would have had a bit more confidence ... to punish rogue bank chiefs where the situation demands. As one senior banker tells us, 'a one size fits all rule does not often work well.... Our view is that, while the CBN governor has got most of the big things right so far in his turbulent nine-month tenure, one must always be wary of a government official with power to do almost anything. We will remain vigilant.'

Predictably, the affected CEOs – Jim Ovia of Zenith Bank, Tony Elumelu of UBA and Akinsola Akinfemiwa of Skye Bank –accepted the decision with apparent equanimity. Jim Ovia made no definitive public comments and Tony Elumelu decided to leave it to the experts to interpret (see Nwachukwu and Fatade 2010).

Concern about the CBN's new central approach to regulation was not solely about whether it would have a beneficial impact on the economy, but about the Central Bank's capacity, or lack of it, to administer effectively the flurry of command policies being instituted. There was also concern about the attendant moral hazard that could be created by poor administration and weak implementation of these policies by the overwhelmed executives of the regulator. In January 2010, the new governor of the CBN admitted, at the *Economist* CEO Agenda Conference, that the CBN did not have the internal capacity to implement the intensive banking supervisory programmes the regulator had commenced. Alongside the tougher approach to bank surveillance was the concurrent need also to announce its own internal targets, so that it could be publicly measured, which critics claimed the new CBN leadership was not so keen on. (See, for instance, Ashimi 2010, citing the publicly disclosed internal targets and self-assessment set by the United Kingdom's Financial Services Authority, even in operational areas such as recruitment of specialist and supervisory staff, which was an input into the overall effectiveness of the FSA's Supervisory Enhancement Programme.) According to Ashimi (2010), 'Changing policies and penalising the supervised is not the end of the cleansing of the financial system, it is just a means to an end.... Since Sanusi knew that the CBN lacks the internal capacity to implement a more intrusive risk based policy, should he not have commenced his tenure with internal cleansing and structural building before shaking up the system?' The lack of appropriate disclosure by the CBN of its own internal efficiency and the integrity of its officers was a key weakness, according to Ashimi (2010) and other sources. Areas where analysts expected more public disclosure included internal budgetary allocations and budgetary trends for enforcement activities, staff performance and sanctions against erring staff, and internal capacity-building performance measures, among others.

New prudential guidelines were issued by the Central Bank in the spring of 2010. However, the dynamics of the Nigerian banking industry were now beginning to alter. At the subsequent Bankers' Committee meeting, the bank chief executives began to more vocal. They asserted themselves on policy issues by insisting that the Central Bank expunge from the new prudential guidelines for the banking sector the requirement for banks to make a two per cent provision for their general loan losses (see Nwachukwu 2010). From the bankers' viewpoint, it was counter-intuitive and indefensible that the CBN would still insist on a general loan loss provision of 2 per cent even after a massive clean-up of the banks' loan books. The original clause in the CBN's new prudential guidelines had stipulated that 'banks should make general loan loss provisions of at least two percent of loan portfolio not specifically provided for, in addition to specific provisions, to provide against the unidentified which are known to exist in any portfolio using a systematic method which should be consistently followed from period to period.'

The CBN's rules on provisioning reflected the regulator's top-down approach to regulation, which was non-consultative. The complications associated with the new level of provisioning required for any non-performing loan were reflected in the lack of distinction between commercial loans and project finance facilities. The latter could, for instance, have a two-year moratorium for repayment. The lack of a differential approach to provisioning in the guidelines for these two types of credit facilities meant that, after 90 days, some project loans with longer tenures and repayment moratoria could be classified as non-performing.

7.4 Restructuring

Technically, the interventions of the Central Bank in Nigeria cannot be described as bank restructuring. However, several attempts were made by the Central Bank to alter the operating structure and operating model of banks in Nigeria. Early in 2010, it released a circular on the regulator's intention to discontinue the universal banking regime and move to a segregated banking regime. Banks that still wanted some affiliation with a diversified financial services group in Nigeria would be the option of creating a holding company. This was arguably the first major structural attempt to tackle the underlying causes of the 2009 banking crisis. In the circular BSD/DIR/GEN/CIR/04/012, dated 30 March 2010, the CBN provided three options for banks on one axis (to be either regional, national or international) and two options on another (either to be stand alone commercial banks or to be owned by a bank holding company (or more appropriately a financial holding company)).

The scheduled phasing out of universal banking by September 2011 was contentious and likely to generate controversy with no clear means of validating the economic benefits. On the other hand, the planned review of the Prudential Guidelines for Banks, which had last been done in 1999 and was scheduled review every five years, was viewed by industry analysts as a positive development. The first review of the prudential guidelines was due to be completed by 31 December 2010. While the CBN's directorate of banking supervision had stated that the plan to phase out universal banking was in line with the 'International Financial Reporting Standards and global best practices', critics were of the opinion that the theoretical justification for the change was weak and the justification for using IFRS and 'global best practices' was only an evasion.

For some operators, the key question was whether the plan to phase out universal banking was just another of the CBN's solutions in search of a problem, or was it a properly considered policy option. Even banks that were keen to implement the measures found they generated more questions than answers, as with some other CBN proposals of the day, if they wanted to migrate to the holding company structure (Nwachukwu 2010).

From an industry viewpoint, however, restructuring the banking industry could not be achieved without reaching a resolution of the ownership issues for the eight banks rescued by the Central Bank. It became increasingly evident that the option of a sale to either foreign investors or local banks interested in acquiring the rescued banks was not as easy to implement as the CBN had anticipated. Contrary to the indication by the governor of the CBN, noted in a Bloomberg report on the sale of the rescued banks in February 2010, that 'some transactions could be concluded by April or May', none of the banking transactions had been concluded by then and the likelihood of a resolution in the near future was slim (see Onu 2010a).

The possibility of the Central Bank achieving its plan of completing the restructuring process or sale of the rescued banks by the end of 2010 was also becoming more remote. Meanwhile, banks such as Standard Bank, one of South Africa's – and Africa's – largest banks, continued to position themselves to acquire banks in Nigeria. Standard Bank's deputy CEO was quoted as saying that the bank had 'lobbied the CBN and government for Standard Bank to be the favoured foreign institution in the consolidation process'. According to a *BusinessDay* report (see Anaro 2010), the bank had capital of US$1 billion for international expansion, including into Nigeria, and another US$350 million excess capital in its Nigerian subsidiary, Stanbic IBTC.

However, fundamental conceptual issues about the financial holding companies that the CBN was planning had yet to be fully discussed in all their ramifications. The underlying principle was to 'ring-fence' depositors' money in banks, keeping it from seeping into under-regulated non-banking subsidiaries. The complementary policies were, however, less controversial. These included the risk management guidelines of the CBN, which limited industries with less than a BB credit rating, to a maximum of 10 per cent of the total loan portfolio of a bank. Others included limiting the amount a director or 'significant shareholder' of a bank could borrow from his or her bank to a maximum of 1 per cent of the bank's share capital, except with the prior approval of the CBN. The new guidelines also defined a 'significant shareholding' as a holding of at least five per cent while the maximum credit to all insiders was not to exceed 10 per cent of share capital. While the average laymen and commentators commended the rationale of the CBN's actions, and its apparent decisiveness, several issues were apparent to industry operators. They knew that circumventing most of those rules was never going to be onerous if the CBN machinery was not in itself entirely overhauled. Their argument was that the real problem in the Nigerian banking industry had never really been the absence of adequate rules and guidelines, and that the enactment or pronouncement of more rules without strengthening the enforcement capacity of the CBN would only lead to regulatory constipation.

With the unforeseen delays in the restructuring of the banks, and the need to be seen to be making progress, the CBN appeared to resort frequently to emergency measures. Several credit schemes, including funds for manufacturing companies, from small and medium-scale enterprises to airlines, became the order of the day.

For example, by 17 May, the CBN had introduced another emergency measure, the SME Credit Guarantee Scheme (SMECGS), ostensibly 'in a bid to unlock the tight credit market in the economy and enhance credit to the real sector'. The ₦200 billion scheme was to 'promote and fast-track access to credit by manufactures and small and medium-scale enterprises (SMEs) in Nigeria', and was wholly funded and managed by the CBN.

However, the policy underpinning of the Central Bank's actions remained rather opaque. Many of the CBN's new funds were production inducing rather than consumption inducing. The production-inducing injection of funds implied that the special resources provided by the Central Bank were to be used for financing expansion and augmenting working capital for businesses, as opposed to directly stimulating consumer purchasing power. Even though the production-inducing injection was a shorter and quicker method of Central Bank intervention to stimulate the economy, the real challenge was on the consumption side, and economic theory (see, for instance, Ajakaiye 1992) suggests that a consumption-inducing policy might have been a better response. First, from past experience of how the CBN had handled similar funds in the past, the Central Bank still lacked the capacity to administer any direct intervention in the economy that required selective credit disbursement. The experiences of the SME credit scheme and the agricultural credit schemes of the 1980s and 1990s were glaring cases in point. Secondly, from the perspective of positive economics, increasing access to funds for private consumers, which had been significantly destroyed by the CBN's disruptive policies of 2009, was more likely, *ceteris paribus*, to increase effective demand and ultimately result in increased cash flow, increased output and, hence, increased growth for the private sector.

That the credit incentive schemes and interventions were necessary was not in doubt. What was questionable were the tactical methods adopted by the Central Bank, whose world view and hypothesis about the banking crisis was sometimes based, according to analysts, on the governor's background as a risk manager and not as an economist. According to analysts, such as Bismarck Rewane (see Onu and Ushakang 2010), 'The banking industry was over-bloated and indulged in trading, underscoring the need to right size. The diagnosis of the problem in the banking industry is correct but the prognosis is questionable and therefore one can say that the outcome of the measures is probable.'

The bailed banks' return to profitability, however, seemed to happen faster than the analysts predicted (see Omachonu 2010a). The three-year projection by private sector analysts hinged on three factors: the discovery of hidden pockets of toxic assets; the slowdown in the economy; and the revelations of the abuses and excesses of the turn-around managers imposed by the Central Bank of Nigeria. But, the CBN's spokesperson Mohammed Abdullahi maintained that all the issues related to the troubled banks might be resolved by September 2010.

Irrespective of how the current issues are resolved, Nigeria will still have to decide how to resolve these problems should they arise in the future. One of the dominant interrelated problems facing world banking today is the dilemma in positive economics about how to deal with very large banks whose failure could almost collapse an economy – the 'too big to fail' argument – and the corollary issue in normative economics of whether bailing out banks with taxpayers' money is credible, efficient or equitable., The further question is: 'How does the government protect bank depositors without protecting bank creditors and greedy bank managers, given that deposit insurance is only a last resort?' Several ideas have been suggested, which could be largely categorized into the three options by Paul Tucker, Julie Dickinson and William Poole, respectively (see, for example, Jackson 2010.) The first option, by Paul Tucker of the Bank of England, suggests a beefed-up version of the special resolution process, whereby the regulator takes over a failed bank, and expeditiously works with creditors or arranges a debt–equity swap to strengthen the balance sheet. The second option, proposed by Julie Dickinson, Canada's head of financial supervision, in the *Financial Times*, is that banks issue securities with an embedded convertible coupon which could be triggered to equity if the regulator took control. The third, by William Poole, former president of the St Louis Fed, is that banks mandatorily issue 10-year papers, with staggered maturity profiles, equal to a tenth of their liabilities. The yield on the paper, and the market appetite for the paper at the point of rollover, would determine whether the bank would have to shrink its balance sheet.

In Nigeria, much of this argument has not so much been about the mechanisms of intervention but more about the equity and efficiency of using taxpayers' money to bail banks out and about the process for determining how much and when that intervention should be made by the government.

Restructuring bad debts: the asset management company

In 2004, the then governor of the Central Bank, Chukwuma Charles Soludo, had proposed, as part of his 13-point agenda, the creation of a classified asset management company (AMC) in Nigeria to serve as a clearing-house for non-performing risk assets of commercial or universal banks. However, the creation of the AMC in Nigeria did not materialize in the first three years of Soludo's tenure, and became more difficult after 2007, when a new president was sworn in. After a new governor of the CBN was appointed in May 2009, and 10 out of the 24 banks in the banking system were put on a watch list, the Central Bank accelerated the drafting of the AMC bill and the creation of the company.

The CBN drew on the lessons of the Asian crisis in the 1990s, after which some countries, including China, created centralized classified debt resolution companies for banks, popularly called asset management companies. AMCs typically have four key objectives: helping to restore the loan quality of originating banks; centralizing the disposal of non-performing loans (NPLs); providing alternative and faster options for resolving the NPL stock of the banking industry; and selling some NPLs through either securitization or open auctions. The Nigerian Asset Management Company was designed to be similar in essence and operations to the Chinese AMCs (see Cousin 2007). Operationally, the AMC would acquire the toxic assets in exchange for cash, which would increase the liquidity of the banks and reduce their debt overhang. As of April 2010, Nigerian banks had suffered a diminution in their risk assets to the tune of an estimated ₦9 trillion (US$60 billion), while only ₦1.5 trillion (US$10 billion) had originally been provided for, creating a potential loss of about ₦7.5 trillion (US$50 billion).

In principle, the Nigerian AMC is empowered to purchase non-performing assets from financial institutions or banks, such that the original bank borrower now becomes indebted to the AMC (See Eghobamien (2010). In the purchase of the NPL, the AMC would have paid the bank a 'fair' value for it, thus providing liquidity to the bank. Key lacunae in the AMC bill and other related publicly disclosed policies of the AMC, as disclosed by the CBN, include:

- silence on the pricing or valuation of the assets and the mechanics of the operations of the AMC;
- non-recognition or clarification of the role of the extant Investment and Securities Tribunal in dealing with disputes arising from assets purchased by the AMC;
- silence on the details of eligible assets or asset classes that the AMC can purchase.

The AMC bill also attempts to revolutionize the law relating to the sale and purchase of financial assets. It also extends the liability of directors on the board of a company to one of almost strict personal liability where a loan to the director's company is classified by the Central Bank as non-performing.

With an estimated ₦1 trillion (US$6.7 billion) needed to recapitalize the distressed banks, and a base case scenario that only 50 per cent of the face value of the toxic assets or non-performing loans would be recovered within the first 10 years of the asset management company, several issues arose as to the efficiency of using taxpayers' money for this purpose.

Finance minister Olusegun Aganga, an ex-Goldman Sachs managing director, cautioned: 'My concern was that if you are going to put money into it, wherever that money comes from, it is taxpayers' money. I am the one that should account for taxpayers' money. So I have to make sure taxpayers get value for it and I am not taking that responsibility lightly. So wherever I source the money, I have to look at it properly and ensure the interest of the Nigerian people, not just the banking sector' (see, for instance, Omachonu 2010b). Technically, the toxic assets that the rescued banks had on their books consisted of genuine loans that had been fully disbursed to genuine investors for shares on the NSE as well as phantom loans which banks used to fund capital-raising and purchase their own shares. Given the rock bottom value of some of the stocks, buying the toxic assets that constituted these problems would imply purchasing them at greater than their market value. This introduces the need for a detailed pricing mechanism, on which the CBN is as yet silent. This view is reinforced by Razia Khan, the African economist for the global Chartered Bank: 'If it is to recapitalise or partially recapitalise banks, then it (the AMC) would have to buy the assets at a greater-than-market value. Is there a moral hazard involved in doing this? Absolutely yes. But that is precisely the reason why regulation then needs to be tightened' (quoted in Omachunu 2010b).

Beyond the moral hazard problem, several other operational issues would need to be straightened out by the Central Bank if the AMC in Nigeria is to achieve its stated objectives. In early July 2010, the president of the Federal Republic of Nigeria had yet to give his assent to the Asset Management Corporation of Nigeria (AMCON) bill, which had been unanimously passed by the National Assembly on 23 June. Even when assent was given, experts believed that the AMCON would face legal challenge in court because of lacunae in the bill, and because of issues about the way in which the Central Bank took over the management of the eight rescued banks. How proactively the Central Bank manages these issues will determine how quickly the process of restructuring the loan portfolio of the banks can commence.

By November 2010, the executive leadership team of the Asset Management Company of Nigeria (AMCON) had resumed work in Abuja, Nigeria, several months after the president had given assent to the AMCON bill and about three weeks after their screening by parliament. Expert opinion is that another six months would be required to assess the progress of AMCON.

8
The Road Ahead: Sustainability of Bank Reforms

8.1 The future challenge

The objective of any banking reform is to enable citizens to have wider access to credit and financial services in an efficient and sustainable way. Any other focus of reforms can only be short-term, tentative, or otherwise misguided. In a developing country where growth has been anaemic, and the average citizen cynical and impatient due to the inability of past governments to fulfil their promises, the success of a reform effort will depend on the transparency of the reformer – to prove that there is no hidden agenda – and on an ability to demonstrate a long-term road map to galvanize public interest. On the other hand, if the reform effort is largely dependent on the charisma or personality of the reformer – be it the president or the governor of the Central Bank – achieving reforms can be volatile, laborious, and often discouraging.

In more mature economies, where macroeconomic indicators are more reliable and more generally available, reforms are better calculated and better thought through and allowances are made for policy biases. However, some of the financial sector reforms in Nigeria have been adversarial efforts rather than corrective, collaborative initiatives.

Just as the temporary successes recorded by the Failed Banks Tribunal sent the villains into hiding for a single business cycle – approximately seven years – before another crop of well-educated *nouveaux d'ecole* emerged as bank CEOs, it is uncertain how entrenched the current Nigerian banking reforms might be. Even if they become established, several questions remain about how systematic the reforms are, and how well thought through they have been, if they are to serve as learning points for other West African countries and promote Nigeria's quest to be one of the two key hubs for capital coming into Africa.

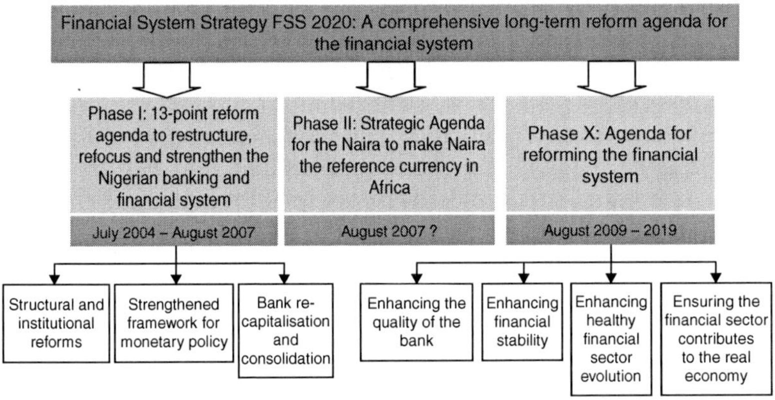

Figure 8.1 Overview of the Nigerian banking sector reforms 2004–10

As Mwega (2002) suggests, 'financial sector reforms are particularly difficult because of the powerful vested interests that have been created through high government intervention over the years.' Brownbridge and Harvey (1998), in a study on the impact of financial reforms in African economies, found that 'the greater the structural changes in the banking system caused by government intervention, the more difficult it was to achieve the objectives of financial liberalization by simply reversing the earlier policy changes.'

In Nigeria, the potential for the banking reforms to have the structural impact that would encourage the banks to support maximum real sector growth and economic development is not borne out by history. Greater emphasis will have to be placed on market-driven mechanisms underpinned by the country's laws. At an operational level, some analysts have, for instance, questioned whether the manner of the Central Bank's takeover of the eight rescued banks, and the dismissal of their executive and managing directors, might not run into stormy legal waters, thereby delaying the ability of the Central Bank to restructure the banks and hence the industry. On a more fundamental level, others have queried whether the drastic actions of the Central Bank in disciplining defaulting bank directors and borrowers, even without the judgement of the courts, and in allegedly threatening suspects with fire, brimstone and jail terms without legal or administrative due process, would result in the improved behaviour the Central Bank wishes to achieve. In the 1990s, for instance, the Abacha military regime established the Failed Banks Tribunal to try promoters and directors of banks alleged to have failed. These draconian actions by the government, which used the Failed Banks Tribunal to arrest and detain about 160 senior bank executives in high-security prisons in Nigeria over an eight-year period, with subsequent blacklisting by the Central Bank, did not prevent the emergence of another generation of banking crooks immediately afterwards, from 2002 to 2009. Similarly, it is not certain that the Central Bank's activities naming and shaming suspects as criminals, even before their trials, will in itself correct the future behaviour of the next generation of bankers or serve as deterrents to bankers a decade down the line. On the contrary, as was observed with the Failed Banks Tribunal, while a ruthless and draconian approach to bank reform might yield short-term results and send the 'bad bankers' into hiding for a while, the results are often counterproductive and detrimental to the influence of the regulators in the future. In the case of the Failed Banks Tribunal, a special extraordinary tribunal, some of its judgements were later found to be 'null, void, and of no effect and the conviction set aside as if they never occurred' on appeal to the regular courts, including the Supreme Court, the highest court in the land,. By 2006, five judgements relating to directors of the so-called failed banks of the 1990s had been given by the law courts, including the Court of Appeal and the Supreme Court, each of them in favour of the bank directors. In most instances, the judgements in favour of the criminalized bank directors were largely based on the violation of their fundamental human rights at the Tribunal and the fact that the their conviction had not followed the due process of the law. The ultimate effect of this was that the next generation of bankers of the early 2000s learnt nothing from the draconian clean-up efforts of the 1990s, except to find smarter ways to break the law and stay ahead of the Central Bank. Any reform effort that does not seek to inculcate better behaviour in the operators through the proper mechanisms has a limited likelihood of success.

Even though no one could doubt the rationale for the 2009–10 banking reforms, very few players, even among the regulators, had fully anticipated the complications and increased responsibility that come with such a massive effort. Experts are unanimous that as an economic manager of approximately cabinet-level rank, the governor's duty is to uphold the integrity of the information and market signals generated by Nigerian banks, to uphold the stability of the banking system and to allow things to take their legal course. However, irrespective of the irrational exuberance of the market operators, some expert commentators, in their discussion of the two most recent governors of the Central

Bank, suggest that they should have displayed more circumspection. Many still argue that a more experienced governor, even while confronting entrenched banking interests, would have kept his counsel, relied more on good advice, without compromising his own convictions, and avoided the sort of personal exchanges and references that Sanusi often became caught up in. He would have announced his policy more guardedly and in a more structured way, as most reserve bank chiefs worldwide would do.

The CBN under Sanusi had won the war. But the 2009 reforms had created more questions than answers. Did the end justify the means? What would be the eventual price? What would happen to the foreign institutional rights that had been trampled upon in the takeover of the banks, and to the confidence of the international community? How would the local and foreign core investor nations respond to being sidestepped? How would the international investment community assess Nigeria's banking reforms in a world of increasing adherence to the rule of law and order, as opposed to a world of regulatory threats, and the creation of scapegoats? Were the reforms just about sanitizing one aspect of a system or a holistic reformation that put the entire system on a path of self-sustained growth? Or, would the system be subject to drastic regulatory hijacks each time it faltered or the regulator failed in his or her responsibility for pre-emptive surveillance? If the ultimate objective of the reforms were to engender sustainable banking sector growth and stability, while stimulating savings mobilization and private sector credit allocation, would the Sanusi reform programme deliver any marked improvement by 2014 on the dismal reform records of many African countries? This is when his term as governor of the CBN would be over and Nigeria only six years away from its vision of being one of the top 20 countries in the world? Finally, were the central banking and market reforms only about risk management (that is, 'de-risking' banks) or were they about statesmanship and crafting structural, sustainable growth-inducing policies in collaboration with other regulators and the fiscal arms of government?

This book does not attempt to provide all the answers but has sought to articulate the issues concisely and to suggest the multifaceted dimensions of the polity and economy in which our banking system must operate for any financial sector reform to be long lasting.

Given the Nigerian operating environment, several other considerations will influence the ultimate playing out of the banking reforms: the sustained growth of the Nigerian economy; the deepening of the financial markets; the continued independence of the CBN; the degree of interference from politicians in CBN decisions; the incorporation of a vision of reform in the work of central bank employees below the deputy-governor; and, ultimately, the character of the next governor of the CBN. Since Nigeria's return to democracy in 1999, the Senate's basic criteria for evaluating governors of the Central Bank have been too narrow – competence and moral character. (See, for instance, Ken Foskett *Judging Thomas: The Life and Times of Clarence Thomas*, (William Morrow/Harper Collins, New York, 2004) p. 184.) Apart from the difficulty a fledgling Senate will have in effectively appraising the professional competence of a governor of the Central Bank in a postmodern economy, other soft factors, such as the nominee's ideology, personal and policy temperaments, and world view are also critical in selecting future incumbents of that exalted office. Other commentators have noted the importance of further soft issues: the maturity to deflect intrusive questions; the restrained wisdom to be silent or soft-spoken about the needless controversies stirred up by opponents; and the humility and magnanimity needed by a governor of the Central Bank to push his deputies forward and talk more of what 'we' are doing as a 'team' and less of himself and his personal aggrandisement. This may call for the nominating agency of the executive arm of the government – in Nigeria, the presidency – to work with future nominees to this office on areas they can refine, even when they may already seem to be satisfactory in terms of competence or moral integrity.

The sustainability of bank reforms globally depends at present on two areas of progress: first, the governance issues concerned with kick-starting and continuing a sustainable reform agenda; and, second, the soundness of the reforms' ideological underpinnings. If that underpinning is weak, the reforms will run into the ground no matter how willing successive governments are to continue a reform agenda,

The second point is critical because many of the capital requirements and reporting standards that African countries, such as Nigeria, seek to adopt may have been formulated to further the interests of advanced countries and powerful market players. Claessens *et al.* (2004), for instance, suggests that many of these standards are set at the expense of the developing economies. Notably, there is often a misleading assumption that the causes of emerging market foreign investment crises lie with the emerging market economies themselves, and can be attributed to their weak institutions and inefficient practices.

On the contrary, some of the banking sector policies, ostensibly designed to prevent systemic failure, were only self-protecting. For instance, the Failed Banks decree and the Prudential Guidelines, in operation between the mid-1980s and the mid-1990s, were designed to prevent banks from collapsing and not necessarily to support the growth of the economy. Incidentally, due to the regulators' lack of capacity to update those documents regularly, particularly the Prudential Guidelines, the policies ended up neither limiting bank over-exposures and abuses, nor supporting the growth of the economy. In terms of the balance between international and national policy obligations in the face of market shocks, adverse volatility, and other international systemic shocks, the existing system tends to limit the discretionary policymaking of developing countries. The enhanced monitoring and transparency provisions of the Basle II accords, and other similar proposals, are designed to ensure that the investment climate conforms to the preferences and expectations of Western investors. The new proposals also ignore the overwhelming evidence that many successful developing or emerging market economies (and indeed EU countries) developed under some form of financial repression and not full openness or free market orientation.

The level of development of democratic and market systems is also contributory. We are witnessing USA versus EU models in the West, and India versus China models in the East. While democracies tend to have a greater ability to entrench economic or banking reforms than one-party states, one-party governments can sometimes move faster. The assertion that a democracy's decisions are more durable in this regard becomes questionable. With the failure of the 'self-regulating' markets hypothesis as proposed by the evangelical US advocates of free markets in banking, and widespread criticism of the UK's Big Bang deregulation, banking reform is set to be an ongoing process in future. The new approach to the 'expanded scope of regulation', as proposed by US Treasury Secretary, Tim Geithner, already has an 'overhaul' component in US domestic regulation, which involves setting up systemic risk regulators that would regulate institutions not by what they are but by what they do, giving government powers to regulate crossover or hybrid financial institutions such as hedge funds and other non-bank investment vehicles.

Simultaneously, the new era of global regulation, in which the US would no longer monopolize the position of president of the World Bank and the Europeans would give up their control of the post of managing director of the IMF, will begin to usher in new perspectives on dealing with the dangers and excesses of capitalism, from which African countries might do well to learn.

As for the transatlantic, perhaps trans-industry, debate over whether to push for deeper fiscal stimuli or to focus on regulation, the leading view of Indian economist and prime minister, Manmohan Singh, suggests the way forward for African countries. In Prime Minister Singh's view, there needs to be an umpire to ensure that developed countries honour their pledges but the world needs a new monitoring body, an 'expert crew' either inside or outside the IMF to ensure stimulus measures are 'sustained and maintained'.

In Nigeria, banking reforms and the advent of universal banking, which created some of the problems of the recent Nigerian banking crisis, have always borrowed from global trends and parallels. The G-20 summit of March 2009 discussed expanding the global regulatory system to match the size and complexity of the financial system. Apart from the reactive and rather inverted nature of this proposition, it also lacks an understanding of both economic and financial history. Bank assets reaching phenomenal proportions at the turn of the century (UK, US$11.31 trillion/£7.9 trillion; South Africa, US$300 billion; Nigeria, US$100 billion), from £1.2 trillion in 1990 to £3.2 trillion in 2000 – with a good proportion coming from securities-related investments. Complex connections between commercial banking and securities trading had reached a delicate and intricate state. Adopting the Glass–Steagall Act approach and breaking large banks into their separate businesses, which worked during the US Depression, might appear to be a positive step but other fundamental issues remain to be tackled. Without them some of the CBN's policies might amount to 'regulatory plagiarism' à la Bismarck Rewane (Rewane is a financial commentator, economist and Managing Director of Financial Derivatives Limited in Nigeria), or 'regulatory abuse'. Modernizing the Nigerian banking sector inevitably requires removing some of the obnoxious legacy of practices that Nigerian banks have enjoyed.

For instance, Nigerian banks earn an average of ₦16.5 billion gross from what is called Commission on Turnover (COT), which is typically an *ad valorem* tariff paid at a standard rate of 0.5 per cent of any amount withdrawn from a *naira* current account.

Beyond the specific themes, one main abnormality of the current CBN reforms is the absence of a rich policy debate based on empirical exchanges. This leaves much of our national banking policies to the discretion of one man, the governor of the Central Bank, whose personal whims or professional misjudgements, no matter how sincere his intentions may be, could leave the nation with sub-optimal policies.

A bank reform is no doubt inevitable, and globally both politicians and regulators, and indeed practising bankers, have conceded the need for intervention. Indeed, nobody should underestimate the scale of the rot in the Nigerian banking system between 2000 and 2009, nor the multiplier effects, and the economic damage they have caused. However, if future governors of the Central Bank do not abide by due process and sustainable reform practices, the resulting alienation of the investment community, and the watering down of our respect for capital rights, may end up debasing our collective integrity – the very essence of banking – notwithstanding the rot that caused the reforms. Despite the best of intentions, the governor may have blind spots. The success of bank reforms could, therefore, lie in the quality of robust evaluation of the reform alternatives, which in part depends on the intellect and conviction of the deputy-governors of the CBN, some of whom are little known to the public.

Besides core policy issues, several others still remain. For example, ethnic issues have challenged the implementation of reforms in other sectors. A case in point is the civil service reforms initiated by the head of the civil service of the federation, Steve Oronsaye in mid-2009, which faced severe setbacks due to intransigent permanent secretaries. Examples of the stiff opposition to reforms, some with ethnic undertones, include the case in which the permanent secretary and head of the National Assembly Service Commission (NASC) (the clerk who doubles as head of the legislative service) was reported as refusing to comply immediately with the Oronsaye's new retirement policy (*The Guardian*, 11 October 2009). Another instance was the head of an agency under the Federal Ministry of Health, who, rather than retire in compliance with the policy, chose instead to go to court. He also attempted to persuade another senior government official of cabinet rank to issue an official memo to counter the orders of the head of the civil service.

As well as ethnic issues, there is the need to reinvigorate the manpower base. Most regulatory agencies are weak, stymied and lack the capacity to run with the vision of reforms laid out by top or executive management. As of 2005, for instance, it was reported that the majority of workers in a large government-owned corporation Nigerian National Petroleum Corporation (NNPC) were over 50 years of age. Thirty-one per cent of them were nearing retirement, with only a mere 2 per cent of the entire workforce less than 30 years old, and the average age of employees close to 50 years. The worrying reality is that this picture applies to several other government agencies attempting to take forward transformational change.

Effective funding of the reforms has also always been a challenge. Out of an estimated government budget of ₦4.07 trillion, an estimated ₦680 billion is spent on petroleum subsidies, amounting to ₦1.5 times the entire capital spending of the federal government. Another ₦1.7 trillion, or close to 50 per cent, is spent on salaries and wages for federal civil servants, so that a large chunk of the federal budget is expended on recurrent expenditure, mainly salaries and wages. This leaves little for capital spending and medium-term funding injections into the banking system, in a country where domestic savings by individuals and businesses are low.

A situation in which more than half of the federal government's budget is recurrent expenditure has also been linked to the stifling of the growth of the banking system, with much liquidity passing through that provides cheap money with multiplier effects, and hence high inflationary potential. On the other hand, low capital expenditure has limited the deepening of the financial markets, constraining the room for the innovative growth of capital market products. Between 2004 and 2009, the neoclassical relationship between interest rates and bond prices seemed to have been lost in the management of the economy, partly due to the weak relationship between the various heads of the financial regulators. However, there was more coordinated interaction between at least some of the seven key financial, regulatory or policy agencies in Nigeria – the Central Bank of Nigeria, the Securities Exchange Commission, Nigerian Deposit Insurance Corporation (NDIC), National Insurance Commission of Nigeria (NAICOM), National Pension Commission, Debt Management Office (DMO) and Federal Inland Revenue Service – in working with the federal Ministry of Finance towards the end of March 2010. That month, Nigeria experienced a major inter-ministerial and inter-agency collaboration, which led to the removal of taxes on corporate debt issues and reduced transaction fees, making it more cost-efficient to raise capital on the domestic bond market at lower coupon rates (*BusinessDay*, 25 March 2010). This laid the ground for stronger financial intermediation.

More recently, the economic outlook described by the Ministry of Finance suggests that '...the macroeconomic environment is expected to further gain additional momentum and there will be enhanced real GDP growth performance in view of the on-going and envisaged structural reforms'.

While there is no doubt that there are ongoing reforms in Nigeria, the 'structural' nature of some of these reforms will continue to be questioned until future reformers learn from the failures and successes of past reform efforts.

8.2 Key success factors for reformers in Nigeria

Character of the reformers

Many of the reformers in Nigeria have emerged from the burning crucible of their personal experiences, often supported by a spiritual, not necessarily religious, drive or fervour.

Based on our limited study of the reform process, it appears that four key factors are critical for a successful reform in any sector in Nigeria

1. Initial leadership support – empowerment by a disinterested leader, usually the president, vice-president or governor of a state in Nigeria, is often all that is needed for the take-off of any reform initiative.
2. Sound prior understanding of a sector – tackling the problem at source and taking policy action with prominent implementation almost immediately upon assumption of office is a key success factor for most reform efforts. Successful reformers have all had a detailed understanding of the issues, have known what political opposition they could face and how to navigate that terrain. They have known what priority areas to tackle first. In Nigeria's pluralist society, and with its high levels of poverty, there are always many well qualified but relatively poor semi-professionals who would flood any political appointee with ideas, initiatives and suggestions, sometimes self-servingly. Without a deep first-hand understanding of the sector in question and the ability to differentiate between a multitude of advisors, it would be difficult for any reformer to take action. Most reformers in Nigerian governments have their action plans defined for them before they begin their first day in office, and only use advice for modifying rather than defining their blueprints. It is this sound understanding of the sector that enables them to dive deep into the root cause of the problem within their first few months in office without chasing shadows.
3. Character is important, often backed by a greater then usual spirituality or religious faith. While religious belief has often been abused on the continent, and in Nigeria in particular, and though it may be difficult to discern genuine faith-conscious professionals from self-serving people, most of the successful reformers, from Oronsaye to Dora Akunyili to Sanusi, are people with a strong personal religious belief or spirituality.
4. Passion is necessary. For Akunyili, for instance, there were two key motivators – integrity, reflected in her returning £12,000 (*The Guardian*, 4 October 2009), and the death of her sister Vivian, who died in 1988 after using fake drugs. This engendered in Akunyili a great zeal to get rid of counterfeit drugs. She was able to get the proportion of expired, substandard, counterfeit or unregistered drugs in Nigeria down from 60 per cent to less than 30 per cent in 5 years, even though most of the fake drug barons were from her ethnic part of the country. This was a significant achievement as, in 2002, the WHO had reported that 70 per cent of medicines in Nigeria were fake. The National Agency for Foods and Drug Administration

(NAFDAC) estimate was 41 per cent. By 2008, NAFDAC's estimate was 16 per cent. Independent observers, such as Bate and Ayodele (2009), observed a decline in failure rates of antimalarials from 32 per cent to 18 per cent by 2009. These results were due to several factors, but they included improved controls, surveillance and prosecution of counterfeiters by NAFDAC

In the drug war, for instance, Akunyuli, as director-general of NAFDAC, identified the genesis of the massive fake drug problem. Even though fake drugs have been here since the 1960s, it was clear that their increase was traceable to several clear factors – including the exit of the multinational pharmaceutical companies in the 1990s and the emergence of cheap pharmaceutical factories in India and China that were willing to compromise standards. She used her background knowledge of the sector and her prior experience working as zonal secretary of the Petroleum Trust Fund between 1997 and 2000. This gave her a good understanding of the drugs sector and of government bureaucracy, which enabled her to drive a focused plan of action for drug control in Nigeria (see an interview with Dora Akunyuli in *The Guardian*, 17 April 2005). This understanding of government bureaucracy was pivotal to the agency identifying and collaborating with all stakeholders in the war against fake drugs. Holistic inter-agency solutions were then developed, across all stakeholder groups, including banks. For instance, banks were notified not to prepare financial importation documents for drug importers without NAFDAC clearance.

Nuhu Ribadu, of the Economic and Financial Crimes Commission, maligned by many (including the fraudsters, public officers and their cronies that he targeted), has been celebrated abroad for leading a war, which was globally adjudged a huge success, against financial fraudsters and economic saboteurs. He endured constant innuendo, and there were allegations that every case he prosecuted was tainted by politics, and that he was being used as a wild dog by the civilian president to attack his political opponents. But, even critics could not doubt that Ribadu assisted in establishing the anti-corruption fight and that he built an institution that outlasted him, his choleric and outspoken behaviour notwithstanding.

Many of these crusaders and reformers received international acclaim. Ribadu, after less than two years in office, had already been invited to address the World Bank Congress in Singapore in 2006, was in a dialogue with the then UN Secretary-General, and had won *ThisDay* Man of the Year in 2005. But, their effective communication with key influencers in the domestic economy often contributed much to the continuity of their reform efforts. Despite Ribadu's notable achievements, his greatest challenge still remained convincing a section of the Nigerian community that the anti-graft war was not selective.

For Oronsaye, who was from the private sector and a former accountant with Peat Marwick Ani Ogunde & Co, a firm of chartered accountants which had once had the KPMG franchise in Nigeria, reforms need to be subtle, strategic and with as little media uproar as possible. Stephen Osagiede Oronsaye, who became head of the federal civil service in Nigeria in 2009, the country's most senior and ostensibly most influential civil servant, had served as personal assistant to his former boss, the minister of finance in the 1990s, until 1998. Subsequently, from 1999, he was permanent secretary under the Obasanjo civilian regime, largely in the State House, as permanent secretary and principal secretary to the head of state, where he developed an unparalleled understanding of the State House machinery. Selected from a shortlist of five candidates – which also included Dr Hakeem Baba Ahmed (believed to be the most senior permanent secretary by tenure, having been appointed to that grade in 1998), Dr Goke Adegoroye, Prof. Dapo Afolabi and Dr Raheem Ogunbambi, a former research fellow at the Institute of International Affairs (Akanbi and Olaleye 2009). Oronsaye won by a narrow margin.

Interestingly, of the five candidates short-listed for consideration, four had PhDs, in a well-educated civil service that was reputed to have over 28 PhDs at the director and permanent secretary level – an ironical contrast in a nation with a poorly skilled civil service. It suggests a well-qualified top-heavy structure but a mediocre middle management and a thinning, undertrained lower management. The implication of this is that, for the reforms to be sustainable, there are renewal issues for the civil service in Nigeria and for semi-autonomous public agencies alike.

Lessons from other countries with the same heterogeneous polities and ethnic complexities would help Nigeria. In India, for instance, the approach of using insider radicals to reform the system has been found to yield more sustainable economic results than the Nigerian practice of introducing neophytes, who inherently lack a long-term perspective to drive through central banking reforms. Manmohan Singh, an economist trained in Cambridge and Oxford, who had previously worked in government, academia, the United Nations and as head of the Reserve Bank of India, before serving as finance minister of India from 1991 to 1996, presided over the opening-up of India's economy with free market reforms. He is widely respected as the architect of India's economic liberalization. Without a strong political base, he had to relax or abandon the overbearing state controls, helping to unleash entrepreneurism, robust growth rates and boost public finances. The disadvantage to such reform policies is that the reformers always have to strike a balance between dramatic restructuring, which has an element of surprise, and a participatory approach, which has theoretically better outcomes but may be hijacked by vested interests.

During many of Nigeria's earlier reforms, as in many other developing countries, there were vested interests who wanted to maintain the *status quo ante* and alleged that measures had been introduced without full public debate and, at times, outside the constitution and the rule of law. In attracting officers of international quality back to Nigeria, the Obasanjo administration granted two cabinet ministers extra-statutory salaries: US$247,000 and US$120,000 to the finance minister, Okonjo-Iwealla, and the foreign affairs minister, Olu Adeniji, respectively. This compares with the ₦794,085 (approximately US$70,000) salary per annum stipulated in the Certain Political, Public and Judicial Office Holders (Salaries and Allowances etc) Act No. 6, 2002. While the media uproar about the remuneration of these public officers was eventually calmed, creating flexible but transparent remuneration options for non-partisan, non-corrupt, reform-oriented individuals, who want to assume public office, is sometimes a challenge in developing countries. For many, the pressure is not the remuneration when in office, but pensions to enable them to maintain the same standard of living after leaving public office.

8.3 Comparative lessons

Were the Nigerian banking reforms of an orthodox deregulation and market-driven *laissez-faire* kind, as advocated by orthodox development economists and multilateral institutions, or did they take a more unorthodox, re-regulation, command-and-control approach? There are several parallels with other countries, and with a number of programmes of financial reform in other developing countries, which may be compared to the Nigerian experience. Historically, Nigeria's economic growth has often been compared to that of Venezuela and Malaysia, because of their similarly intensive use of natural resource and their hetero-cultural complexities. Sometimes India, due to its complex ethnic mix, as well as its land mass and demographic profiles, is compared. On the other hand, many of these comparator countries have been able to avoid the 'resource curse' (a phenomenon where oil-rich countries or countries with abundant natural resources become complacent in developing other critical revenue sources, sometimes leaving the resource-rich country worse than their counterparts without abundant mix of natural resource), 'Dutch disease', and the vicious economic cycle of Nigeria. Due to the striking similarities between the institutional situation and policy malpractice in the Venezuelan banking crisis of the 1990s and the Nigerian banking crisis of 2008–9, one could attempt to draw some lessons from the Venezuelan experience.

Unlike Venezuela, whose banking crisis was closely related to the intervention and control of the country's second largest bank, the Nigerian banking experience did not carry the same risk from the dominance of a single bank. However, after the implementation of a multiple exchange rate system in the 1980s, banks in both countries found trading and arbitrage in foreign exchange operations highly profitable to the disadvantage of real sector lending. Severe deficiencies in banking supervision became glaringly obvious after it was discovered that banks had loaned money to themselves and to their subsidiaries, and had disbursed many short-term loans without any second-way-out (SWO) (second way out is an alternative means of recovering your loan in the event the first way out or initial cashflow fails) for the loan.

Overall, as in the Venezuelan experience of the 1990s, the Nigerian banking crisis of 2007–9 reflected a complex interplay of factors that might cause and precipitate a financial crisis. In Nigeria, the crisis appeared to have been spurred on by the abrupt way regulations were imposed and the ineffectiveness of financial supervision. One useful distinction (see, for instance, Vera 2001) is to separate the underlying institutional and macroeconomic factors that could make the financial system vulnerable (the underlying causes) from the actions taken to guide decision making (the precipitating factors). Vera suggests that the actions taken to guide decision making (the right economic policy actions) might help to remedy or soften the impact of a decline. They could also help to counter serious weaknesses in financial structures and industry lapses.

In Nigeria, the precipitating factors for the banking sector crises appear to have been almost as serious as the underlying causes that perpetuated it. The painful reality of the Nigerian economic development and planning process, and indeed of the Nigerian banking reforms, was that for a long time the Central Bank did not have a robust and quantitative macroeconomic framework. In the absence of a testable framework that was relatively scientific and value-free, it was almost impossible for any meaningful quantitative modelling to be done, especially when there was no institutional capacity to do so at the Central Bank before the Soludo years. As Folarin Alayande has suggested, in relation to the institutional planning problem in Nigeria, 'convenience, not conviction' has often dictated the choices our economists have made. By 2005, shortly after assuming office as governor, Soludo's key focus was to build such a modelling capacity at the Central Bank in order to support the existing research capabilities of the regulator. However, while this was begun, the benefits have yet to be fully realized.

In the *Economist* of 18–24 July 2009, an article entitled 'Modern Economic Theory – Where it Went Wrong and How the Crisis is Changing It', re-examined the theoretical underpinnings of many current economic policies and found them to be rather subjective. It suggested that central bankers need a more fact-based approach towards policymaking. This puts the job of economic planners and central bankers in the spotlight and makes them increasingly responsible for exercising their judgement more effectively. Accolades are certain to come to those who operate with restraint and exercise careful judgement. By the end of 2009, for instance, Ben Shalom Bernanke, chairman of the US Federal Reserve, had been chosen as *Time* magazine's Person of the Year 2009 (*Time* magazine, 16 December 2009). Mild-mannered and soft-spoken, like many effective central bank governors the world over, Bernanke's views were non-partisan and ideologically neutral but they were also methodical, data driven and based on the up to date innovative thinking (*www.Time.com*).

On the other hand, compared with most earlier governors of the CBN, the personalities of the two appointed in Nigeria in 2004 and 2009 tended to reflect some hypomaturity. For instance, Bernanke helped to oversee the financial stress tests that finally calmed the markets without any sensationalism or giving media interviews describing the main culprits as criminals. Apologists for the sensationalist governors at the CBN often attribute their exuberance to the underdeveloped markets and unruly operators they regulated However, historical evidence suggests that the long-term benefits of a financial sector reform that is not coordinated or aligned to the principles of natural justice are often limited.

One key lesson remains. As in some other jurisdictions, boards considering appointments to the office of governor of the CBN should examine a range of composite factors, including policy temperament and personality, and not just professional CVs and political affiliations.

8.4 Big themes: action plan for sustainability

The CBN Act and the structure of regulation in Nigeria reflect the overcentralization of power at the centre in the federal authorities, as with many other policies. The governor of the CBN is vested with too much power, which makes him liable to major policy gaffes as a result of misjudgement if he is too little supported by internal self-correction.

Ever since the exit of Victor Odozi, a deputy governor at the Central Bank in the 1990s, many analysts have believed that the powers of the CBN deputy governors have been inadvertently whittled down, given the character of the assertive governors since 2003, exposing the country excessively to their individual temperaments.

By 2009, the demerits of a strong governor of the CBN, who is keen on his own area of expertise – monetary policy for Soludo, and risk management and banking supervision for Sanusi – had become obvious. In 2004, this hindered balanced economic management and there were several instances of the monetary policy regulator, the CBN, not acting in concert with other financial sector regulators or with the fiscal authorities, notably the Ministry of Finance.

The central issue in the 2009 bank reforms was the conflict between optimizing general welfare (systemic assurance of the banking system) versus personal freedom (recognizing that the banks were legal persons with their own constitutional rights and governance mechanisms). Similar to the ice-cream versus umbrella argument, the issue remains how we strike the right balance.

Ever since the 1950s to the 1970s, when Nigeria adopted a British-style regulatory approach, it has failed to keep up with international developments in financial regulation. In the UK, the Financial Reporting Council (FRC) was the independent regulator responsible for promoting confidence in corporate reporting and governance, until this structure was altered in mid-2010. While it provided broad-spectrum regulation and surveillance, the nature of the surveillance, albeit often criticized, is to support enterprise and investment and enhance the UK's strength in competitive international markets. In the context of the global economic downturn, the FRC's responsibilities were also increasingly important in fostering the confidence needed for recovery.

The challenges facing financial services companies were described in the Turner Report, which articulately outlines the problems that have beset the regulation and supervision of financial service companies in the UK. They are still as true for Nigeria as they were for the UK.

First is the macro-prudential problem. Bank examiners in Nigeria have traditionally found it difficult to see the wood for the trees, or have simply chosen to turn a blind eye. Individual supervisors have traditionally spent too much time dealing with problems, bank by bank, and individual regulators have tried to attack these problems sub-sector by sector, instead of on a coordinated macro basis. In the UK, this required a deliberate 'rebalancing' of the tripartite authorities – the FSA, the Bank of England and the Treasury, whose regulatory system Nigeria copied in the post-independence days (the Financial Services Authority in the UK was established in 1997) – Nigeria needs the same; indeed, there is also an imperative to come up with a deliberate policy of 'productive overlap'.

Second is the very weak and corrupted 'idea procurement' process between independent financial services regulators. Even though Nigeria's laws have established the regulators as independent and autonomous (the CBN for banking, NAICOM for insurance and the SEC for capital markets), the scope for voluntary joint investigations in today's era of universal banking, or even for a coordinated exchange of ideas or rigorous public challenge of them, was lacking until a semblance of it was introduced by the governor of the CBN in the last quarter of 2009.

Third is the geographical problem of universal banks operating in different countries. This is even more of a problem across regulatory boundaries, for instance: a large Nigerian bank with a wholly owned securities trading firm in Nigeria; and a fully licensed UK bank, and an insurance underwriter in another African country as subsidiaries. The reality is that until 2007 very few, if any, Nigerian banking groups had detailed group transfer pricing models. Hence it was difficult to identify a consolidated financial statement that reflected the true and fair position of each of the segments of the business.

Fourth is the critical issue of capital adequacy and its implications for liquidity, risk management and the cost behaviour of Nigerian banks. With one of the highest equity to asset bases in the world at the end of 2008, Nigerian banks created their own self-inflicted asset pricing bubble, largely uncorrelated with the bubble in the West. This 'fundamental intellectual mistake', to quote Sir Callum McCarthy, that all we need are 'bigger banks' or 'stronger regulators' without seeking to create a market mechanism that works, will need to be corrected. Finally, there is the issue of inter-regulator protocols for mergers, acquisitions and liquidations. A disastrous case in recent Nigerian financial service industry history is Spring Bank, in which different regulators adopted different policy positions. When confronted with the mess, the new governor of the Central Bank played safe by responding that the merger had received court approval. Discussions about inter-agency approaches are often fragile, especially because the SEC and NAICOM have some unwritten responsibility for administrative oversight from the Federal Ministry of Finance, while the Central Bank is to all intents and purposes fully autonomous of the ministry. It is critical that one body, perhaps the Central Bank, takes the lead role in developing a coordinated protocol for these issues, rather than waiting for another system failure.

Borrowing from Sir Callum McCarthy's summary of his review of the British regulatory landscape (*Financial Times,* 1 April 2009), the Central Bank is not a regulatory island even though it enjoys a prominent position as one of Nigeria's most powerful regulators. A trade-off of improved effectiveness of surveillance, but a perception of less independence, would be worth making. Whether the Central Bank adopts that 'first among equals' role, and whether other regulators accept the CBN's leadership in these areas, would depend, more than anything else, on the tact and character of the CBN leadership in driving change even on matters not expressly devolved to it in its enabling Act.

Furthermore, regulators need to define what real reforms are and what they are not. Not every regulatory clean-up or knee-jerk reaction by a regulator to correct its own earlier acts of negligence is a reform. A reform has to be a coordinated programme of actions that are linked to one another, involving fundamental improvements in the structure, practices and behaviour of an industry or government, and correcting abuses, malpractices and inefficiencies with the aim of creating a new structure and form.

Regulators are of one or two types – competitive or conservative. Competitive regulators intend to achieve a globally competitive local market. Conservative regulators are risk-averse or risk-neutral, and are more focused on preserving the integrity of the local system and maintaining the soundness of the current industry.

Sanusi's strange mixture of radicalism, with its curious blend of idealism (all banks must have clean books and no non-performing loans immediately) and internationalism (we prefer foreign investors to take over our stressed banks) was, actually, similar to the non-participatory style of his predecessor. Several lessons remain to be learnt by the Nigerian authorities as to the process of selecting the right governor of the CBN, with a combination of both a striking intellect and a balanced temperament.

8.5 Conclusion

On the evidence, Nigeria can still have hope. Overall economic growth, and the commendable containment of depositors' losses in the Nigerian banking crisis, suggests that, with more collaboration between financial sector regulators and the development of the capacity to make positive, fact-based policies, real and sustained financial sector growth is probable in the medium term. It is certain that Nigeria will become Africa's largest economy by 2020, (or 2025 at the latest). Nigeria's main objective should be competing on efficiency and not just size. Abolishing baseless, but instinctive, practices, such as the 'excess crude account', whereby Nigeria currently saves any oil revenue above a benchmark price, and migrating to more transparent fund options such as a sovereign wealth fund (SWF) are imperative and urgent. This would create more opportunities for financial service institutions in a true free market economy. According to plans by the minister of finance, the SWF would include a stabilization fund to shield Nigeria from volatile oil prices and also a basket for inter-generational savings. Hopefully, the SWF would also insulate government windfalls better from profligate political administrations. For instance, the Excess Crude Account (ECA had about US$20 billion in 2007, when the former president came to power in May 2007, but only US$3 billion three years later. Furthermore, an SWF would better insulate the banking system, and indeed the entire financial system, from the recklessness of wanton government spending and from the injection of liquidity into the system even when the economy has limited capacity to absorb it.

However, there are even more fundamental questions about the extent to which banking reforms would stimulate economic growth, and whether a recovery will lead to sustained growth for Nigeria.

Whatever the answer, one thing is certain: future policies and policy responses have to be more formally coordinated, unlike in the past, when the CBN took bold actions and financial services regulators acted almost independently. It is evident that most of the structural progress that has been recorded in the financial system has happened through inter-agency cooperation and continuous consultation, as opposed to the practice by which the CBN tries to dominate and overemphasizes its autonomy even at the risk of killing off the policy or alienating other governmental agencies pivotal to the success of the reform. These inter-agency successes include efforts to make Nigerian bonds more competitive. Nigeria cannot afford to adopt a guiding principle of 'whatever it takes', similar to that practised by the G-20's central bankers in 2008–9, to rejuvenate its financial markets and sustain its growth. However, Nigeria will need a clear framework to enable it build consensus around the approach to be adopted should we have another asset-price bubble before 2020. Currently, neither Nigeria nor any of the West African countries have a robust macroeconomic model to build medium-term quantitative scenarios. We need to be able to decide, for instance, whether we should allow an asset-price bubble to play itself out, or use monetary policy and regulation to achieve quantitative easing.

We need also to take a view of regulation. The notion of the CBN as a policeman, or as a division of Special Branch fully equipped to catch financial terrorists and banking industry hijackers, even at the risk of breaking the laws of the land, needs to change. Critics have argued, for instance, that the last two incumbents of the office of governor of the Central Bank of Nigeria have acted with a narrow understanding of their powers, which led to them taking a legalistic approach to them rather than using their office to realise a new regulatory landscape. That kind of neoclassical power-based view of regulation is giving way globally to a postmodern approach of subtle regulation, where the focus is on the instruments of control as opposed to the targets of control and the ego of the regulator. In the new reality of community policing and coordinated regulation, financial services regulators in Nigeria need to work towards a better understanding of the real drivers of market failure, rather than mere institutional failure. These are two different issues, both conceptually and practically. For instance, to paraphrase a leading Nigerian investment banker, one of the key reasons for the stress of the banking system in Nigeria in 2008–9, apart from the often-cited executive greed of bankers and poor corporate governance, may have been that many of the operators, including that generation of bank general managers, managing directors, and the regulators had limited, if any, real understanding of asset-backed lending in volatile markets. Most of the senior bankers in the Nigerian banking industry, from general managers to executive directors and managing directors, were taught credit based on cash flow-based lending, where the first-way-out (FWO) was cash flow and the second-way-out (SWO) was asset sale. The similarities between these two kinds of lending were subtle but fundamental enough to sink a bank, which most bankers were reluctant to admit. One kind required greater collateral assets, the other more asset-pricing skills and valuation skills. Unfortunately, the regulators never seemed to discern the changing signs of the times until the banking collapse of 2009. This was made worse by the fact that in Nigeria an, efficient securities market has not yet developed so any asset price bubble creates greater 'noise' and 'degrees of error' than would happen in most advanced markets, where it is actually difficult to spot.

One potential long-term major limitation to the growth of the banking sector is the country's economic inequality, which will continue to make banking economically attractive only in certain regions and to certain customers or demographic segments. A single index that best captures the most depressing view of Nigeria is the inequality index, which, at 0.48 per cent, is one of the highest in the world. This inequality index reflects a composite of the three devils of corruption, poor infrastructure and unemployment, which most commentators and the Western media seize on. Nonetheless, historical evidence and contemporary international economic data suggest otherwise, promising better prospects. When India launched its economic and banking reforms in 1991, there were doubts among experts in multilateral banks and multilateral development institutions and among Western sceptics whether those reforms would be continued by successor governments. Twenty years later, India has had a handful of governments, yet none has reversed those far-reaching reform initiatives.

According to the governor of the CBN, in his lecture at Bayero University in Kano, Nigeria, in February 2010, 'What we have done in the Central Bank, is to fire the opening salvo in what could potentially be a revolutionary battle against the nexus of money and influence that has held this country to ransom for decades...'.

Will Nigeria's future regulation follow the 'caring capitalism' ethos and sponsor a culture of 'ethical corporate governance', or will we have a fascist or populist regulator? It may be true, as Governor Sanusi suggested, that some bank CEOs have an animal spirit and need to be punished, and that the battle against the nexus of money and influence requires more than gentlemanly regulation. However, discretion is the better part of regulatory valour. History teaches us that the most respected and successful regulators are firm, yet have a Socratic openness. Regulators who fail in this see their legacies unravel quickly and come unstuck shortly after they leave office. As the philosopher George Santayana quipped, 'Those who cannot remember the past are condemned to repeat it.'

Although the success of the Nigerian economy and the stability of the financial system are certain, the timing is not. Ultimately, two factors will influence this: the character of the next governor of the Central Bank – whether radical or conservative – and the legitimacy of the FSRCC in implementing and enforcing cross-sectoral reforms across banking and capital markets. The congruence between the CBN and the other financial service regulators in terms of strong constitutional and legislative backing and mature collaborative surveillance by the regulators will also matter. Empowering the FSRCC may well be the Nigerian banking sector's final turbo-charged take-off into self-sustained growth.

Epilogue

Going by popular sentiment, the Nigerian banking reforms had begun to win commendable acceptance, both locally and internationally by mid-2011, two years into the term of office of the governor of the Central Bank. As well as commendations from multilateral institutions, the governor had received several international and local awards, including a number of honorary doctorates[1] from well-known local universities. (*ThisDay,* Monday 21 March, 2011). In January 2011, Sanusi Lamido Sanusi was named African and Global Central Banker of 2011 by the *Banker Magazine,* the same magazine which had serenaded his predecessor five years earlier. By April 2011, *Time* magazine had listed Lamido Sanusi as one of the 'World's 100 Most Influential People' (Perry 2011), describing him as a 'veteran of an often corrupt banking system ... who said he was "cleaning up not just banking, but all of Nigeria"'. Another Nigerian entertainment group, the Silverbird Group, had awarded him the 2010 Man of the Year Award for his courageous reforms.

In the international financial community, the President of the African Development Bank (AfDB), Donald Kaberuka, in an interview in December 2010, said that 'Governor Sanusi Lamido Sanusi has done a marvelous job ... I am confident and fully support what Sanusi is doing' (Ikokwu 2010).

Meanwhile in Nigeria, exactly 16 months after the launch of Sanusi's banking reforms, a former CEO of one of the rescued banks, and a very prominent citizen from one of the country's leading industrial dynasties and ostensibly from one of its most illustrious families, was sentenced on 8 October 2010 to 18 months imprisonment after a plea bargain involving the forfeiture of cash and assets totalling over ₦150 billion (approximately $1billion US dollars). The former CEO of Oceanic Bank was also convicted of a bank and securities fraud by the Federal High Court in Lagos. However, one major conviction and six to seven notable decisions notwithstanding, several hurdles remained as obstacles to pursuing the CBN-led reforms. On Monday 25 October 2010, two weeks after the conviction of one of the bank CEOs, the Federal High Court affirmed in another major victory for the governor of the (CBN) that he did have statutory powers to appoint and remove any bank chief executive or director. The ruling was based on section 35 sub-section (2) (d) of the Banks and Other Financial Institutions Act (BOFIA). This empowered the governor to remove or appoint people, notwithstanding anything in any written law or contained in the memorandum or articles of association of any bank.

After several delays, the Asset Management Corporation of Nigeria (AMCON) was established in July 2010 and empowered under the AMCON Act 2010 and the AMCON Guidelines to acquire the eligible bank assets of qualifying financial institutions. Within a short period, the new AMCON, under the leadership of a former vice-president of Goldman Sachs, had bought margin loans at fair market value for ₦770 billion, It received assets that were worth more than that as a guarantee, in its mission to recapitalize some of the under-capitalized banks, returning them to a position attractive enough to attract new investors. The reforms had taken on a new momentum, with 21 of the nation's 24 banks selling their non-performing loans to AMCON (Oronsaye 2010). However, the issue of CBN's and AMCON's claim to legal 'ownership' of the banks, the extent of CBN's authority for the initial injection of funds, and AMCON's for the subsequent acquisition of non-performing loans and recapitalisation, remained to be tested in the law courts. The managing director and chief executive officer of AMCON, Mustapha Chike-Obi, maintained in an interview with *ThisDay* (Akanbi 2011) that '... AMCON may or may not be the majority owner of the banks ... I want to tell them that those banks have negative shareholders' funds. If the Central Bank did not retain their licences and guarantee their deposits, those banks would have been wound down by now' On the other hand, some of the shareholder interest groups disagreed.

The Central Bank governor seemed to have won the battle, and was quoted at IMF meetings in October 2010 that he was sure that the CEOs of other rescued banks would be disciplined. Nonetheless, assessing the success of the reforms implementation was still a little premature. It may have been glaringly obvious to some that a number of bank chiefs had apparently 'emptied the vaults' when the financial system was sick and the regulators were looking the other way but those allegations were yet to be substantiated in a law court. The diagnosis and prognosis for the financial system *imbroglio* remained uncertain to many analysts.

For the healthy banks that had not been condemned by the joint CBN/NDIC audit of 2009, the full-year financial results for 2010 revealed mixed results. Six of the 14 banks had published results which did not meet analysts' expectations, while another six had showed remarkably improved performance over the previous financial year ended December 2009. Lending for quarter one in 2011 also appeared sluggish despite AMCON's purchase of bad loans, raising the old argument about the true drivers of bank performance in Nigeria.

Was this a case of performance-conduct-structure or structure-conduct-performance? The CBN position was closer to the latter, maintaining that the emergence of universal banking had provided an avenue for corrupt bank executives to channel funds from one subsidiary to another, thereby permitting banks to create the erroneous impression that individual entities in the banking group were liquid. According to this argument, correcting these structural inefficiencies would lead to improved transparency and greater intrinsic performance. The consequent unbundling of many of the nation's large banking groups was underway between 2010 and 2011 while some of the banks, such as Guaranty Trust Bank, decided to spin off their non-bank subsidiaries. However, the Central Bank of Nigeria's position – that the country's purportedly 'illegal' universal banking regime contributed substantially to the 2009 banking crisis – was disputed. The Minister of Finance, Mr. Olusegun Aganga, a distinguished Goldman Sachs alumnus, continued to maintain the opposing position that the adoption of universal banking in Nigeria was not the 'cause' of the regulatory deficit in the financial system, but it was the 'inadequate regulatory architecture which cannot currently cope with the innovations introduced by universal banking in the financial industry' (Anaro 2010). To date, I am not aware of any empirical study of the degree of causation or correlation between the universal banking system and the banking crisis, so this matter remains highly conjectural and subject to interpretation.

Meanwhile, the rapid changes in the global financial system, and in the UK financial system which the Nigerian banking system had borrowed from in its early post-colonial years, were making increasing demands for Nigerian regulators to keep up. In the United Kingdom, the new Conservative government was proposing key changes to financial services regulation in mid-2010 with the announcement of the scrapping of the Financial Services Authority (FSA) in June 2010 (Peace 2010). The FSA had been established in 1997 during the early days of the Labour Party's tenure, stripping the Bank of England of some of its powers to regulate financial institutions. However, the Conservative government's plan to scrap the FSA did weaken the arguments of proponents for the separation of banking supervision and monetary policy formulation in Nigeria.

The calm between the storm

Amongst the accolades for the banking reforms, a few discerning analysts still argued that any reform that does not change the structure or performance of an industry can only be transitory. A few extreme critics like Ayibu Alewu, in a sarcastic back page article entitled 'CBN Set to Develop Its Own Poultry Farm' (See *ThisDay* Monday 4 July 2011, p. 72), believed that the CBN was meddling in real-estate businesses and other external activities while advising banks not to do the same. He cited several sectoral intervention funds of the CBN and the CBN's dabbling in non-core activities outside its primary mandate, such as building a world-class 'hotel and conference centre'.

How far indeed has the banking system moved away from the 1991 banking era when many banks obtained banking licences with borrowed capital (₦40 million for a merchant bank and ₦50 million for a commercial bank) raised through questionable commercial papers spuriously for investment grade companies, and then diverted to the Central Bank to procure a banking licence, as attested to by a deputy-governor of the Central Bank? (Encomium, 6th Anniversary Commemorative Edition, July 2003, Lagos. Article/Interview with Azuh Arinze titled 'Wema Bank's md Tunde Lemo Discloses the Calamity That Almost Truncated His Career', pp. 78–80). How well would the Central Bank of Nigeria, the National Deposit Insurance Corporation (NDIC) and the Asset Management Corporation of Nigeria handle the transition of the bridge-banks that were created when the CBN and NDIC nationalized three of the rescued banks in August 2011 in very curious circumstances?

By May 2011, the apparent renewed interest in Islamic banking on the part of the leadership of the Central Bank, and the claims and counter-claims as to the true motives of the CBN's Islamic banking scheme, was also raising several issues as to the objectivity or sensitivity of the Central Bank. The Governor's opponents interpreted his actions from a religious and ethnic viewpoint. His argument remained that non-interest banking has economic merits in its own right and had been sponsored by the former CBN Governor who was a Christian.

One argument was most aptly captured by Eghes Eyieyen who wrote that 'with the proposed introduction of Islamic banking, the CBN plans to foist on the nation, a needless controversy'(See for instance article titled 'Islamic Banking: CBN May Face Fresh Litigation Hurdle' by Obinna Chima, page 29 *ThisDay* Wednesday 29 June 2011 Vol. 16 No. 5910). Meanwhile, the CBN leadership continued to maintain that the non-interest banking initiative was part of the CBN's plans to increase financial inclusion for Nigerians. One fact did become clear from this avoidable controversy: the theoretical and empirical underpinnings of many of the Central Bank's decisions were seldom communicated well. It made it difficult for an objective observer or analyst to quantify the costs and benefits of the CBN's programmes.

Another issue was remuneration. According to the CBN deputy governor Kingsley Moghalu, 'Clearly we do not think the CBN should be setting the pay for directors of commercial banks. I believe what the speech was trying to do was to call attention to the risks of remuneration based only or mostly on short term profit targets' (the speech refers to the that by a representative of the CBN Governor at a conference where he highlighted the fact that unduely high remuneration of bankers should be checked). This suggested that the CBN's policy was only to

Table E1 Indicative annual compensation figures for selected Nigerian banks (USD equivalent)**

Designation	Global equivalent	Average guaranteed pay	Average range for variable pay/ bonus (+/–15%)
Graduate entry-level	Analyst	14,474	2,895
Officer	Associate	27,632	11,053
Manager	Manager	59,211	23,684
Assistant General Manager	Assistant Vice-President	118,421	71,053
Deputy General Manager	Vice-President	157,895	94,737
General Manager/ Divisional Director	Executive Vice-President	197,368	197,368

**Randomly selected banks as at 2009.
Note: USD $/₦152; banks have widely varying approaches to bonuses, variable pay and performance pay.
Source: Random sampling with bank employees across various banks and various levels.

'provide guidance' on remuneration. (See 'CBN Will Not "Legislate" on Bankers' Pay' by Festus Akanbi, *ThisDay*, Sunday, 19 June 2011, p. 25.)

Regulatory intervention notwithstanding, the heated debate about whether Nigerian bank executives were overpaid relative to their counterparts in other African banks continued to brew. Many of the media reports were flawed and made comparisons with dissimilar countries (see 'Bank Directors and Fat Salaries' by Nicholas Ibekwe, *Next on Sunday*, Sunday 10 July 2011), Nonetheless, the fundamental issue of whether bankers are overpaid in bonuses for the risks they take is a widespread concern, even though the facts suggest that banking is not the highest-paid sector in Nigeria (see Table E1).

There have also been allegations of a spurious increase in the profitability of the rescued banks. Some of them have been accused of hiding multi-billion *naira* losses in deferred taxes, essentially through carrying deferred taxes on their books through flexible interpretation of the prudential guidelines (see 'Rescued Banks Hide Multi-billion *Naira* Losses in Deferred Tax' by Anthony Osae-Brown, *Businessday* Monday 11 July 2011).

Challenges ahead

Legal battles in court by various stakeholder interest groups, and the limits on the regulatory capacity of the Central Bank itself to administer the new banking regime effectively, as envisioned by Sanusi, continue to pose key challenges to Nigerian banking reform. By early 2011, the disputes about the sale of the rescued banks continued unabated. Some concerned shareholder groups were questioning the authority of the management teams appointed by Central Bank of Nigeria to sell the shares of their banks or to enter into merger or acquisition agreements. Alternatively, they challenged the transparency with which it was being done. For instance, one of the shareholder interest groups alleged that the suspension of four of the directors from a particular ethnic group at Finbank Plc, which was one of the rescued banks (Thisday 2011), in order to achieve the sale of that bank to another bank was unwarranted. Questions about the imminent sale of one of the rescued banks to another bidder, which submitted the lowest bid, instead of the highest bidder, were also raised. In the case of Union Bank, the Federal High Court in Lagos granted in April 2011 the plea of an institutional shareholder of one of the rescued banks, Union Bank of Nigeria Plc, restraining a potential core investor from acquiring the bank, based on the plaintiff's deposition that the bank's existing shareholders had not been consulted on the recapitalisation (*Thisday* 2011B).

Notwithstanding the assertions of the Central Bank of Nigeria's deputy governor in charge of financial system stability, Dr. Kingsley Moghalu, that the number of banks in the country would have been reduced to 20 by the end of 2011, actual legal and operational realities suggested a less optimistic scenario for the second round of Nigerian banking consolidation in the twenty-first century. (Crusoe 2011)

Several potential core investors placed adverts in the newspapers announcing that they had signed Memorandums of Understanding (MOUs) with some of the eight rescued banks. For example, Vine Capital Partners and Phoenix Acquisition Company Limited announced an MOU with Afribank, and African Capital Alliance Consortium with Union Bank. It was reported that the Central Bank of Nigeria had warned in April 2011 that 'whereas the trend of signing an MOU among the rescued banks was welcomed and shows the intrinsic value that investors see in Nigerian banks, the exercise can only lead to actual transactions if and when CBN issues no-objection (approval) and other regulatory approvals are met' (Chima 2011). This happened amidst the unabated 'noise' of the anonymous activist group Renaissance Professionals, which continued to sponsor wild attacks on the CBN's process of facilitating the appointment of core investors to the rescued banks (Renaissance Professionals 2011). They questioned the authority of the CBN to facilitate these appointments through its selected financial advisers, as well as the capitalization of some of the special purpose vehicles that were selected 'ahead of more notable international and local firms including ....the Standard Bank Group'.

Despite the adverse headwinds in the banking sector and the poor recovery in the stock market, there was a successful general election, leading to the swearing of a new administration under President Goodluck Jonathan in May 2011, and a favourable macroeconomic climate. Prospects for growth in the Nigerian economy, and indeed the banking sector, were looking increasingly bright. Despite the rating downgrade by Fitch of Nigeria's outlook in October 2010, which was challenged by the Finance Minister, Standard & Poor still rated the country a "B+/ B", based on its strong balance sheet and a stable prospects, albeit with a 'high political risk'. Meanwhile, the new director-general of the Securities and Exchange Commission, Arunna Oteh, who was a former vice-president at the African Development Bank, and the new director-general of the Nigerian Stock Exchange, Oscar Onyeama, who was an ex-American Stock Exchange (AMEX) and New York Mercantile Exchange (NYMEX) member, had both settled into their new roles and were trying to turn around the Nigerian capital market system.

In the run up to the 2013 milestone for Nigeria's journey to its Vision 20:2020 – of building a world-class financial system and one of the 20 largest economies in the world by 2020 – several imperatives face the economic team. However, the outstanding questions dwarf even the imperatives. Can Sanusi go down in history as a leading economic statesman, and not just an activist or reformist? Will the Central Bank be able to improve economic coordination with the Federal Ministry of Finance and the Office of the National Economic Adviser and National Planning Commission? Can they combine to achieve the near-perfect synchronization that enabled Rubin, Greenspan and Summers to avert a global economic meltdown after the decade of 1987–97 (*TIME Magazine* 1999)? Can the Nigerian economic management team deliver a co-ordinated policy mechanism, in symphony with the Central Bank helmsman, that can rival South Africa in the race to be the economic 'giant of Africa' by the year 2020?

Ultimately, the fundamental question will be whether the institutional pragmatism that has been adopted by the recent regulators of the nation's financial system will be able to deliver sustainable economic results? Or, would the results be better if the reforms were underpinned by a more conservative objectivist philosophy?

Despite the tumult in the Nigerian banking industry in the decade between 2001 and 2010, a few banks, including at least one of the 'Big Four' banks and several of the mid-sized banks, still maintained their integrity and were loyal to the values of strong corporate governance. They continue to provide a beacon of hope for the self-correcting banking market in Nigeria. If nothing else, they remain a lasting testimonial to the strong underlying resilience of the Nigerian financial system.

Appendix

Classification of credit and investment ratings into investment grade and non-investment grade by global rating agencies

	Moody's	Fitch's	S&P
Investment Grade	Aaa		AAA
	Aa1		AA+
	Aa2		AA
	Aa3		AA–
	A1		A+
	A2		A
	A3		A–
	Baa1		BBB+
	Baa2		BBB
	Baa3		BBB–
Non-Investment Grade	Ba1		BB+
	Ba2		BB
	Ba3		BB–
	B1		B+
	B2		B
	B3		B–
	Caa1		CCC+
	Caa2		CCC
	Caa3		CCC–
	Ca		CC
	C		C
			D

Moody's Bonds rated Ba are adjudged to have speculative elements with the protection of interest and principal payments not being safeguarded during both good and bad times over the future.

S&P (Standard and Poor's) Obligations rated BB are adjudged to face major ongoing uncertainties or exposure to adverse business, financial, or economic conditions that could adversely impact the obligor's capacity to meet its financial commitment on the obligation.

Notes

1 Banking Reforms in Emerging Markets: An Introduction

1. Simply defined, adverse selection refers to a market process in which unfavourable results occur due to information asymmetries between lenders and borrowers. Because lenders are not well informed about borrowers and their activities, there is the risk that lenders will most likely lend funds to borrowers who will default on loan repayments. Moral hazard, on the other hand, refers to the risk that the borrower will not repay funds lent to the lender after the transaction has been concluded, and, therefore, the lender suffers loss.

2 The Nigerian Banking System: The Case for Reforms

1. Based on a speech delivered during the former World Bank president's tour of Africa, 2005–6 (Paul Wolfowitz in Nigeria, *This Day* 17 October 2006).
2. Based on a paper presented by EFCC chairman, Nuhu Ribadu, at the 7th Guest Lecture series of the Financial Institutions Training Centre, August 2006 (*ThisDay*, 13 August 2006, p. 24).
3. See, for instance, ThisDay, vol. 11, no. 4,165, 16 September 2006, and front page of *ThisDay*, Saturday 12 August 2006, vol. 11, no. 4,130; Globacom: EFCC Arrests Babangida's Son.
4. According to a professor and former head of department of economics at the University of Lagos, Professor Ayo Ogunseye, then president of the Lagos Chamber of Commerce and Industry, consulted a team of experts in economics to run econometric models as to whether the official and parallel markets would converge in the medium term, as was claimed by certain government officials. The findings were negative. Ironically, almost 20 years later, civilian president Olusegun Obasanjo still promised to harmonize the two rates.

4 Does Size Matter? The Quest for Transnational Banks

1. Head of Agreement: A non-binding document outlining the main issues relevant to a tentative partnership agreement. An informal agreement between two parties seeking to form a partnership outlining the rights and responsibilities each would have in the partnership. Heads of agreement are intentionally vague and are usually the first step toward a full contract. Negotiations continue after the MOU is signed. Heads of agreement are similar to a memorandum of understanding for partnerships, but heads of agreement are not enforceable in a court of law, unlike an MOU.

6 Politics of Banking Reforms

1. In the period between November 2009 and January 2010, the author held brief interviews with two retired CBN directors in Abuja on their views of the banking crisis and the CBN's handling of the crisis. Discussion with three former directors of the Central Bank. Abuja. On/around Tuesday 18 August 2009.
2. $2.8 billion is at an exchange rate of $/₦148.
3. 1 USD = ₦150.

7 Corporate Governance and Restructuring

1. The $2.8 billion is at an exchange rate of $/₦148).
2. In the period between November 2009 and January 2010, the author held brief interviews with two retired CBN directors in Abuja on their views of the banking crisis and the CBN's handling of the crisis. Discussions with three former directors of the Central Bank. Abuja. On/around Tuesday 18 August 2009.

Epilogue

1. These honorary docorates included an honorary doctorate in business administration from the University of Nigeria, Nsukka, in February 2011, an honorary doctorate from Bayero University, Kano, in March 2011, and an honorary doctor of laws from the University of Jos in March 2011.

Bibliography

Abati, R. (2005) 'Kupolokun's NNPC', *The Guardian* Newspaper (Lagos: The Guardian), Sunday 17 April, p. 52.

Abimbola, A. and Eugene, A. (2005) 'EFCC Arrests Tafa Balogun: May Be Arraigned Thursday', *ThisDay* Newspaper (Lagos: ThisDay Newspapers Limited), 30 March. www.nigerianmuse.com/nigeriawatch/officialfraud/?u=Tafa_Balogun_arrested.htm

Abubakar, S. (2009) 'Nigerian Bank Nigeria CBN Central Bank of Nigeria – Unity Bank Thinking Out of The Box' (Abuja: Daily Trust), 10 November.

Aburime, T. U. (2008) 'Determinants of Bank Profitability: Company-Level Evidence from Nigeria', *Lagos Journal of Banking, Finance and Economics.*

Accessbank (2010) http://www.accessbankplc.com/whoweare.aspx (accessed 2 February 2010).

Adebowale, Y. and Momodu, S. (2009) 'Retrenchment Fever Grips Banks, Oil Companies: Loans To Customers Dry Up', Nigeria Best Forum, 5 September.

Adeniyi, O. (2004) 'Can Soludo Save the Nation', *ThisDay* Newspaper (Lagos: ThisDay Newspapers Limited), 2 May.

Aderinokun, K. (2009) 'Why We Embarked on Radical reforms on Banks', *ThisDay* Newspaper (Lagos: ThisDay Newspapers Limited), 11 October, p. 10.

Adibe, J. (2002) 'The Wrong Man for an Impossible Mission', *Financial Times*, 8 February.

Adibe, J. (2009) 'Sanusi: Radical in a Conservative Job', *BusinessDay* (Lagos: BusinessDay), Friday 4 – Sunday 6 December, p. 12.

Afribank (2010) http://www.afribank.com/dynamicdata/Historicalbackground.aspx (accessed 12 February 2010).

African Development Bank (ADB) (1994) *African Development Report.*

Africa Report (1994) 'To Tell the Truth Is Risky Business in Nigeria', *Africa Report*, Jan/Feb.

Afrinvest Nigeria (2007 and 2008) 2007 Review, 2008 Market Outlook.

Agbaje, O. '*Udo Udoma* and the sec Chairmanship', *BusinessDay*, Wednesday, 10 March, p. 48.

Ajakaiye, D. O. (1992) 'Challenges of the Nigerian Banking Sector: A Macroeconomic Overview', *New Nigerian Bank Economic and Business Review*, vol. 1, no. 1, June.

Ajibade, A. (2010) 'Fighting Margin Facility with One Voice', *The Nation* Newspapers (Lagos: The Nation), 24 March.

Akanbi, F. (2011), 'AMCON in No Hurry to Sell Debtors' Assets', *ThisDay Newspaper* (Lagos), Sunday 13 February 2011, pp. 28–29.

Akanbi, F. and Olaleye, O. (2009) 'As Amma Pepple Retires On June 16... 5 Perm Secs Jostle for Head of Service Post', *ThisDay* Newspaper (Lagos: ThisDay Newspaper Limited), Sunday 7 June.

Akinola, I. (2010) '*Okereke-Onyiuke* Eases Elakama Out in Stock Exchange Power Play: NSE Council Meets to Endorse His Retirement', *BusinessDay*, Monday, 1 March.

Akio, T. (2009) 'The Economist Briefing "Losing its Shine"', *BusinessDay Newspaper* (Lagos: BusinessDay Newspaper Limited), 14 December.
Alayande, F. (2004) 'Rent-Seekers in the Banking Hall', *ThisDay* Newspaper (Lagos: ThisDay Newspapers Limited), 14 July.
Alayande, F. (2004) 'Now Let's Have Serious Banking', *ThisDay* Newspaper (Lagos: ThisDay Newspapers Limited), 11 July.
Alayande, F. (2010) 'Corporate Governance: Current Developments and Challenges', a paper presented at the annual conference of the Institute of Chartered Secretaries and Administrators in Nigeria: Sheraton Hotel in Lagos in September 2010.
Alayande, F. (2010) 'Corporate Governance: Current Issues and Challenges', Seminar Paper presented at the National Conference of the Institute of Chartered Secretaries and Administrators at the Sheraton Hotel, Ikeja, Lagos.
Alayande, F. (2010) 'Nigeria's Corporate Governance Coded: The Missing Links', *BusinessDay*, 18 January.
Alayande, F. (2010) "Leadership Succession and Bank CEOs: Options for Nigerian banks". BusinessDay, Lagos, Sunday, 04 July.
Alesina, A. and Summers, L. (1993) 'Central Bank Independence and Macro-Economic Performance: Some Comparative Evidence', *Journal of Money, Credit and Banking*, vol. 25, no. 2, pp. 151–62.
All Africa Global Media (2009) 'Nigeria: Banking on Agriculture in Kwara', All Africa Global Media, 2 December.
Al-Yousif, Y. (2002) 'Financial Development and Economic Growth: Another Look at the Evidence from Developing Countries', *Review of Financial Economics*, vol. 11, no. 2, pp. 132–52.
Anaro, B. (2010), 'Universal Banking Not Cause of Banking Crisis, Says Finance Minister', BusinessDay (Lagos), Tuesday 17 August 2010, p. 4.
Anaro, B. (2010) 'Is BOFIA Superior to Shareholders' Power on Appointment on Banks' MD', *BusinessDay* (Lagos: Business Day), Monday 25 January.
Anaro, B. (2010) 'Nigerian Banks in Sight of Standard Chartered Bank's $1.4bn Acquisition War Chest', *BusinessDay*, 01 June.
Arestis, P. and Demetriades, P. (1997) 'Financial Development and Economic Growth: Assessing the Evidence', *The Economic Journal*, vol. 107, no. 442, pp. 783–99.
Arestis, P., Demetriades, P., and Luintel, K. (2001) 'Financial Development and Economic Growth: The Role of Stock Markets', *Journal of Money, Credit, and Banking*, vol. 33, no. 1, pp. 16–41.
Aryeetey, E. and Hyuha, M. (1991) 'The Informal Financial Sector and Markets in Africa: An Empirical Study', in A. I. Chhibber and S. Fischer (eds): *Economic Reform in Sub-Saharan Africa* (Washington DC: The World Bank).
Ashaka, K. (2006) *Sunday Sun*, 3 December, vol. 3, no. 194.
Ashimi,T.(2010) 'Runny Yolk May Soil Sanusi's Egg Poaching', in 'Watching the Watchdog', *ThisDay*, Tuesday, 30 March, p. 11.
Atje, R. and Jovanovic, B. (1993) 'Stock Markets and Development', *European Economic Review*, vol. 37, nos. 2–3, pp. 632–40.
Ayadi, O. F. and Hyman, L. (2006) 'Financial Liberalization and Price Rigidity in the Nigerian Banking System', *Managerial Finance*, vol. 32, no. 7, pp. 557–68.
Ayodele, T. (2009) 'Is War against Bad Medicine Paying Off', *ThisDay* Newspaper (Lagos: ThisDay Newspaper Limited), Sunday 2 August.

Bagachwa, S. D. M. (1994) *Financial Integration and Development in Sub-Saharan Africa: A Study of Formal Financial Institutions in Tanzania* (Mimeo).
Baier, S., Dwyer, G. P., and Tamura, R. (2003) 'Does Opening a Stock Exchange Increase Economic Growth?', *Federal Reserve Bank of Atlanta Working Paper.*
BankPHB (2010) http://www.bankphb.com/index.php (accessed 23 February 2010)
Bate, R. anBain, J. S. (1956) *Barriers to New Competition* (Cambridge, MA: Harvard University Press).
Beck, T., Cull, R., and Jerome, A. (2005) 'Bank Privatization and Performance: Empirical Evidence from Nigeria', *Journal of Banking and Finance*, vol. 29, nos. 8–9, pp. 2355–79.
Beck, T., Dermiguc-Kunt, A., and Levine, R. E. (2000, 2007) *A New Database on Financial Development and Structure* (Washington, DC: World Bank).
Beck, T., Levine, R., and Loayza, N. (2000) 'Finance and the Sources of Growth', *Journal of Financial Economics*, vol. 58, nos. 1–2, pp. 261–300.
Bekaert, G., Harvey, C., and Lundblad, C. (2003) 'Does Financial Liberalization Spur Growth?', *Working Papers- Duke Fuqua School of Business*, pp. 1–51.
Benhabib, J. and Spiegel, M. (2000) 'The Role of Financial Development in Growth and Investment', *Journal of Economic Growth*, vol. 5, no. 4, pp. 341–60.
Berger, A. N. (2000) 'Efficiency of Financial Institutions: International Survey and Directions for Future Research', in P. T. Harker and S. A. Zenios (eds) *Performance of Financial Institutions: Efficiency, Innovation, Regulation* (Cambridge UK: Cambridge University Press).
Berger, A. N., Hunter, W. C., and Timme, S. G. (1993) 'The Efficiency of Financial Institutions: A Review and Preview of Research Past, Present, and Future', *Journal of Banking and Finance*, vol. 17, pp. 221–49.
Brownbridge, M. (2000) 'Financial Regulation in Developing Countries', *Journal of Development Studies*, vol. 37, no. 1.
Brownbridge, M. and Harvey, C. (1998) *Banking in Africa: The Impact of Financial Sector Reforms since Independence* (Oxford: James Currey).
Brownbridge, M. and Kirkpatrick, C. (2000) 'Financial Regulation in Developing Countries', *Journal of Development Studies*, vol. 37, no. 3, pp. 1–24.
Bottomline (2009) 'Interview with Remi Babalola', *Bottomline* Magazine, 4 June.
BusinessDay (2009) 'Flawed Conception', *Financial Times*, quoted in *BusinessDay Nigeria*, Tuesday 20 January, p. 42.
BusinessDay (2009) 'Exploiting Crisis to Build New Banking Structure', *BusinessDay*, Monday 14 December.
BusinessDay (2010) Thursday 25 March, p.1.
BusinessDay (2010) 'Code of Conduct for Capital Market Operators and Their Employees', *BusinessDay*, Monday, 10 May, p. 50 .
Business News and Articles (2009) 'Shareholders Desperate to Reclaim Troubled Banks', StockNewsLine.com, Monday 2 November.
Caporale, G., Howells, P., and Soliman, A. (2004) 'Stock Market Development and Economic Growth: The Causal Linkage', *Journal of Economic Development*, vol. 29, no. 1, pp. 33–51.
Central Bank of Nigeria (various years) *CBN Annual Reports.*
Central Bank of Nigeria (various years) *CBN Annual Reports and Banking Supervision Reports.*
Central Bank of Nigeria website (2007) www.cenbank.org

Central Bank of Nigeria (2008) *Annual Report* (Abuja: Central Bank of Nigeria, CMA).
Chapple, S. (1990) 'A Sequence of Errors? Some Notes on the Sequencing of Liberalization in Developing Countries', *UNCTAD Discussion Papers*, no. 31.
Chima, O. (2011), 'Afribank Signs MOU with Vine Capital', *ThisDay Newspaper* (Lagos), Vol. 16, No. 5826 of Wednesday 6 April 2011, P. 56.
Citibank (2010) http://www.citi.com/citi/global/index.htm (accessed 23 February 2010), http://www.citi.com/citi/global/nga.htm (accessed 2 February 2010).
Claessens and Underhill (2004) 'Basle II Capital Requirements and Developing Countries: A Political Economy Perspective on the Costs for Poor Countries of Rich Country Policies', *Conference Paper.*www.sgir.org/conference2004/papers
Collins, J. (2009) *How the Mighty Fall* (New York: HarperCollins Publishers).
Cronje, J. J. L. (2003) 'The Efficiency of South African Banks: A Non-parametric Approach', *South African Business Review*, vol. 7, no. 1, pp. 32–40, Sabinet Online.
Crusoe, O. (2011), 'CBN: 20 Banks May Remain By June', *ThisDay Newspaper* (Lagos), Thursday 20 January 2011, p. 4.
DeGregorio, J. and Guidotti, P. (1992) 'Financial Development and Economic Growth', *World Development*, vol. 23, no. 3, pp. 433–48.
De Haas, R. (2004) 'Law, Finance, and Growth during Transition: A Survey', *The Economist*, vol. 152, no. 3, pp. 375–402.
Diamondbank (2010) http://www.diamondbank.com/careers/our-bank.html (accessed 23 February 2010).
Demetriades, P. (1997) 'Financial Markets and Development', in M. El-Erian and M. Mohieldin (eds) *Financial Development in Emerging Markets: The Egyptian Experience*, Cairo: Egyptian Center for Economic Studies (San Francisco: International Center for Economic Growth).
Demetriades, P. and Hussein, K. (1996) 'Does Financial Development Cause Economic Growth? Time-Series Evidence from 16 Countries', *Journal of Development Economics*, vol. 51, no. 2, pp. 387–411.
Demirguc-Kunt, A. and Levine, R. (1996) 'Financial Constraints, Uses of Funds, and Firm Growth: An International Comparison' (Washington DC: World Bank. Mimeo).
Djiwandono, J. S. (1999) 'Central Banking Reform in Indonesia', paper presented at the Regional Central Banking Reforms in the Context of World Reform Workshop, November 9–10, Hong Kong
Djiwandono, J. S. (2000) 'Bank Indonesia and the Recent Crisis', *Bulletin of Indonesian Economic Studies*, vol. 36, no. 1, pp. 47–72.
Dornbusch, R. and Reynoso, A. (1993) 'Financial Factors in Economic Development', in R. Dornbusch (ed.) *Policymaking in the Open Economy: Concepts and Case Studies in Economic Performance* (Oxford: Oxford University Press).
Driffill, J. (2003) 'Growth and Finance', *The Manchester School*, vol. 71, no. 4, pp. 363–80.
Dymski, G. (1999) *The Bank Merger Wave: The Economic Causes and Social Consequences of Financial Consolidation* (Armonk/London: M. E. Sharpe).
Ecobank (2010) http://www.ecobank.com/aboutus.aspx (accessed 2 February 2011).

Eghobamien, O. (2010) 'Banking Sector Reforms: A Guide to the Asset Management Corporation Bill', *BusinessDay*, Thursday, 13 May, p. 33.

Emenuga, C. (2002) *African Voices on Structural Adjustment: A Companion to Our Continent, Our Future* (IDRC/CODESRIA/Africa World Press). Available from: http://www.idrc.ca/en/ev-56356–201-1-DO_TOPIC.html

Equitorial Trust Bank (2010) http://www.equitorialtrustbank.com/about.html (accessed 23 February 2010).

Fama, E. (1965) 'The Behaviour of Stock Market Prices', *Journal of Business*, vol. 38, no. 1, pp. 34–105.

Fama, E. (1970) 'Efficient Capital Markets: A Review of Theory and Empirical Work', *Journal of Finance*, vol. 25, no. 2, pp. 383–417.

Famakinwa, S. (2006) 'Breaking the DSTV Monopoly', *ThisDay* Newspaper (Lagos: ThisDay Newspapers Limited), 12 August, p. 64.

Fidelity Bank *Annual Report and Financial Statements 2009.*

Financial Standard (2004) 'CBN Slams N1b Fine on UBA', *Financial Standard* Newspaper (Lagos: Financial Standard Newspapers Limited), 15 March, vol. 5, no. 21.

Financial Times (2009) 'Britain Is not a Regulatory Island', *Financial Times*, Lagos, Wednesday 1 April, p. 13.

Finbank (2010) http://www.finbank.com.ng/about_us/about_us.asp?parent=3&id=78 (accessed 2 February 2010).

First Bank of Nigeria plc (2009) *Annual Report & Statement of Accounts 2009.*First City Monument Bank (2010) http://www.firstcitygroup.com/newfcmb/about/company/corporate.aspx (accessed 11 February 2010).

Fortune (2010) 'SMEs List Constraints On Access To Credit', Fortune News (Abuja: Fortune News), 22 April.

Gartner, M. (2004) 'Monetary Policy and Central Bank Behaviour', in K.R. Charles and S. Friedrich (eds) *The Encyclopedia of Public Choice, 1000.*

Ghali, K. (1999) 'Financial Development and Economic Growth: The Tunisian Experience', *Review of Development Economics*, vol. 3, no. 3, pp. 310–24.

Goldsmith, R. (1969) *Financial Structure and Development* (New Haven, CN: London: Yale University Press).

Graff, M. (2003) 'Financial Development and Economic Growth in Corporatist and Liberal Market Economies', *Emerging Markets Finance and Trade*, vol. 39, no. 2, pp. 47–70.

Greenspan, A. (2008) *Financial Times* Economists' Forum, March.

Greenwood, J. and Jovanovic, B. (1990) 'Financial Development, Growth, and the Distribution of Income', *Journal of Political Economy*, vol. 98, no. 5, pp. 1076–1107.

GuarantyTrustBank (2010) http://www.gtbank.com/about-gtbank/our-bank/corporate-profile.html (accessed 11 February 2010).

Hardy, D. C. (2006) *Regulatory Capture in Banking*, IMF Working Paper WP/06/34, published January 2006, http://www.imf.org/external/pubs/ft/wp/2006/wp0634.pdf

Hawkins, J. (1999) *Bank Restructuring in South-East Asia* (Basel: Bank for International Settlements).

Hesse H. (2007) 'Financial Intermediation in the Pre-Consolidated Banking Sector in Nigeria', *World Bank Policy Research Working Paper*, no. 4267.

IFC WB Group Private Sector Resources-Concentration Ratio (deposits).

Iheduru, O. C. (2010) 'Soludo's Exuberance or Sanusi's Populism in 2010?' *BusinessDay*, Thursday, 07 January.

Ikhide, S. I. and Alawode, A. A. (2001) 'Financial Sector Reforms, Macroeconomic Instability, and the Order of Economic Liberalization: The Evidence from Nigeria', *AERC Research Paper* #112, African Economic Research Consortium.

Ikokwu, C. (2010), 'Risk of Debt Stress for Nigeria Very Low', *ThisDay Newspaper* (Lagos), Sunday, 5 December 2010, p. 112, http://234next.com/csp/cms/sites/Next/Home/5628486-/ (Source: 234next website; retrieved 8 October 2010 07:23pm).

Imoyo, A. (2010) 'New Stock Exchange CEO, Eds to Emerge in July', *BusinessDay Weekend*, Friday 21–Sunday 23 May, vol. 9, no. 98.

Inanga, E. L. (1995) 'Financial Sector Reforms in Sub-Sahara Africa', paper presented at the XI World Congress of the International Economic Association, December 18–22, Tunis.

IntercontinentalBank plc (2010) http://www.intercontinentalbankplc.com/portal/general/aboutus.php?pid=34&mode=content (accessed 23 February 2010).

Isik, I. and Hassan, M. K. (2002) 'Technical, Scale and Allocative Efficiencies of Turkish Banking Industry', *Journal of Banking and Finance*, vol. 26, no. 4, pp. 719–66.

Jackson, T. (2010) 'Too Big to Fail' Debate Makes Move in Right Direction', *Financial Times*, 12 April.

Jayaratne, J. and Strahan, P. (1996) 'The Finance-Growth Nexus: Evidence from Bank Branch Deregulation', *The Quarterly Journal of Economics*, vol. 111, no. 3, pp. 639–70.

Kassimatis, K. and Spyrou, S. (2001) 'Stock and Credit Market Expansion and Economic Development in Emerging Markets: Further Evidence Utilizing Co-integration Analysis', *Applied Economics*, vol. 33, no. 8, pp. 1057–64.

Khan, A. (2000) 'The Finance and Growth Nexus', *Business Review* (January), Federal Reserve Bank of Philadelphia, pp. 3–14.

Koivu, T. (2002) 'Does Financial Sector Development Affect Economic Growth in Transition Economies?', paper presented at the Nordic Conference in Development Economics, 10 April, Bergen, *BOFIT Discussion Papers*.

Kolapo, Y. (2009) 'Global Crisis: I Did Not Say Nigeria Was Immune –Soludo', *The Punch* (Lagos: The Punch), Thursday 5 February.

Kuforiji, K. (2006) Telephone Interview with Rhythm 93.7 August.

Laffont, J. J. and Tirole, J. (1991) 'The Politics of Government Decision-Making: A Theory of Regulatory Capture', *Quarterly Journal of Economics*, pp. 1,089–127.

La Porta, R., Lopez-de-Silanes, F., Shleifer, A., and Vishny, R. (1998) 'Law and Finance', *Journal of Political Economy*, vol. 106, no. 6, pp. 1133–55.

Leadership (2009) 'CBN's Disclosure Requirement for Banks: The Facts', Leadership Newspapers, Monday 17 August.

Lee, C. and Wong, S. (2005) 'Inflationary Threshold Effect in the Relationship Between Financial Development and Economic Growth: Evidence from Taiwan and Japan', *Journal of Economic Development*, vol. 30, no. 1, pp. 49–71.

Levine, R. (1997) 'Financial Development and Economic Growth: Views and Agenda', *Journal of Economic Literature*, vol. 35, no. 2, pp. 688–726.

Levine, R. (2002) 'Bank-Based or Market-Based Financial Systems: Which is Better?', *Journal of Financial Intermediation*, vol. 11, no. 4, pp. 398–419.

Levine, R., Loayza, N., and Beck, T. (2000) 'Financial Intermediation and Growth: Causality and Causes', *Journal of Monetary Econnomics*, vol. 46, no. 1, pp. 31–78.

Lipumba, N. H. I. (1994) 'Africa beyond Adjustment', *Overseas Development Council Policy Essay*, no. 15.

Lohor, J. (2007) 'FG Suspends Naira Redenomination', *ThisDay* Newspaper (Lagos: ThisDay Newspapers Limited), Saturday 25 August, vol. 12, no. 4,508, pp. 1–6.

Mauro, P. (1995) 'Corruption and Growth', *Quarterly Journal of Economics*, vol. 110, no. 3, pp. 681–712.

Mbamalu, M. (2009) 'Q & A with Ola Vincent', *The Guardian* Newspaper (Lagos: The Guardian), September.

McKinnon, R. (1973) *Money and Capital in Economic Development* (Washington DC: The Brookings Institution).

Minier, J. (2003) 'Are Small Stock Markets Different?' *Journal of Monetary Economics*, vol. 50, no. 7, pp. 1593–604.

Modigliani, F. and Miller, M. (1958) 'The Cost of Capital, Corporation Finance, and the Theory of Investment', *American Economic Review*, vol. 48, no. 3, pp. 261–97.

Modigliani, F. and Miller, M. (1961) 'Dividend Policy, Growth and the Valuation of Shares', *The Journal of Business*, vol. 34, no. 4, pp. 411–33.

Mohamed, M. M. (2008) 'Evaluating the Performance of Top African Banks Using Data Envelope Analysis', *World Review of Entrepreneurship, Management and Sustainable Development*, vol. 4, no. 4, pp. 345–65.

Morck, R., Shleifer, A., and Vishny, R. (1988) 'Management Ownership and Market Valuation: An Empirical Analysis', *Journal of Financial Economics*, vol. 20, pp. 293–315.

Mwega, F. M. (2002) 'Financial Sector Reforms in Eastern and Southern Africa', in Mkandwire, T. and Soludo, C. C. (eds) *African Voices on Structural Adjustment: A Companion to Our Continent, Our Future* (Ottawa, Canada: International Development Research Centre, IDRC).

Next (2009) 'Government Agencies Have Shown Fairness in Recruiting Personnel', *Next Sunday* Newspaper, Sunday 27 September, p 7.

Next (2010) 'Is the CBN Too Powerful?' *Next* newspaper, Sunday, 24 January, p. 13.

Next on Sunday (2009), Sunday 9 August, vol. 1, no. 32, p.1.

Next on Sunday (2009) 'Government Agencies Have Shown Fairness in Recruiting Personnel', *Next On Sunday*, Sunday 27 September.

Nissanke, M., Aryetey, E., Hettige, H., and Steel, W. F. (1995) *Financial Integration and Development in Sub-Saharan Africa* (Washington DC: World Bank. Mimeo).

Nokuthala, S. (2005) 'Cost and Profit Efficiency of South African Banks', Unpublished MBA Research Report, University of Witswatersrand.

Norbrook N. and Lawal L. (2009) 'Nigerian Banks – Signs of Life', *The Africa Report* (Lagos: The Africa Report), no. 17.

Nwachukwu, C. and Fatade, W. (2010) 'The True Test of My Leadership Has Just Begun', *Next On Sunday*, 24 January, p. 4.

Nwachukwu, O. (2010) 'Banks Get More Relief as CBN Expunges 2% Loan Loss Provision Guide', *BusinessDay Wednesday*, 19 May.

Nwogwugwu, I. (2009), 'CBN Sacks Five Bank CEO's, Injects N400b', *ThisDay Newspaper* (Lagos), 14 Aug 2009.

Nwoji, C. (2010) 'Economy: Performance Indicators Hit Lowest Ebb in Q1' (Abuja: *The Champion*), 29 March.

Ogiemwonyi, V. (2010) 'Udo Udoma's Chairmanship of SEC: A Time for Clear Thinking', *BusinessDay*, Thursday, 04 March.

Ogunkoya, D. (2010) 'Foreign Chief Executives Return to Blue Chip Firms', *Next On Sunday*, Sunday, 31 January, p. 10.

Ogunwale, K. (2009) 'Investment: Information as Critical Ingredient', *Stock World*, 9 December.

Ojeifo, S. (2009) 'Nigeria: Bajomo – Bailout Fund Didn't Need Appropriation', *ThisDay* Newspaper (Lagos: ThisDay Newspapers Limited), 11 September.

Ojowu, O. (2007) 'The Strategic Agenda for the Naira and Other Issues', *ThisDay* Newspaper (Lagos: ThisDay Newspapers Limited), Sunday 26 August, p.42.

Okike, E. N. M. (2007) 'Corporate Governance in Nigeria: The Status Quo', *Corporate Governance: An International Review*, vol. 15, no. 2, pg. 173–93.

Okwe, M. (2007) 'World Bank Offers Assistance on New Naira Policy', *The Guardian* Newspaper (Lagos: The Guardian), Sunday 19 August, vol. 25, no. 10,488, p.1.

Olawuni, T. and Akintola, K. (2010) 'Distressed Banks need N1 trn for Recapitalisation', *BusinessDay*, Friday 19–Sunday, 21 March, p. 3.

Omachonu, J. (2010) 'Bailed Banks Return to Profitability May Take 3 Years – Analysts: Projection Contrast with cbn's September Target', *BusinessDay*, Wednesday, 10 March.

Omachonu, J. (2010) 'Analysts Raise Moral Questions Over Purchase of Toxic Assets by Asset Management Company- Takeover of Insider Related Margin Loans Is Waste of Public Funds', *BusinessDay*, Tuesday, 22 June, p. 4.

Onu, E. (2010) 'Comply With Governance Code, CBN Tells Banks', *ThisDay*, Wednesday, 12 May, vol. 15, no. 5, 498, p. 42.

Onu, E. and Ushakang, J. (2010) 'Keeping to Banking Reforms', *ThisDay*, Wednesday, 12 May 2010, p. 31.

Onwuka, N. (2009) 'Nigeria: House Tackles CBN Over Banks' Bailout', *ThisDay* Newspaper (Lagos: ThisDay Newspapers Limited), 3 September.

Opie, R. (trans) (1934) *The Theory of Economic Development* [Schumpeter, A. (1912) *Theorie der wirtschaftlichen Enwicklung* {Leipzig: Dunker and Humblot}] (Cambridge, MA: Harvard University Press).

Orjiako, C. (2009) 'The Era of Militant Banking', *ThisDay Newspaper* (Lagos: ThisDay Newspaper Limited), Monday 14 September, vol. 14, no. 5,258, p. 18.

Oronsaye, S. (2010), 'Asset Company Takes Over Debts of 21 Banks', *234 Next* (Lagos), 31 Dec 2010.

Osae-Brown, A. (2010) 'Audit of Nigerian Banks: Questions, Questions, Questions...', *Bank Loan*, 26 February.

Oshikoya, T. and Ogbu, O. (2002) 'Financial Liberalization, Emerging Stock Markets and Economic Developments in Africa', in Mkandawire, T. and Soludo, C. (eds) *African Voices on Structural Adjustment* (IDRC/CODESRIA/ Africa World Press).

Pagano, M. (1993) 'Financial Markets and Growth: An Overview', *European Economic Review*, vol. 37, no. 2–3, pp. 613–22.

Park, Y. (1993) 'The Role of Finance in Economic Development in South Korea and Taiwan', in Giovannini, A. (ed.) *Finance and Development: Issues and Experience* (Cambridge: Cambridge University Press).

Park, Y. (1994) 'Korea: Development and Structural Change of the Financial System', in Patrick, H. and Park, Y. (eds) *The Financial Development of Japan, Korea and Taiwan* (New York; Oxford: Oxford University Press).

Patrick, H. (1966) 'Financial Development and Economic Growth in Underdeveloped Countries', *Economic Development and Cultural Change*, vol. 14, no. 2, pp. 172–89.

Patrick, H. (1994) 'Comparisons, Contrasts and Implications', in Patrick, H. and Park, Y. (eds) *The Financial Development of Japan, Korea and Taiwan* (New York; Oxford: Oxford University Press).

Peace (2010) 'Credit Fiscal Policy to the Rescue', *BusinessDay*, Monday, 17 May, p. 16.

Peace (2010), 'More Thoughts on Financial Regulation', *BusinessDay* (Lagos), Monday 21 June 2010.

Perry, A. (2011), 'The Most Influential People in the World', *Time Magazine* (US), Vol. 177, No. 17, 2 May 2011.

Penrose, E. (1995) *The Theory of the Growth of the Firm*, 2nd edn (New York: Oxford University Press Inc.).

Renaissance Professionals (2011), 'CBN and the Grand Cover-Up: How to Buy Your Own Bank', *ThisDay Newspaper* (Lagos), vol. 16, no. 5826, Wednesday 6 April 2011, p. 17.

Revzin, P. (1984) 'British Labor Unions Begin to Toe the Line, Realizing That the Times Have Changed', *The Wall Street Journal*, 23 November.

Ribadu, N. (2006a) 'The Seventh Guest Lecture series of the Financial Institutions Training Centre', *ThisDay* Newspaper (Lagos: ThisDay Newspapers Limited), 13 August, p. 24.

Ribadu, N. (2006b) 'Why We Moved Against Transcorp', *ThisDay* Newspaper (Lagos: ThisDay Newspapers Limited), 16 September, vol. 11, no. 4,165.

Rioja, F. and Valev, N. (2004) 'Does One Size Fit All? A Re-examination of the Finance and Growth Relationship', *Journal of Development Economics*, vol. 74, no. 2, pp. 429–48.

Robinson, J. (1952) 'The Model of an Expanding Economy', *The Economic Journal*, vol. 62, no. 245, pp. 42–53.

Rousseau, P. and Wachtel, P. (2002) 'Inflation Thresholds and the Finance-Growth Nexus', *Journal of International Money and Finance*, vol. 21, no. 6, pp. 777–95.

Saint-Paul, G. (1996) 'Demand-driven Financial Development', in N. Hermes and R. Lensink (eds) *Financial Development and Economic Growth-theory and experiences from Developing Countries* (London and New York: Routledge).

Santomero, A. M. and Eckles, D. L. (2000) 'The Determinants of Success in the New Financial Services Environment', *FRBNY Economic Policy Review*, pp. 11–23.

Sanusi, L. (2010) *The Nigerian Banking Industry: What Went Wrong and the Way Forward*, Kano: Convocation Square, Bayero University.

Schultz, C. (1999) 'Monetary Policy, Delegation and Polarization', *The Economic Journal*, University of Copenhagen. www.res.org.uk/society/mediabriefings/pdfs/1999/April/schultz.pdf

Senbet, L. W. and Otchere, I. (2006) 'Financial Sector Reforms in Africa: Perspective on Issues and Policies', in F. Bourguignon and B. Pleskovic (eds) *Annual World Bank Conference on Development Economics: Growth and Integration* (Washington DC: The World Bank), pp. 81–119.

Shan, J. and Morris, A. (2002) 'Does Financial Development "Lead" Economic Growth?', *International Review of Applied Economics*, vol. 16, no. 2, pp. 153–69.

Shaw, E. (1973) *Financial Deepening and Economic Development* (New York: Oxford University Press).

Shleifer, A. and Summers, L. (1989) 'Breach of Trust in Hostile Takeovers', *NBER Working Paper*, no. 2342.

Shleifer, A. and Vishny, R. (1998) 'A Model of Investor Sentiment', *Journal of Financial Economics*, vol. 49, pp. 307–43.

Singh, A. (1997) 'Financial Liberalization, Stock Markets and Economic Development', *The Economic Journal*, vol. 107, no. 442, pp. 771–82.

SkyeBank (2010) http://www.skyebankng.com/ (accessed 3 February 2010).

Smith, A. and Aigbe, K. (2010) 'The Nigerian Banking Sector... What Next?' (UK: The Chapel Hill Denham Group).

Sobodu, O. O. and Akiode, P. O. (1996) 'Managing Banking Policy and Bank's Financial Condition under Deregulation in Nigeria: Impact Analysis Using Logit Regression Model', *Interim Report* Presented at AERC Workshop, Nairobi, Kenya.

Sobowale, D. (2009) 'Political Implications of the Banking Sanitisation – Rule of Law and Banking', *ThisDay* Newspaper (Lagos: ThisDay Newspaper Limited), Sunday 6 September, p. 27.

Soludo, C. C. (2004) 'Consolidating the Nigerian Banking Industry to Meet the Development Challenges of the 21st Century', speech by the Governor of the Central Bank of Nigeria, Professor Chukwuma Charles Soludo, on 6 July.

StanbicIBTC (2010) http://www.ibtc.com/portal/site/nigeria/menuitem.2792be962d90f70440ff36313367804c/?vgnextoid=d63d12778d4f8110VgnVCM100000337608c4RCRD (accessed 3 February 2010).

SterlingBank plc (2010) http://www.sterlingbankng.com/aboutus/aboutus.aspx (accessed 3 February 2010).

Stein, H., Ajakaiye, O., and Lewis, P. (2002) 'The political economy of financial liberalization in Nigeria', in H. Stein, O. Ajakaiye, and P. Lewis (eds) *Deregulation and Banking Crisis in Nigeria* (New York: Palgrave Macmillan), p. 23.

Stigler, G. (1971) 'The Economic Theory of Regulation', *Bell Journal of Economics*, vol. 2, pp. 3–21.

Sulaiman, T. (2007) 'Cadbury Nigeria Sued by Investors Over Accounting', *The Times* of London, 12 March. Available from: www.thetimes.co.uk (accessed 11 November 2010).

Sutton, J. (2005) *Market Structure: Theory and Evidence*, London School of Economics, Journal of Industrial Economics symposium of 1987.

Thangavelu, S. and James, A. (2004) 'Financial Development and Economic Growth in Australia: An Empirical Analysis', *Empirical Economics*, vol. 29, no. 2, pp. 247–60.

'THE NEW CBN: Transparent Regulators or Crafty Manipulators', *ThisDay* Newspaper (Lagos: ThisDay Newspaper Limited).

The Banker (2005, 2006 and 2007) Annual Publications.

The Guardian (2005) 'My Unending War with Drug Fakers', *The Guardian* Newspaper (Lagos: The Guardian), Sunday 17 April, p. 22.

The Guardian (2008) 'Senate Panel Halts Recapitalisation of Broking Firms', *The Guardian* Newspaper (Lagos: The Guardian), Thursday 13 March.

The Guardian (2009) *The Guardian* Newspaper (Lagos: The Guardian), 6 September 2009, pp. 18–19.

The Guardian (2009) *The Guardian* Newspaper (Lagos: The Guardian), Sunday 4 October, vol. 27, no. 11, 239, p. 1.

The Guardian (2009) *The Guardian* Newspaper (Lagos: The Guardian), Sunday 4 October, pp. 17–18.

The Guardian (2009) *The Guardian* Newspaper (Lagos: The Guardian), Sunday 14 November, p. 11.

The Guardian (2009) 'CBN's Reforms- Economic Sabotage or Bank Sanitisation', *The Guardian* Newspaper (Lagos: The Guardian), Tuesday 1 December, p. 26.

The Guardian (2009) *The Guardian* Newspaper (Lagos: The Guardian), Sunday 11 October, vol. 27, no. 11, 246.

The Guardian (2010) 'Sanusi Indicts CBN Managers Over Banking Crisis, Pledges Sanctions', *Guardian*, 8 July.

The Guardian On Sunday, Interview with Mr. Gamaliel Onosodes.

Time Magazine (1999), 'The Committee to Save the World – The Three Marketers', New York, February 1999, pp. 18–26.

The Nation (2007) 'The Money', *The Nation*, Wednesday 14 November, p. 13.

The Punch (2008) 'Council Restructures Stock Exchange', *The Punch*, Thursday, 23 October, vol. 17, no. 20, p. 1.

The Week (2005) Cover Story, 'Arrest of The Godfather'.

ThisDay (2005) 'The Foreign Debt Controversy', *ThisDay* Newspaper (Lagos: ThisDay Newspapers Limited), 13 March.

ThisDay (2006) 'Globacom: EFCC Arrests Babangida's Son', *ThisDay* Newspaper (Lagos: ThisDay Newspapers Limited), 12 August, vol. 11, no. 4,130.

ThisDay (2008) 'Wema Bank: NDIC Report Indicts ex-MD', *ThisDay* Newspaper (Lagos: ThisDay Newspapers Limited), Sunday 9 March, p. 29.

ThisDay (2008) *ThisDay* Newspaper (Lagos: ThisDay Newspapers Limited), Wednesday 7 May, p. 35.

ThisDay (2009) *ThisDay* Newspaper (Lagos: ThisDay Newspapers Limited), Thursday 20 August, vol. 14, no. 5,233.

ThisDay (2009) *ThisDay* Newspaper (Lagos: ThisDay Newspaper Limited), Sunday 6 September, p. 22.

ThisDay (2009) *ThisDay* Newspaper (Lagos: ThisDay Newspaper Limited), Thursday 5 November, p. 6.

ThisDay (2009) *ThisDay* Newspaper (Lagos: ThisDay Newspapers Limited), Sunday 15 October.

ThisDay (2009) *ThisDay* Newspaper (Lagos: ThisDay Newspapers Limited), Sunday 25 October, vol. 14, no. 5,299.

ThisDay (2010) 'Sanusi's Stakes in Rescued Banks to Be Sold by May', *ThisDay*, Friday, 12 February.

ThisDay (2010) *ThisDay* Newspaper (Lagos: ThisDay Newspapers Limited), Tuesday 20 April, vol. 15, no. 5,476.

Tsangyao, C. (2002) 'Financial Development and Economic Growth in Mainland China: A Note on Testing Demand-following or Supply-leading Hypothesis', *Applied Economics Letters*, vol. 9, no. 13, pp. 869–74.

Uffot, E. (2009) 'Sanusi's Reform: The Unintended Effects', *Newswatch* Magazine. Sunday 4 October.

United Bank for Africa (UBA) (2002) *Annual Report and Accounts*.

United Bank of Nigeria (2010) http://www.ubagroup.com/group/genericpage/351 (accessed 23 February 2010).
Valderrama, D. (2003) 'Financial Development, Productivity, and Economic Growth', *FRBSF Economic Letter*, no. 18. Available from: http://www.frbsf.org/publications/economics/letter/2003/el2003-18.html
Villanueva, D. and Mirakhor, A. (1990) 'Strategies for Financial Reforms', *IMF Staff Papers*, vol. 37, no. 3, p. 50,936.
Violaine, C. (2007) *Banking in China* (New York: Palgrave Macmillan).
Wachtel, P. (2001) 'Growth and Finance: What do We Know and How do We Know It?', *International Finance*, vol. 4, no. 3, pp. 353–62.
Wema Bank Plc (2010) http://www.wemabank.com/newWema/CMSContent.aspx?PageId=20&PageName=CorporateInformation (accessed 2 February 2009).
Wolfowitz (2006) 'Nigeria Has Lost $300 Billion to Corruption: Ribadu is a Remarkable Man', *ThisDay* Newspaper (Lagos: ThisDay Newspapers Limited), 17 October.
World Bank (1989) *World Development Report* (Washington DC: Oxford University Press).
World Bank (1994) 'Adjustment in Africa: Reforms, Results and the Road Ahead', *World Bank Policy Research Report* (New York: Oxford University Press).

Index